CW01511588

For my son Finn
Learn from my mistakes
Be inspired by my successes
Make every second count

ISBN -13: 9781481805322
ISBN – 10: 1481805320

WHEN THE GOING GETS TOUGH... IT MAKES A GOOD BAR STORY!

The extraordinary adventures of an ordinary man

By Ben Church

ABOUT THE AUTHOR

This book recounts Ben's adventures as a single man between leaving school and getting married. He has been a teacher of Geology and Geography since 1989.

He is still travelling, mostly leading groups of teenagers on month-long expeditions in Africa, South America and South East Asia. These adventures will be covered in his next book.

Ben is a keen photographer. If you want to see the photos that document his adventures, visit :

www.benchurch.com

Adventures in the book

www.flickr.com/photos/benchurch/sets

Adventures since the book

www.benchurchphotography.com

Art photos for sale

ACKNOWLEDGMENTS

Thanks to my editors, Wendy Church and Cally Oldershaw.

Thanks also to all of my family for their continued support of my adventures and the countless friends who have joined me in so many of my ridiculous exploits.

CONTENTS

Chapter 1 THE GREAT BRITISH BIKE RIDE

John O'Groats to Land's End
The Adventure Begins

It took an incredible total of twenty-three hours to travel 1,100km from Norwich to Thurso by train. Thankfully, it didn't take long to cycle the 30km from Thurso to John O'Groats where I pitched my tent and crashed out early, well and truly knackered by my marathon journey and heartily glad, finally, to have finished my A-levels.

The Great British Bike ride, a sponsored event to raise money for Friends of The Earth started with a big breakfast - essential for a hard day on the road. I have to confess that on the second day I bought myself a bigger bowl! We finally set off just after nine o'clock with a few of the obligatory "me-me" photos next to the John O' Groats road sign. The skies were dull and overcast, so I started out at a pretty good pace. The cycling was good, with some hard hill climbs. What goes up must come down and the climbs were rewarded by superb freewheeling descents with many entertaining hairpin bends. After cycling a total of about 110km, we arrived at the campsite near Helmsdale just after four in the afternoon. It was a good, but fairly basic site right next to the sea. The evening was convivial, with a campfire on the beach and entertainment provided by the weird and wacky Natural Theatre Company whose offbeat humour was to keep us entertained throughout the ride, however exhausted we might be. A really good spirit of togetherness was quickly developed among the 120 cyclists taking part.

The second day was a relatively easy 64km ride. I found that I was getting into the steady rhythm needed to climb the longest and steepest hills. Essential stops for Mars Bars and tea resulted in cafés becoming surrounded by bikes leaning against the walls - sometimes as many as thirty at a time! That evening, the campsite was in a pleasant situation next to a loch at Bonar Bridge. The downside was that the whole area was covered in cowpats! After pitching up and having a good meal, most of the group descended on a local pub for a great evening, with beer, some guitar playing, and lots of laughs.

Even after the excesses of a night in the pub, it wasn't too bad getting on the road the next morning. The day started with an 8km hill climb which sweated out any lingering traces of a hangover. At a super little café, I stopped for a break and chatted with a young couple, Mike and Alison, who were doing the ride on a tandem which reached frightening speeds going downhill, especially with their two year old son on the back!. At our campsite at the Rugby Club, I broke my record for speedy tent pitching and couldn't resist a quick spin on a petrol-engine go-cart on a nearby track - speed freak or what!

The fourth day was an absolute belter! We set off from Inverness amidst a cacophony of horn-blowing (we'd all been given tacky plastic devices for this purpose). I ended up cycling with a group of fourteen - previously I'd been on my own or in groups of two or three. Many were Aussies and Kiwis, ubiquitous travellers - always easy companions with an endless stream of entertaining tales. Half way down Loch Ness we stopped at a cafe on a boat.

Nearby, was a guy in a hut who'd devoted the last nine years of his life looking for Nessie, the Loch Ness Monster. He had a few interesting photos, but I left unconvinced.

The next section of the ride has become one of the most enduring memories of the whole trip: climbing up and over the mountains, a long hard ascent, repaid by the spectacular scenery of pine and deciduous woods, crags, valleys, and moorland. The descent on the other side was an adrenalin-inducing white-knuckle ride at terminal velocity. However, immediately after one exceptionally sharp hairpin bend, negotiated while bombing along at a good speed, we had a minor pile-up when we encountered a closed gate across the road. Thankfully, there was no damage to cyclists or bikes. At 550m, on the top of the moor, we cycled through cloud, which was an eerie experience. When we dropped out of the mist we were met by blazing sun and we stopped by an isolated mountain stream for a refreshing skinny-dip. We'd slipped into a relaxed and flexible routine with many tea and Mars Bar stops which became the flavour of the whole end-to-end ride. After pitching up at Kincraig in the evening, I estimated that We'd covered about 120km.

The next day, I travelled with the same group, covering a gruelling 130km. The first half of the ride was an unpleasant struggle along the A9, battling against an unforgiving headwind, though we shared the brunt of it by slipstreaming each other. My cycling style was changing - at home, in flat Norfolk, I'd tended to pump around in high gears; now I found that cruising in a fairly low gear was the most effective approach to touring. I was getting used to hills too - I hadn't had to walk up one so far. At the end of the day, it was good to unwind with a Scottish ceilidh in a local pub, even if it meant not getting to bed until the early hours of the morning.

The prescribed route to Edinburgh was a pretty easy 90km dotted with several superb descents which we positively roared down. We crossed the Forth Bridge *en masse* to please a gaggle of press photographers. I was in my element! It was good to have a day off in Edinburgh, doing much needed laundry (shades of the classic Levis advert). Having a few beers and a good boogie at a disco laid on by the Edinburgh Friends of the Earth rounded off the day in style. I enjoyed meeting Cathy who was only sixteen – I was an old man of eighteen! She had come on her own, bringing her cycling club's tandem - an interesting way to get to know people!

Back on the road the next day, we cycled on to Coldstream and kept mainly to quiet country lanes. There was one particularly good hill climb, Liberton Brae (gradient 1 in 7), which I took in my stride. We arrived in Coldstream just in time to become part of the local Carnival which was quite a hoot. In the evening Julian, a laid back Aussie, led a wonderful group meditation - a great mental tonic and a good preparation for the next day's laborious journey to Hexam battling relentless headwinds.

The road onwards to Richmond was long, hard, and hilly. On the way, I stopped in Stanhope and indulged in the delights of a 'stottie' (a flat, round loaf or bun typical of the North east). Leaving Stanhope, I very nearly lost my wallet - it must have fallen out of one of my bags as I leaned into a bend. Luckily, a passing motorist spotted it and gave it back to me. This made me feel really good, but the exhilaration of getting of getting up the 1 in 7 hill was the cream on the cake!. After that though, it was grim cycling up on the moors for a while - I was alone and struggling. At one point, I was defeated by a brutal hill and had to get off to push – I'd finally reached the boundary between pride and stupidity! I made a welcome tea stop in Eggleston and met the rest of the group for a sociable afternoon of less challenging cycling. In the evening, we camped at a beautiful site overlooked by Richmond castle and enjoyed a few pints of top quality Theakston's Old Peculiar in a friendly pub just up the hill from our camp.

The 'Wensleydale day' was wonderful, second only the outstanding Loch Ness experience. Four of us followed a minor road running parallel to the busier road on the set route. The highlight was the Garsdale Station Road, an enormously steep hill; most of us had to dismount and push. The Natural Theatre Company pulled off a rib-tickling stunt at the top; we arrived, panting, to find a chap standing there in a white boiler suit with a wash-basin and towels strapped to his front and a water tank on his back, asking if we needed a wash and brush-up! A few hundred metres further on they had set up an impromptu roadside bar - a tray of drinks appeared from behind a wall on the end of an extended arm! Descending the other side of the hill was possibly the fastest I've ever been on a bike, maybe even reaching speeds as high as 70kmph. Unfortunately, one guy, Bruno, came off on a tight bend and lost a fair amount of skin - a nasty case of 'road rash'. After that, it was great to have a night relaxing by the campfire under a clear and starry sky.

The road to Liverpool was rather boring, with long sections following fairly busy main roads which seemed to be heavily strewn with glass. Arriving in Liverpool was depressing as we cycled through some run-down areas. However, the mood was lightened by a mock anti-bike demonstration by the Natural Theatre Company. The next day we were given a police escort to the ferry across the Mersey, which was a good laugh and made us feel important. Then we forged onwards and out of Liverpool to just beyond Shrewsbury, riding the last couple of kilometres through the rain to our rather damp and dreary campsite.

Shrewsbury to Brecon was good. Riding Hergest Ridge was splendid and reminded me of the Mike Oldfield song of the same name, making me appreciate the probable inspiration for it - long leafy lanes bounded by high hedges and glorious green tunnels of foliage. The day ended with a breathtaking downhill ride into Brecon followed by a good swim in the pool near our campsite.

I left Brecon late, accompanied for a few minutes by a chap dressed in a spotless black suit, complete with bowler hat and white gloves. This was topped by a bizarre addition, a silver stocking mask (courtesy of the Natural Theatre Company), which made him look like an extra from Doctor Who. The ride from Brecon to Caldicot was only about 70km or so and the tiny leafy lanes were a joy. It was good to have time for a long relaxed picnic lunch down by the river at Usk - I gorged on sticky buns. Little did I know that seven years later I would land a job at Monmouth Comprehensive School, only 20km away, where I would work for twenty years. Towards the end of the day, I took a detour from the set route, following minor roads from Shirenewton to Caldicot. There was one particularly memorable 5km hill climb followed by an exhilarating 5km descent. My effort was rewarded with adrenalin, locked elbows, glazed eyes, and a fixed grin!

The route from Caldicot to Bath was quiet and pleasant, much of it following disused railway tracks that had been cleared to provide an excellent network of cycle paths. We camped just outside Bath at Boyd farm at the top of a cruel hill, a punishing end to the day. I cycled down to the station to meet my then girlfriend, Teresa. While she took the bus up to the campsite, I struggled back up the hill on my bike and we spent a great evening around the campfire listening to a good local folk band. The next day, it was good to wander around Bath, a city first established as a spa by the Romans. We admired the ancient remains and the elegant Georgian architecture until Teresa had to take a bus back home. I went for a swim in the Bath Lido, an open- air swimming pool which was absolutely freezing and in the evening, we all went to a party hosted by the Bath Friends of the Earth group which led to a wobbly ride back to the campsite on a traffic-free cycle track.

We left the next morning and made for the interestingly named Kingsbury Episcopi (the word 'episcopi' is Latin for 'of the bishop'). We stopped in Wells, the smallest city in England, with its magnificent cathedral and unique moated Bishop's Palace and then on to Glastonbury whose early history is linked with its dominant landmark, the Tor, which I enjoyed climbing. The atmosphere was thick with mysticism. There are claims that Joseph of Arimathea brought the boy Jesus to Glastonbury and that, years later, after the crucifixion, he returned with the Holy Grail which, legend has it, is buried beneath the Tor. The town grew up alongside the Abbey whose history goes back to a Celtic monastery dating back to 500 AD. In later years I made many annual pilgrimages to the legendary Glastonbury music festival, but that night we made our own music at the campsite. It was on a cider farm and copious quantities of devastating scrumpy were consumed, resulting in bleary eyes in the morning, only partly cured by strong black coffee.

Another good day of cycling took us to Exeter where we camped at the Art College. I rode on my own for much of the time, though I joined some of the others at lunchtime to pig out on 'real' coffee and lots of cakes. Despite a little rain the following day, the ride over Dartmoor was beautiful, with a welcome stop for lunch at the top in Two Bridges. After camping in an isolated field near Tavistock we set off for Truro. We took plenty of long stops and little did I know then that Truro was to become my home twenty eight years and many travels later! The campsite at the end of the day was in Chacewater – a village whose beautiful name comes from the term 'Chase or hunting ground near to a stream'. This was the only commercial campsite we stayed at on the entire trip and it wasn't too bad.

The last day of the ride was bracing. We cycled through the, to us, strangely named Praze on Beeble which means 'meadow on the river Beeble'. Everyone met at the Wreckers Inn at lunchtime. A group of us (thirteen men and five women) left early and cycled a few hundred metres up the road where we stripped off and finished the last couple of kilometres of the ride as a cycle-streak. Unsurprisingly, we got a mention in the tabloid newspaper, *The Sun*! There were crowds of grockles (tourists) and much fun when we finally arrived at Lands End after cycling 2,000km. There was a heady atmosphere. I felt truly elated! Although it was raining, we all felt great and celebrated in style with glasses of champagne all round followed by a huge cream tea. We camped at Penzance Rugby Club and had a noisy farewell party, royally entertained by the Natural Theatre Company and FREE BEER before saying 'goodbye'.

It was then back home to Norfolk, to prepare for my next big adventure – studying for a Geology degree at Birmingham University.

Chapter 2 MIDGES TO MUD LOGGING

The Isle of Skye and Beyond

In my first year at university, I spent eight weeks on the Isle of Skye doing a geological mapping project of a 25km^2 area that formed the basis of my Birmingham University Geology degree dissertation. I stayed in the Broadford Bay youth hostel where, at one point, there were sixteen geologists and a total of thirty on the island. It didn't take long to establish an effective daily routine, conducting fieldwork for seven or eight hours a day, then inking in my maps, checking my notes, and labelling specimens in the evenings. After a week, I'd had a lucky break: I was offered the job of Assistant Warden for the summer. This meant staying a couple of weeks longer than I'd planned. As a student on a niggardly grant, £50 a week made it all seem worthwhile. The best thing, however, was having a rent-free room of my own. It was a relief not to be woken up at dawn every morning in a dormitory that seemed to accommodate plastic-bag-rustling 'boy-racer' cyclists, setting off early to burn off another 160km plus a day.

The variety of people passing through the hostel was amazing and led to many interesting exchanges. I learned how to say: 'Have you got a sheet sleeping bag?' in Japanese, Italian, French, Dutch, and German! I met a lot of real characters, including a Glaswegian itinerant jewellery salesman who was very much like the Scottish comedian Rab C Nesbitt. He managed to poach some trout one day and cooked them up for supper accompanied by a tin of ravioli – unusual, but delicious! One night, after a few drams too many, he returned from the pub to find the hostel locked. He ended up sleeping in the drying room, amidst muddy smelly boots and damp half-washed laundry.

Working on the beach was hazardous at times and seagulls and oystercatchers frequently mobbed me, especially while I was having my lunch. However, I only really began to suffer when I'd finished the easy job of mapping the coastal exposures and headed inland. Most of the inland exposures were in stream sections where there was a prolific insect population. For me, it was not being bitten that was the problem, it was the psychological warfare. In Skye the midges are invincible, simply by virtue of their numbers. Myriads surround you, buzzing into every orifice - eyes, ears, nose, and mouth. One day, I met a fellow geologist wearing a wide-brimmed hat with bright yellow net curtain draped over it to keep the little buggers off. There were a few windless days when the midges were so bad that 'mozzies stopped fieldwork'. However, the really nasty bugs were the 'clegs' or horseflies and being bitten by one of those was like being stabbed with a dart.

Another hazard of fieldwork was that it often involved a lot of walking through heather, the home of the dastardly sheep tick. This gruesome little bug latches onto you and sucks your blood, its body swelling as it takes its fill. If you inadvertently brush it off, it may leave its jaws embedded in your flesh which can result in a septic wound. I remember the swarthy Glaswegian warden of the youth hostel sitting on the stairs, surrounded by an enthusiastic international audience, as his wife extracted a tick from his leg admonishing him not to be a wimp. One day, there was a blood-curdling scream from the showers, followed by a towel-clad figure streaking up the stairs. I later heard that this geologist had discovered a sheep tick in his groin - he never did tell us how he got rid of that one!

A visit to the Portree Highland Games provided a pleasant break. We were treated to the rousing music of the pipes (shades of my grandfather) and to skilful Highland Dancing competitions. The sporting competitions were amazing, especially the heavy events. Hulking tartan-clad locals impressed us with the caber toss which involved the competitor balancing a tapered pine pole or log (holding the thinner end) and charging forward to toss it so that it somersaulted, the wider end hitting the ground first. The winner was the one whose throw was closest to the ideal twelve o'clock position on an imaginary clock. In the stone put (as opposed to the shot put), the competitor lobbed a 12kg rock. The Scottish hammer throw was astounding - a 7kg round metal ball was attached to the end of a shaft just over a metre long and the hammer was whirled about the head and thrown as far as possible over the shoulder. The weight throw was even more jaw-dropping. Here, the athletes attempted to toss a weight (it's been known to be as heavy as twenty-five kilograms!) over a 4.5m horizontal bar using only one hand, but it was the good old tug-of-war that captured for me the spirit of the games - an impressive spectacle of true grit, with none of the polished toned muscles of the vain bodybuilder, just the brawny products of a hard life farming 'on the hill'.

I had a break from fieldwork for a few days when my girlfriend Bridget, a dentistry student from the University of Birmingham, came to visit me. We took the post bus from Broadford to Elgol. It didn't move for half an hour after boarding, but we were in no hurry and it was interesting to eavesdrop on the conversations of our fellow passengers and get a flavour of day-to-day life of the island. We had a scenic drive with much stopping and starting - it took just over an hour and a half to travel fifteen miles! After a leisurely boat trip and indulging in some gorgeous cream gateau we set off at an easy pace along the coast path to Camasunary where we camped in an idyllic location, nestling at the foot of the looming Black Cuillin Mountains. The following day, we did a long walk into the heart of the dark and brooding gabbro peaks. Walking along the coast, we came to the famous 'Bad Step', a vast slab of rock which blocks the path. It has to be crossed by walking along an almost horizontal crack; one careless step could have meant a swift slide down into the sea below. Bridget gallantly teetered around it and before long we were having a brew stop at the bay of Loch na Leachol where, wandering on the beach, we found hundreds of jellyfish washed up like some kind of failed alien invasion.

We walked along the western bank of Loch Curuisk, pausing to drink from the clear streams of pure water that cascaded down the mountains, then climbed up from the end of the loch, intending to head west over the ridge and down to Glenbrittle. As we gained height, we found abundant lucky white heather and huge tasty bilberries. However, the cloud base lowered and before long visibility was reduced to no more than ten metres. The ascent to the ridge looked a bit hazardous on the map, so we decided to err on the side of caution and retraced our steps from Sgurr na Banachdich back down to Loch Coruisk. Our campsite at the southern end of the loch was somewhat windswept, but at least that kept the midges off; they'd been truly unbearable earlier.

After a lazy start the next day, we walked along Allt a Choire Riab-haich, leaving the footpath to follow the side of Loch Choire Riab-haich, then due north to Meall Deorg and down Glen Sligachan. We stopped at the Sligachan Hotel for a well-earned drink and were entertained by the weird contorted reflections of the mountains in the curved windows of the bar. Then we hitched back to the hostel and feasted on barbecue beans and hot dog sausages which tasted as good as a gourmet meal in an expensive hotel – hunger really is the best sauce!

A few days later, we hitched back up to Portree. Our first lift was with a young woman who was working as a theatrical adviser for the N.W. Highlands and Islands. It sounded as though it was an interesting occupation and involved a lot of travelling. She said she'd got through four cars in a couple of years due to winter snowdrifts, sheep, and summer tourists (she put the last two in the same category). A twenty minute wait at Sligachan was spent standing by the road in the blazing sun watching a couple of Golden Eagles flying high and soaring on the thermals in the distance. They were great, but didn't compare with the eagle we had seen at much closer range a few days before while on the Red Cuillin.

After another lift we arrived in Portree. I felt pretty queasy as soon as I'd stepped out of the car and before long I was really struggling with an awful headache, shivering, cramps, and gut-wrenching nausea. It seemed incredible that on the notoriously cold and damp Isle of Skye I'd managed to experience heat exhaustion! I put it down to having what, for me, was an uncharacteristically short haircut! The only cool place to lie down was the churchyard, which seemed pretty appropriate considering how I felt. It was a couple of hours before I felt able to catch a bus back to Broadford and to go to bed with a couple of Aspirin. Loads of water, sugar, and salt, together with a few hours' sleep soon put me right. However, I must admit to wingeing quite a bit throughout. Mercifully, Bridget mopped my brow and looked after me, though for a long time she didn't let me forget what a wimp I'd been. . . .

As my stay on the Island of Skye was drawing to a close it seemed fitting to commemorate the hallmark of the summer - the midges. I put together a design showing a pair of hairy legs with feet clad in walking boots dangling from a cloud of insects with one waving arm brandishing a geological hammer and the other flailing at God's little creatures. The body and head of the human figure were represented by balls of swirling insects (I am no good at drawing faces). When I got back to Birmingham, I got thirty T-shirts printed with this design and posted them off to the geology students who'd ordered them during my last few days on Skye. The caption read 'Bloody Midges! Skye Geologists 1984'.

I marked the end of my university studies by attending the legendary Live Aid concert of 1985 at Wembley Stadium followed by a glorious summer travelling by Inter- Rail around Europe with my girlfriend Bridget.

Real Life beckoned and my first job was with Exploration Logging, known as 'Exlog'. It began with a two-week training course in Windsor where I found myself sharing a room with Stuart Deveraux, one of the geology students I'd met on the Isle of Skye the previous summer. Exploration Logging was a service company on the oil rigs which specialised in formation evaluation, less glamorously known as 'mud logging'. Very simply, this involved the collection, testing, and description of samples of rock chippings as the exploration well was being drilled. The job provided plenty of opportunity for travel and significant time off. This was the ideal moment to seize such an opportunity - I was young, free, and single and, as yet, had no responsibilities.

Windsor was followed by safety and survival instruction in Aberdeen which proved to be a curious mixture of something like an army assault course and the old TV game show *'It's a knockout'!* The first couple of days were spent at a fire station. Search and rescue exercises in a building that was a maze of rooms, tunnels, and ladders proved to be a lot more difficult than one might think - especially when it was pitch dark and we were wearing breathing apparatus, which is both heavy and bulky. To add realism, the following day we did a similar exercise, but in a building where gas burners were turned on (we could feel the top of our ears burning!) Smouldering pallets were added thus creating a dense smoky atmosphere. I began to appreciate just how hard a fireman's job is! We also had a go at working with a variety of different fire hoses, using both foam and water. The power of the jet from a normal fire hose was mighty. It took two people to hold it safely. If one of them had let go, the person left holding the heavy brass nozzle would probably have ended up getting swiped with it, resulting in an arm being snapped like a twig.

We had a number of lectures on safety and first aid. These were accompanied by a gruesome set of slides that had the audience grimacing. We learned that many of the guys who had worked on the drill floor had fingers missing where they'd caught them in a chain wrench; the result of which was the finger being pulled off at the knuckle - ouch!

The next couple of days were spent jumping into an icy swimming pool with an over-effective wave machine, trying to right capsized life rafts and rescuing dummies. This was made more difficult by the fact that we were being sprayed with high-pressure hoses. . . . The fun really started when we had to practise in the helicopter-ditching simulator. We were told that you mustn't get out until the bubbles stopped swirling around. If you were to get out too early in a real accident you'd stand a good chance of being cut in half by the rotors. However, such fine timing is easier said than done when you've just been dropped from a great height and spun around while firmly strapped in with several other 'victims' all equally keen to get out as fast as possible. Later in the course, we were set free from the security of a building or simulator to spend a day on the real-life waters of Aberdeen Bay getting used to handling lifeboats, setting off flares, and performing rescues.

After two weeks of the rigours of the safety and survival course, I was pretty tired and was looking forward to a rest, but this was not to be. The following Monday I was sent off to spend a week as a trainee on a rig called the *West Venture* in the Norwegian sector of the North Sea. After a long journey involving trains, planes, and taxis, I eventually flew out from Kristiansund on a forty-minute helicopter flight. Most of the choppers I travelled in were big Sikorsky S-61s which are incredibly noisy and not very comfortable, especially when you're sweating in an ungainly survival suit that weighs several kilos. Subsequently, I found out that two weeks later the sister rig had had a 'blow-out' when an uncontrolled release of gas under high pressure had resulted in an evacuation with people jumping into a sea that had become a maelstrom of bubbling foam.

The *West Venture* was smaller than I'd expected. It was an exploration rig and as such wasn't as large as a production platform. The exploration rigs were either jack-up rigs with legs that could be adjusted to suit the water depth (up to about 100m) or, if situated in deeper water, they were floating and semi-submersible with large pontoons anchored to the sea bed. Most of them were triangular and only about 100m across. They usually accommodated about sixty men and, very rarely, one or two women, many of them working for different companies. The quality of life varied enormously, but it was usually fairly basic as far as accommodation and food were concerned. It was usual to spend two, three, or four weeks at a time on a rig; the period was known as a 'hitch' and involved working twelve hour 'tours' or shifts, without any days off.

The Exlog units were like small laboratories and varied in size from palatial (8m long), common in the North Sea, to squalid (5.5m long). In the larger units there was a crew of two: a mud logger and a computer engineer. In the smaller units, the mud logger worked alone for twelve hours a day. Offshore, I worked in both large and small units. All the units I worked in onshore were of the smaller variety. There wasn't much to do during the twelve hours when not working. On North Sea rigs there was usually a video room, but the videos were almost always those the shops couldn't rent out. There was also a multi-gym and maybe a table tennis table, if you were lucky, but good intentions to work out regularly usually evaporated after a couple of days. I spent most of my free time reading, listening to music, writing letters, thinking, and reflecting on my life, the universe, and everything else.

My second hitch wasn't much use as a training exercise, though it typified the unpredictability of the job. I was told that I'd be working onshore in Scotland for three weeks and would be back in time for Christmas. In the event, I worked for five weeks of twelve hour shifts and got home on the 27th of December.

My third training hitch was on the *Maersk Endeavour*, a rig in the Danish sector of the North Sea. I'd been told that I'd be offshore for three weeks, but actually, I was only on the rig for six days. This unpredictability was something I was to get used to. For the next couple of years I never knew where, when, or for how long I'd be working. This didn't do an awful lot for my love life! In fact, my university romance with Bridget came to an end, though we've always kept in touch.

During this hitch I experienced my first big storm offshore, the 'Great Storm' of October 1987. Massive waves up to 25m high kept swallowing up the supply boat. I don't know how the crew on those boats can survive such severe conditions. The winds were gusting up to 200kmph and blew sea spray horizontally across the platform.

One chap got blown over and bruised his kidneys badly enough to have to spend a night in the sick bay. It was impossible to get any sleep as the legs of the jack-up rig were screaming with metal fatigue as we were buffeted repeatedly by the waves. It was quite a night!

After three training hitches I was officially qualified, though I didn't feel very confident. It was a couple of months before I was called up to go on my first 'real' job. The oil industry was in a major slump and I only got about six weeks of work during my first six months with Exlog. During this time I was paid a 'retainer' which wasn't very much at all; even when I was working I'd only take home about £500 a month. Unfortunately, mud logging is one of the worst paid jobs on the rigs, on one rig in the Norwegian sector we were earning the same as the cleaners, despite our degrees and training. However, when I was offshore I couldn't spend any money and as I didn't have a house, a car, or a steady girlfriend, I was able to save.

We were supposed to work two weeks on, followed by two weeks off, in the North Sea, though it never worked out to be as regular as that. However, it was good to have time off. I often got home after a hitch, emptied my rucksack, re-packed it, and stuck out my thumb to cadge a lift up to Derbyshire where I'd work for a week or so at an outdoor pursuits centre based at Edale Youth Hostel. It was called S.E.A.L. Guides and later evolved into the Rocklea Activity Centre based in Hathersage. I was an instructor in climbing, caving, mountain biking, or hill walking during the day and it was my job to 'entertain' everyone in the pub in the evenings. I enjoyed this instant social life every night. I was able to burn the candle at both ends. I worked hard and played even harder because I was always able to catch up on sleep once I got back on a rig. I was constantly on the move during the time I worked for Exlog and for a couple of years I never spent more than ten days in one place apart from when I was working.

I did my first two 'real' hitches on the *Arch Rowan* in the UK sector of the North Sea, off Great Yarmouth. The rig was drilling into salt, so oil-based mud was being used. This was horrible stuff as you had to wash the samples first in diesel and then in detergent. After two weeks of this my hands were a flaky mess, even if I wore gloves and used a barrier cream. Drilling in salt did have its advantages, though, because whenever the drill string was run in or out of the hole it would inevitably get jammed. It often took several hours of 'jarring' or pumping down 'pills' of water to get it going again. This meant a lot of time in 'logging position number one', i.e. sitting around with your feet up, drinking coffee, and listening to music or incredible bullshit stories from anyone who happened to be there. On one rig in the North Sea which had an American crew, mostly from Texas, the mud engineer told more tall tales than most, so we rigged up a red light and a buzzer that would go on at the flick of a hidden switch - the 'bullshit detector' had been born!

After the *Arch Rowan,* I did a week-long hitch on the *Treasure Scout.* During the latter half of the year I had had the steadiest period in my career with Exlog when I did four two-week hitches and a couple of individual weeks on the sister rig, the *Treasure Saga*, in the Norwegian sector. I then did a couple of two week hitches on the *Deep Sea Bergen* and one on the *Polar Pioneer.* The *Polar*

Pioneer was drilling north of the Arctic Circle and as it was February I didn't see daylight during the whole time I was on the rig. I did, however, get to see the unearthly beauty of the *Aurora Borealis* - The Northern Lights.

The following spring I was transferred to the overseas division of Exlog and started to work onshore in what promised to be more exotic locations. The first of these jobs was a month near Deir ez Zoir in the middle of the Syrian Desert. After a night in Damascus, I took a five-hour bus journey through seemingly endless desert - mile after mile of emptiness. At Al Farat, the rig company representative, Bob, drove us to the site in a large Chevrolet pick-up. I was somewhat disconcerted by the presence of an armoured car when we arrived, but the soldiers just stood around and looked bored and not particularly prepared for an 'incident'.

The facilities at the rig site were Spartan to say the least. The accommodation comprised a handful of cabins that were reminiscent of the huge metal containers used for transporting goods by ship. There were no recreational amenities. Sometimes I used to lie on top of my cabin reading, but the sun was so intense that I never lasted outdoors for long. Occasionally, I'd go for a walk away from the rig until I could only just see the derrick and then back again across the featureless, stony desert. The only living things seemed to be lizards, dung beetles, and mangy-looking wild dogs that frequently kept me awake at night. Camel herds passed the site from time to time; you would normally smell them before you could see them!

The workload was variable and when there wasn't much to do, a twelve-hour shift on my own became an exercise in killing time. I wrote letters and read. Countless hours were spent fly-swatting or watching the dung beetles that occasionally flew into the unit, spinning around on their backs until they managed to right themselves, and then flew off, appearing embarrassed by their aeronautical incompetence. The food on this rig was appalling. I think they must have had a cookbook entitled '101 Ways to Cook a Camel'. There were no green vegetables at all, so I made a point of eating oranges every day to avoid getting scurvy. It was unbearably hot during the day and pretty cold at night.

After twenty-eight days of twelve-hour shifts and a couple of spectacular sandstorms that turned the whole sky an alarming orange, I was glad to leave the rig, especially as I'd been lucky enough to cash in my flight home and thus be able to spend three weeks travelling overland back to Britain.

Chapter 3 A FUNNY THING HAPPENED ON MY WAY HOME FROM WORK . . . .

Syria to the UK

With the money from my cancelled flight, I was able to buy an InterRail ticket that would take me back to the UK from Istanbul. The Exlog Company man gave me a lift to the base camp and I was then able to catch a bus to Damascus.

Once there, I risked life and limb in one of the big battered 1950s American beasts of cars which served as taxis. The aggressive driving style often adopted by taxi drivers the world over was amplified here, as were the constantly used horns. I enjoyed many hours strolling around the Hamidah Souk, the old market. It felt like being in a time warp that took me back several hundred years. It was a cornucopia of sensory delights. I was bombarded from all sides by exotic colours, sounds, and smells. There were legion stalls selling fabrics of every describable hue, alongside vendors touting a glittering array of gold and silver jewellery. Many were calling out to advertise their wares, constantly trying to outdo their neighbours. I was the only western face in the teeming crowd. It was odd to notice that everyone, regardless of how well-dressed they might be, wore scruffy down-at-heel shoes. There were countless small coffee shops where men flashed smiles glinting with gold teeth and supped at little glasses of strong, sweet, black coffee. Women glided past in amorphous black gowns, their faces hidden by veils. Hidden in streets near to the main souk, I discovered many a tiny workshop where craftsmen made anything from shoes to wooden stools, from brassware to pottery.

I didn't take many photographs as I felt it would have been intrusive; I was just happy to soak up the medieval atmosphere of the place. However, I did take a couple of shots and when doing so got talking to two brothers who were friendly and keen to practise their English. I ended up having tea with the entire family. Their home was a peaceful refuge from the frantic noise and dust. Three stories of rooms with balconies overlooked an open courtyard stocked with bright well-tended plants. I was introduced to the boys' mother and sister, neither of whom could speak English but their warm hospitality made me feel welcome and at ease. Before long, the mother had suggested that I might want to marry her daughter; this was met with huge mirth by the two brothers.

I left Syria on a night bus which took ten hours to arrive at Antakya in southern Turkey. By the time I arrived, I was starving and quickly found a street vendor selling hot spicy bread which I savoured with thick, black coffee. Other customers were young lads covered in oil and grease who looked as though they'd been born in the garages where they worked. The bus station was the centre of intense comings and goings long-distance coaches and local mini buses had roof racks piled high with all manner of produce - I even saw one with a loudly protesting goat tied aloft. In the afternoon, I decided to board another bus and travelled through the night to Denizli, where I took a *'Dolmus'* (minibus) to Pamukkale. During the hours of daylight, I marvelled at snow-capped mountains surrounded by lush green valley plains. I was pleasantly surprised at how easy it was to travel around Turkey on public transport.

It was good to arrive at Pamukkale early in the morning and after wandering around, I sat on a hill overlooking the village watching the place beginning to stir. I took a rest and wrote my diary, occasionally looking up to watch the slow but deliberate meanderings of a shepherd and his flock. Later, I went to the little museum, which was reasonable, but nothing special. However, my main reason for visiting Pamukkale was to see the travertine cascades, terraces of carbonate minerals left by flowing water. I wasn't disappointed. The travertine was like a glittering iced cake – massive, but at the same time delicate.

My next stop was Selcuk, where I found a clean, cheap, and friendly little pension. The museum there had some exquisite artefacts recovered from the nearby ancient Roman city of Ephesus, including the spectacular statue of Artemis retrieved from the Temple of the Goddess in Ephesus. I also visited the castle which glowed with shades of warm orange as the sun went down. The walls were massive and built with stones, bricks, and mortar which were reinforced by fifteen towers, all still intact. The castle dated from the Byzantine as well as the Ottoman periods and inside there were paved streets, cisterns, a church, and a mosque. I amused myself by taking a timed self-portrait in a huge stoneware 'Ali Baba' jar as well as taking a few more serious photographs.

As I walked down from the castle, a couple of beaming small children came running up to sell me a pretty bunch of wild flowers. They invited me into one of the ramshackle cottages that nestled below the castle to meet their family. Again, I was made welcome and drank lavish amounts of delicious apple tea which became a favourite of mine while in Turkey. None of the family could speak English but, despite having only narrowly scraped a grade C at O-level German some eight years previously (much to the amazement of my mother who, as a teacher of German, had told me that I was 'beyond salvation!'), I managed to hold a reasonable conversation with the man of the house in pidgin German. Like many Turkish men of slender means, he'd worked in Germany as a *Gastarbeiter* ('guest worker'). The family was obviously very poor and I was pleased when the father offered to polish my rig boots for a few Turkish lire because it gave me an opportunity to express delight and at the same time, help them out without being patronising.

Visiting Ephesus alone at dawn was a magical experience. I particularly remember standing at the back of the 25,000 seat-capacity amphitheatre, imagining times past. The tranquil silence was rudely shattered by a lively school party and I was about to move on when the group became still and one girl took centre stage and sang in a beautiful, clear voice; the acoustics were perfect. When she finished, the thirty kids' applause sounded like a capacity crowd at a stadium gig - incredible!

I enjoyed investigating the well-preserved ruins and had an idyllic doze in the sun for half an hour before looking for somewhere to eat. Passing a cafe, I spotted a European-looking guy eating alone at an outside table and asked him if the food was any good. He invited me to join him. The kebab and salad were great and so was John's company. We got talking about travel plans, found we were both heading the same way, and ended up sharing a hire car to Bodrum. The scenery was stunning and on the way we stopped to marvel at the spectacular sanctuary of Apollo at Didyma, an amazing feat of third century BC engineering and architecture. It had originally been a pre-Greek cult centre with a spring and sacred grove which the Ionian Greeks developed and the oracle continued to be in use until Christianity was established. It was officially closed in 385 AD when a Byzantine church was erected in the temple compound. Sadly, in the 15th century an earthquake left the temple in ruins. When we arrived in Bodrum it was already dark and all the pensions were full, but after spending about an hour cruising around, we eventually found a place to stay in Goldum, three kilometres away.

The next morning, we were pleasantly surprised to find that we overlooked a calm sheltered bay. Later, we went for a slow ramble around the Crusader Castle, an imposing edifice right next to the harbour, built by the Knights of St. John in the early fifteenth century. Having had our fill of that, we headed off towards Marmaris. It was another beautiful drive along tiny country roads with views of the Datca Peninsula. John and I said goodbye in Marmaris. He continued travelling south to Kas and I bought a bus ticket to Istanbul.

While I was waiting for the bus, I had a few drinks at a bar and was highly amused to witness the incredulous laughter of the proprietor when confronted with a tourist sporting a huge, architectural, green Mohican haircut. The owner of the bar and I struggled to communicate in pidgin German which elicited further mirth and when I left, he wouldn't let me pay for my drinks, which was just as well, as they would have cost a bomb!

The hustle and bustle of Istanbul, the largest city in Turkey, was something of a shock to the system. I must admit that for a while, I regretted leaving the peaceful coastal villages. The famous Grand Bazaar was something of a disappointment too, after the medieval souk of Damascus, but it was still fascinating. There were so many brightly illuminated displays of glittering gold and silver jewellery that it made my eyes hurt. It was very much a matter of hard selling, the dealers more aggressive and persistent than anywhere else I'd been. Later, a visit to the Blue Mosque proved to be awe-inspiring. It was an active mosque and got its name from the blue tiles decorating its interior. I also visited the Tokapi palace, the primary residence of the Ottoman Sultans for approximately four hundred years. It housed the largest concentration of gold and jewels I'd ever seen – I was bug-eyed!

Next, I crossed the Galata Bridge and walked alongside the river where fishermen sold their wares directly from their boats which bobbed up and down in the wash of bigger craft passing by. Some of them had open fires on deck to cook fresh mackerel. I tried some – delicious! The reward for climbing the Galata tower was a spectacular view looking out over the hazy cityscape of Istanbul, the gateway to the East. It was good to have the wind in my hair and to think about how many places there still were to visit, how much to see, to do, and to experience in this wonderful world. Later in the day, my wanderlust was fuelled further by conversations with travellers I'd met at the hostel where I was staying. We went out for a delicious Turkish meal together and were kept entertained by a jolly waiter who kept shouting out "Sheeeeeesh Kebab" and waving his enormous cooking knives at passers-by.

The next day started with a breakfast of Turkish honey with fresh locally made yoghurt - scrummy! I visited a barber and experienced a luxurious shave, expertly executed with a cut-throat razor. I then explored the Aya Sophia, an inspiring Byzantine building which was, in turn, once a church, then a mosque, and was now a museum. I continued to the Egyptian Bazaar as well as the Grand Bazaar. 'People watching' (both the stallholders and tourists) was the order of the day. Back at the hostel I chatted with a host of other travellers. The table in front of us piled higher and higher with the shells of salted pistachio nuts as the night progressed. It was good to meet people who were more adventurous than 'capital to capital' Inter-Railers. It was noticeable that many seemed to talk as much about their plans for forthcoming trips as they did about those they had already completed and their current one. In the afternoon I experienced another common facet of travel, the amazing coincidence. I met Simon Palgrave-Moore, a chap I was at school with when I was about ten and hadn't seen since! Quite encouraging that we still recognised one another!

In the evening, I joined Alexandra, whom I had met at the hostel, a stunning lively nineteen-year-old who was travelling around on her own,. We took a taxi to the train station and found seats with an Italian chap who was taking sixteen *Kilims* (prayer rugs) home to sell and a Spanish guy who lived in England. So began a remarkable journey. The night passed fairly quickly, eating and talking. It was frustrating to have to hang around for several hours just before dawn at the Turkish-Greek border, but good to have the opportunity to get out and stretch our legs. Watching spectacular gorges, mountains, and woods unfold before us made the long journey worthwhile. However, there was hassle in Thessaloniki. Apparently, there are usually a few carriages that go all the way from Istanbul to Athens, but for some reason this didn't happen and we had to change carriages at the border. We kept getting moved from one to another which resulted in our reservations no longer being valid. Eventually, we ended up in a cramped compartment full of Greek women shouting and arguing in shrill, piercing voices. Needless to say, we didn't get much sleep; in fact I spent quite a while seeking peace and quiet standing in the corridor. Alexandra and I were both bleary-eyed on arrival in Athens thirty-six gruelling hours after leaving Istanbul. We soon discovered that there was a ferry strike and this caused us both to change our plans. She headed off to Italy and I decided to go on to Delphi. We said our goodbyes and exchanged addresses, though, as is so common with many acquaintances made 'on the road', we never got in touch again.

I left my luggage at the station and strolled around Athens. The Acropolis was covered in scaffolding, seething with school children, and cost a bomb to visit, so I gave it a miss. Instead, I explored the surrounding site which was, in my humble opinion, not a patch on Ephesus. Later, I visited the Archaeological Museum where I especially admired the gold masks from Mycaenae. I sat outside in the sun for a while, watching the pretty yellow and black swallowtail butterflies flitting from one flower to the next. It was good to be free of time constraints and decisions that would affect others - the joy of solo travel!

I took a train to Levadia, but there was no sign of the bus to Delphi and I ended up paying way over the odds for a taxi. For a country so heavily dependent on foreign visitors, I found Greece to be sadly lacking in its service to tourists as far as travel information was concerned. Once I had booked into a hostel in Delphi, I went and found a cheap restaurant where I enjoyed a good *Moussaka* and got talking to an English couple who were on an adventurous walking holiday. They would camp in the middle of nowhere for a few days and then find a hostel to get cleaned up in before setting off into the wilds again.

The following day, I walked over to the ruins but decided that I was 'templed out', so I wandered through meadows of daisies and cool olive groves in the beautiful valley below Delphi instead. It was difficult to believe there were hordes of noisy sightseers less than a kilometre away. It was good to take time out, to stand and stare, just to enjoy being alive and under the sun. On the way back to the hostel, I had my first ice cream in ages and boy, was it good! Luckily, I managed to get a bus all the way back to Athens and eventually found a cheap place to sleep on a mattress on the floor of a large hall. I went out for a meal and a few beers with some lads I'd met at the hostel. They were okay, but a bit too much like rich kids travelling on their dad's dollars, 'trophy-ticking' places off lists, to elicit much respect or interest from me.

I was disappointed not to have enjoyed Athens more, celebrated, as it is, as the cradle of Western civilization and the birthplace of democracy, and as there was a ferry strike I decided to travel on by train and bus to Olympia. We passed through lush olive groves and pretty little streams sparkled as they coursed through rolling hills. It was a good time to be travelling, as many of the trees were full of blossom. In the evening, I met a couple of guys from the hostel I was staying in and we went out for a meal and a few glasses of ouzo - strong stuff! I didn't sleep too well as one of the people in my room was snoring, but what really pissed me off was that two Germans got up at 6 a.m., noisily packed all their gear, and then went back to bed again!

It was restful to be in the quiet ruins of Olympia, surrounded by cherry trees laden with pink flowers and to wonder at the antiquity of the place. It wasn't hard to believe that remains of food and burnt offerings had shown this to have been a site of religious activity for thousands of years, since the tenth century BC, in fact. The ruins themselves had been largely levelled by an earthquake in the third century. However, the size of some of the blocks that made up the columns gave a hint of the once monumental scale of the place. All too soon, however, my musings were shattered when coach-loads of visitors arrived.

It was a real thrill to see the original Olympic stadium, the site of two millennia of sporting history and in the museum, I marvelled at the Ancient Greek helmets, a mixture of artistic beauty and sinister menace. One of the most incredible exhibits was a huge rock weighing 165kg with an inscription saying that a great weightlifter had lifted it above his head - with one hand! This rather put the Highland Games weight lifters who'd impressed me so much on the Isle of Skye, severely in the shade!

From Olympia, I travelled by bus and ferry to Zakinthos on the island of Zante; it was the only ferry still running, thanks to the strike. I was with a young American, Wade, whom I had met in Olympia and it seemed to us that we were the only non-Greeks on the island. Apparently, it usually gets pretty busy in the summer, but we'd arrived well before the tourist season. We found a cheap, clean, little pension run by a friendly elderly couple who could speak about as much English as we could Greek i.e. none! We managed to communicate with gestures and many smiles. The next day, I phoned my workplace Exlog and got the usual: 'We don't know where you will be going, when you will be going, or for how long' response. They didn't need me for the next few days, so I was happy to carry on travelling.

Wade and I took a bus down to Vasilikos, on the relatively remote and rugged southern peninsula. It turned out to be not so much a village, but more a scatter of buildings. We walked down to the beach and scrambled round some low cliffs to the next bay where we found what remained of the Turtle Bay Beach Club. The *'Let's Go!'* guidebook description made this sound like a great place to chill out and party for a few days. However, we were five years too late! It was well and truly closed down. A pity! We decided to go back to Zakinthos where we planned to hire mopeds for the next day. After walking for about an hour, we managed to hitch a lift in the back of a pickup truck and were taken all the way 'home' to our pension. On our return, we received a hearty welcome from the elderly proprietors and Wade and I went out for a companiable pizza, beer, and the attendant bar stories.

Our plans to hire mopeds to explore the island were dashed the next day by torrential rain, so we decided to leave. However, down at the harbour we found a crowd of shouting ferry workers with a megaphone who were very obviously on strike. We dossed around for a while, returning to find a ferry which was to leave at mid-afternoon. On arrival in Killini on the mainland, we enquired about buses to Patras and were told there weren't any. However, to our relief, one arrived ten minutes later! We travelled to Patras together and then went our separate ways.

On the ferry to Brindisi on the Italian coast, I met a bunch of Australian travellers who were really good company. We shared beers and stories before having a surprisingly good night's sleep on deck. On arrival, all passengers with backpacks had to lay them out in customs for the sniffer dog to check. I wondered what would happen if the dog were to cock its leg over someone's pack. I took a train to Milan, together with two of the Australian crowd, Ray and Dave. It was absolutely jam-packed, so we had to sit on little fold-out seats in the corridor. Even though the train was obviously full, there was a constant stream of people battling up and down the corridors looking for non-existent empty seats – an absolute pain in the arse! We were tired and found the high-pitched incessant chatter of the other passengers hard to endure, especially when it carried on deep into the night. It felt as though the Istanbul-Athens nightmare of a train journey was being revisited! On arrival in Milan, I discovered that all the direct trains to Paris were full, so Ray, Dave, and I decided to go via Dortmund - wonderful to have the flexibility of Inter-Rail tickets! There was a four-hour wait in Dortmund, but luckily, there was a warm and reasonably comfortable waiting room where we wrote our diaries and swapped experiences before parting. Travelling is so full of goodbyes.

I got to Paris around 9.30 a.m. and dumped my luggage at the station. The Pompidou centre was my first goal, though I confess that I enjoyed 'people watching' there more than looking at the modern art! Later, I returned to my luggage and set off on yet another improbable journey. Four months earlier, I'd met Lynda at a New Year's party with SEAL Guides at the Edale Youth Hostel where I sometimes did some instructing work; climbing, caving, mountain biking, orienteering and hill walking. We had got on well. She'd mentioned then that she was going to work on a farm near Paris and casually suggested I could visit her, probably assuming that I never would – but I pride myself as being a man of my word, so off I went!

I took a train to Chantilly and managed to find the right bus to the tiny village of Gouvieux, no mean achievement with my pathetic schoolboy French. Somehow, I managed to find the farm and heard loudly bleating lambs as I approached. I followed the sound and there was Lynda and her boss, together with a fellow worker, Will. I just stood there quietly until she looked up and saw me; her face was the proverbial 'absolute picture'!

She was frantically busy tending to all the new born lambs, so I took a much-needed bath which did a miraculous job of revitalising me after seventy hours of travel. I slept in a hay barn, next door to a beautiful horse called Magic, a wonderful experience. Lynda brought me a bite of Pizza and had a good bitch about her employers who, according to her, seemed to be living in the Dark

Ages as far as treating their employees was concerned. Nevertheless, she managed to wangle a few days off and we decided to spend the weekend in Paris.

After getting a lift to Chantilly and having a mosey around, we arrived in Paris in search of cheap accommodation. It proved to be a long search, but I didn't mind as I was in Paris in the sunshine with a pretty girl who was great company and time just didn't matter. We ended up in the *Jardin des Tuileries* where we sat and talked and watched Parisians enjoying the open air and space. The following day, after a traditional French breakfast of coffee and *pain au chocolat*, we went back into Paris and found a cheap, grotty room with a warped wooden floor that was like a rough sea, but it had a certain *'Je ne sais quoi'* and we were just happy to be there. The afternoon was spent wandering around the big market at Port Clignancourt. Seeing so many beautiful clothes made me appreciate for the first time why women spend so much on them. In a carefree mood, we stopped for a *'Pomme d'amour'* (toffee apple!) and then continued our wanderings. On the way back to the Champs Elysees we stopped at one of the Metro stations and stood transfixed for an hour and a half as we watched, listened, and boogied to a superb group of buskers. They comprised four congo and bongo drummers, two guys rapping a rhythm with sticks against a wall, a guitarist, a gangly black male dancer, and a woman who conducted as she danced. There was a large crowd of maybe a hundred people. It was mesmerizing stuff, hypnotic without being boring and we couldn't help dancing to it. Eventually, the police came and moved them on, much to our disappointment as we could happily have stayed for hours. Both of us were practically speechless for a while afterwards, the rhythms had been so good, deep, and soul-stirring.

Later, we went to the cinema to see the mildly amusing *'Crimes of the Heart'* and in the evening we went out for a meal which I couldn't really afford, but I flashed the Amex card anyway. I'd never earned anywhere near the amount needed to qualify for the card, but I had had one from Exlog so I could get flights if I got stranded on a hitch. The next day we had a lazy morning and in the afternoon went to the cinema again, this time to see *'The Golden Child'* with Eddie Murphy which was pretty funny. Finally, we took the train back to Chantilly and enjoyed the pleasant four-mile walk back to Gouvieux. We sat in the hay barn eating Lynda's Easter eggs and then went for a walk down by the river, watching a beautiful pair of pure white swans gliding by.

The next morning, it was time to say goodbye after a happy few days and I set off with absolutely no French money and a full day of travel ahead. As luck would have it, I found a 10 Franc piece and bought a breakfast of baguette and bananas before getting onto a train to Rotterdam. Once in Rotterdam, I followed the instructions to an old school friend's address, but when I arrived I found that there was nobody in except for a blue budgie who was no help at all.

I decided to call it a day and headed for home. On the ferry, I took out my sleeping bag and shook out a flurry of straw from the hay barn before dossing down for a few hours of much needed kip. I'd planned to hitch back to Norfolk from Harwich, but when I found it was only £5 by train I took the easy option and whom should I meet walking home from Norwich station, but Nick Ashford, the guy I'd tried to visit in Rotterdam!

Five days later, I was heading back for another twenty-eight day hitch in the middle of the Syrian desert – arrgh!

After a couple of routine hitches in Syria and one in Turkey, I was sent on a short hitch to Tanzania followed by one in Kenya. I was flown out to the rig in a Cessna 404 which had had most of the seats taken out to make way for freight. As we flew out over the National Park near Nairobi I was enchanted to see ostriches, zebra, and gazelle. We landed surprisingly smoothly on a sandy runway and were instantly surrounded by a crowd of inquisitive local people who seemed to appear from nowhere. After unloading the plane, it was only a ten-minute drive to the site at Galula. Over the next few days, we prepared to move to a new location at Ivuna, 100km away. I met the Exlog guy I'd be working opposite - the legendary 'Crazy Richard'. He was a reasonable enough bloke, but rather eccentric. The American rig crew took the Mickey out of him unmercifully. He didn't have a home in Britain, just a P.O. box number, and spent most of his free time travelling around the countries where he worked.

The Amoco road to the Ivuna site was a badly rutted dirt track. Several of the trucks got stuck and took ages to get going again. At a river crossing, each vehicle was towed across by a bulldozer which took a couple of hours, so I went for a wander. The villages around were small, with little huts made from wattle and daub. There was no obvious game, though there were some beautiful bright blue-green birds that streaked by as flashes of metallic colour and there was a large tree full of monkeys that peered down at me in a highly comical and very nosey manner. Once the river had been crossed, we stopped at the next village and bought a pig to barbecue the following night. While we were there, we met two gorgeous Masai girls who stood very straight and proud. They both had babies, though they only looked about fifteen or sixteen.

The rig site was dusty and inhabited by swarms of blood-hungry mosquitoes. Unfortunately, the kitchen was the last unit to arrive, so food was pretty basic to begin with. The accommodation was even worse than in Syria. On the first night, there was no room for me, so I slept under a mozzie net in the cook's tent. There was no hot water in the shower, no light, and the lavatory door had to be lifted into place. One day we even ran out of water. For the entire two weeks I was on site, I never felt really clean and the mozzies were awful at night. However, the food improved, especially the fresh tropical fruits which included mango and star fruit. I had to work pretty hard on this hitch, as the entire 2,000m borehole had to be drilled in just less than two weeks.

On the way out of Tanzania, we were delayed at Kilimanjaro airport where the official in charge didn't want us to leave. It was something to do with work permits, I think, but in the end a few dollars changed hands and this sorted out the problem.

My first week in Kenya was spent having a great time on standby in Nairobi. I was with Crazy Richard again and an Exlog engineer called John with whom I got on very well. I spent most of the first day looking around the colourful markets and ended up buying an attractive batik for myself, as well as a selection of bronze and ebony bangles to take back as presents for my friends.

Having sorted out a hire car, we visited the Nairobi National Park which proved to be a lot better than expected. Richard had been several times before and reckoned that we were exceptionally lucky to see so much. We saw giraffe, zebra, waterbuck, water buffalo, impala, Thompson's gazelle, warthog, and an adult rhino with its young. At the 'hippo pool' we could leave the car and so we dawdled along next to the creek. There we saw a few hippos, some black faced vervet monkeys, baboons, and some glorious brightly-coloured birds. The fabulous sights were accompanied by fantastic sounds, one insect sounded for all the world like an electric razor. Later, we stopped at a lookout to view the plains below and gazed out at majestic eagles soaring on the thermals.

The highlight of the day for me was spotting a cheetah about 20m from the car. We stopped and watched spellbound as the elegant cat casually loped off. At one water-hole there were hundreds of zebra, water buck, and water buffalo, as well as beautiful white egrets, sacred ibis, and a flock of Marabou storks looking just like ugly old men with their shoulders hunched. It was often possible to get very close to the game, then stop, switch off the engine, and spend twenty minutes or so just watching. At one point, we had to stop for a roadblock of dozing water buffalo and wait for them to get off the road. Inevitably, I got carried away with the camera; I think I took about forty photos.

The car hire was a two-day deal, so on the second day we headed towards Mount Kenya. On the way, we stopped at Karatina to explore the wonderful market. It was vibrant, effervescent with activity and blazing with colour. After some route-finding difficulties we left the main road and drove 15km along a dirt track to Mountain Lodge, near Mount Kenya. It was worth the effort and we spent a couple of hours watching game from the balcony. Then we decided to try to get to Tree Tops game lodge. This proved to be a mistake as it took us so long to find, only to be told that, as we weren't an organized tour booked through agents in Nairobi, we couldn't gain entry. However, simply driving there and then back to Nairobi was a pleasure in itself.

Back at the hotel I suddenly fell ill; just as I left my room to go out for a meal with Richard and John I collapsed. I went straight to bed and within ten minutes I was shivering uncontrollably with a high fever. I felt hot and cold, sweated buckets, had stomach cramps, and spent a lot of time wondering which end to direct towards the toilet! I was delirious and hallucinating for most of the night, which was pretty scary. I felt as though the bed were a small raft on a rough sea and I was constantly about to be tipped off. I think it was a bad dose of food poisoning. Luckily, I felt okay again by the following evening, thanks to copious rehydration drinks.

The hotel Exlog had booked was very noisy and too hot at night, so we moved to another further from the city centre where it was quieter and there was a swimming pool. Next to our new hotel, there was a bar called Buffalo Bill's, complete with saddles on posts which served as stools at the bar. There seemed to be a measure of trade going on between a number of 'ladies of the night' and white businessmen. The food wasn't brilliant, but the beer was good. I left the bar and whiled away a few hours at the famous Thorn Tree Cafe, a popular place for travellers to meet and leave notes for each other.　They also made a particularly good bacon, lettuce, and tomato sandwich.　One afternoon, John and I went to see a two-hour show of traditional dance and music.　The drumming was especially good and enjoyably hypnotic.　It was amazing how the musicians managed to maintain such a strong rhythm even when they were leaping about with extraordinary energy.　The finale was performed by a team of acrobats including one guy who did a limbo under a pole balanced between two normal-sized Coca Cola bottles!

We had a couple of lazy days lounging by the pool and going for leisurely walks in the peace and quiet of the Nairobi arboretum, a haven of calm in a frantic city.　On our last day of standby, we hired a car again and drove to Lake Navasha where we saw good game and one exceptionally beautiful longhaired black and white Columbus monkey.　There were thousands of flamingos which looked rather pale close up, though when a flock of them flew off together it looked like a great pink cloud.　We drove a short distance across the mudflats to get a closer look and very nearly managed to get the car stuck.　Later, when we were driving through one of the more forested parts of the park, a big owl flew low in front of the car, carrying a small monkey. This was a spectacular end to our visit.

The flight to the rig site gave us a superb view of Mount Kenya. The windows had a movable Polaroid plate which made some of the lakes and rivers appear in spectacular shades of metallic green, emerald, turquoise, and blue.　As we landed on the dusty airstrip, ostrich and gazelle fled into the bush.　Apparently, landing had been delayed in the past because of a lion on the airstrip!　When we arrived at the site near Kargi, we found that the facilities were pretty good, even if it was in the middle of nowhere and we had to wait a couple of days before there was any air conditioning. The night sky was breathtaking – I'd never seen so many exquisitely brilliant stars.

One day, ragged bunting was strung up in preparation for a visit by President Moi, who arrived with an entourage of about fifty people. Crazy Richard nearly drove me up the wall with his tidying and polishing and seemed quite put out when the president didn't even come into our unit. He was soon mollified, however, when, before the drilling got started, he and I joined the camp boss to visit Khargi. We drove cross-country through the scrub which was good fun and quite exciting. The village looked pretty desolate, but the people all seemed very happy. The camp boss was recruiting a couple of extra crew for the rig, including a sample catcher for us. The sample catcher would retrieve samples of rock cuttings that were retained by the shale shakers – wire mesh screens through which the drilling mud passed. It was interesting to meet the people and listen to the music of their voices as they chatted in the shade. Most were fairly skinny, though they all seemed pretty healthy. There were a couple of Masai men in full regalia who appeared to be better nourished. Almost all of the men had pierced ears with large holes (1-2cm) and large weighted earrings. They all carried sticks about 1.5m long and a few had spears. Everyone wore sandals made from old car tyres. There was a lot of hand shaking and saying '*Jambo*' ('Hello' in Swahili) and everyone seemed hugely friendly.

I worked on the rig for a couple of weeks until I reached my last twelve-hour tour. I'd phoned the Exlog office on 4th January and quit. I had had a mixed career with the company. On the plus side I have to admit that for much of the time I had had a cushy job, in the sense that I was able to occupy 'logging position number one' for extended periods (i.e. with my feet up). I was also able to travel extensively. On the minus side though, the job was not doing me any good either socially or spiritually; the unpredictability and itinerant nature of the work made it often a lonely existence for someone as gregarious as I am and I felt I should leave while I was ahead.

Luckily, I had managed to save a few thousand pounds so I set off with plans to go travelling for five or six months before returning to the UK to do a teacher training course at Newcastle University.

Chapter 4 HIMALAYAN HIGHLIGHTS

Trekking and white-water rafting in Nepal

I flew on Valentine's Day 1988, as a gesture towards a new beginning, hoping at last, to lay to rest the ending of my relationship with Bridget two and a half years earlier. I'd decided it was time to move on. The Air India flight to Kathmandu was pretty horrendous, as I'd been sick on the plane. There was a twelve and a half hour delay at Bombay (later to become Mumbai) airport where there were no seats to lie down. When we arrived in Delhi, there was some bother with Royal Nepal Airline which delayed my departure and eventually, by the skin of my teeth, I made it onto the last flight to Kathmandu. When finally, I arrived, I overheard an English voice saying that he wanted a taxi into town. I asked if he'd be willing to share with me. This was how I met Alistair and Lise. We squeezed into a battered vehicle and bounced our way through the pot-holed streets to their hotel. This proved to be exorbitantly expensive, so we had a look around the corner and found a more acceptable place to stay for a fraction of the price (55 Rupees a night - about £1.35).

It was marvellous to step out into the streets of the city the next morning, having arrived in the dark and therefore being largely unaware of the delights that awaited me. It was like stepping back into another era. I was surprised by how few tourists there were, having imagined Kathmandu to be a sort of crowded hippy Mecca. I later found out that this was because I'd arrived before the tourist season had begun; a few weeks later and the place would have been teeming. It was easy to hire a beaten-up old push-bike and spend most of the day entertaining myself, stumbling across good places to browse or have a bite to eat. I found that *'Momos'* were appetizing - little hot pastries stuffed with meat. In the midst of a plethora of exotic foods and drinks, there were piles of crates of empty Coca Cola bottles, a sure sign that tourism had been established. The streets were crowded with people, bikes, and dogs. Many rickshaw drivers were plying their trade. I saw one skeletal old man improbably propelling an enormously fat young American tourist. In some of the backstreets, children held a string across the track as tourists tried to pass and in my case attempted, in vain, to muster a toll. When visiting one of the many temples, a little boy clung to my leg, shouting 'One Rupee?' much to the amusement of some passing Japanese tourists. The temples, with their brilliant whitewashed walls and gilded domes, were adorned with huge painted sleepy-looking eyes that seemed to watch you as you passed.

Back in central Kathmandu, I sorted out a trekking permit for Langtang; Alistair and Lise spent hours trying to organise a guide. They just didn't seem to get on terribly well and I wasn't surprised when Lise finally explained the situation. She had been planning to travel with her friend, Charlotte, who had had to delay her departure by a couple of weeks; Charlotte then put Lise in touch with Alistair. I soon decided that she couldn't have been a very perceptive friend .

After a day recovering from the journey to Kathmandu, I set off for the Trisuli Bazaar with Lise, Alistair, and their guide, Anbapu. The bus was crowded, though we did manage to get seats. However, the Nepali buses are built for Nepalis, who tend to be fairly short of stature, so there wasn't much headroom for us. It wasn't as bad as I had anticipated, but Alistair was unhappy and matters came to a head when someone threw up on his leg! Once we'd arrived, Anbapu hired a porter called Jagind for Alistair and Lise and having missed the last bus to Dunche, we decided to start trekking from Trisuli rather than waiting for the first bus the next morning.

Suitably fortified with a giant bowl of vegetable chow mein we started out. It was great to be trekking at last. Anbapu proved his worth by guiding us through a maze of tiny tracks rather than just slogging along the dirt road. Even at this end of the trail, near to Trisuli, I was impressed by the absence of tourists and we only saw two other trekkers that day. I was still finding it difficult to believe I was really in Nepal after months of anticipation. The people were super-friendly, with all the children shouting a chorus of '*Namaste*' ('Hello'), wherever we went. It was good not to hear the cries of 'One Rupee?' so common in the city. Walking in the dark for the last hour, we finally arrived at the Kahotse Hotel which was little more than a hut with candlelight and five hard beds, but we were so tired that it felt like a palace.

The following day was hot and sunny and we took the steep winding dirt track up to Dunche. On the trail we met up with Morden, a Norwegian, and Doug, an Alaskan and walked and chatted with them for some time. As there was something of a communication difficulty with Alistair, I kept my distance. In Dunche we stayed at a place with electric light and a bar, complete with loud music; it was obviously a regular tourist stop so I was glad to leave the next morning. Breakfast was a huge bowl of porridge and some black tea. The day's walk involved much steep climbing, often with steps cut into the more challenging sections. It was good to get off the dirt road and onto the smaller trails, especially when they were carpeted with fragrant pine needles and fringed with bamboo. There were plenty of drink stops throughout the day, the Coca Cola getting more expensive the higher we went. This wasn't surprising when you realise that all supplies are carried in by porters. I soon decided to stick with hot lemon which was a lot cheaper and just as refreshing.

We passed quite a few people carrying huge loads (up to 45kg!) in woven baskets *'doko'* slung on tumplines *'namlo'* – a strap which runs underneath the basket and over the crown of the head, which bears most of the weight. These stocky little people put us to shame; we were carrying state-of-the-art rucksacks and wearing the best boots and clothing modern technology had to offer, while these guys kept up a brisk steady pace with either bare feet or battered plimsolls. 'Walking bushes' often lumbered past. They turned out to be people carrying hefty loads of leaves (animal fodder), again on tumplines. The comical view from behind was a mass of foliage with a pair of feet sticking out at the bottom.

I spent quite a lot of time walking a short way in front of, or behind the others, trying to soak up the immensity and unbelievable beauty of my surroundings - the sheer scale of the mountains was hard to comprehend. At Sybaru we had a meal of vegetables and rice with good Tibetan bread and honey. The bread was cooked in an oven built from clay and fed sparingly with precious firewood. Firewood was in increasingly short supply in this region, especially now that trekking was booming and the local population growing. This was leading to serious deforestation in some areas and causing soil erosion locally, as well as causing flooding as far away as Bangladesh. We heard that due to a Tibetan Buddhist festival, the only lodge that we could have reached that afternoon would have been closed, so we stayed in Sybaru. In the evening I sampled some *chang* (Nepali beer), which tasted like alcohol in stew juice. Later, I sat out on the balcony and wrote my diary, while looking out from the village over an intricate patchwork of carefully tended small terraced fields to the towering mountains beyond. The intensely farmed terraces were an admirable achievement of agriculture and engineering that allowed the people living in these remote valleys to utilise every last inch of cultivatable land available. The twelve-year-old boy who lived in the lodge where we were staying was a real comedian; he showed me a huge spider and told me it was called a *'Wong-Wong'*. I am pretty sure that's not what it was called, but he seemed to find it hilarious, so after that I kept calling him Wong-Wong, much to the amusement of his mother.

The trail above Sybaru was superb. At one point our route involved gingerly walking a new path across an enormous landslide that had moved blocks the size of houses. But for the most part, it was verdant high altitude jungle with numerous cheese plants and hanging mosses and the occasional glimpse of monkeys with cheeky black faces surrounded by a ruff of white fur. Our pace was relaxed and we stopped at a couple of tea-houses along the way. After some delicious pancakes at the *Bamboo Lodge* I had a rather invigorating shave in the freezing snowmelt river. Some of the lodge signs had endearing misspellings such as 'Welcome to hotel Bridge side lovely, fooding and lodging available here', 'Tibetian Hotel and Lodge, here is come to many peoples'. However, the best entertainment was provided by the menus with 'Porriege with musily', 'hot drinki chocolat', 'pencacks', and my favourite – 'bowld eggs'.

Later, I got a 'second wind' and felt charged with adrenalin as I walked the last hour or so of the trail on my own. It felt great, a real 'natural high'. *The Riverside Lodge*, a solitary building in a quiet spot next to the river, was a welcome sight at the end of the day. Later, the others joined me and we drank vegetable soup followed by a double egg omelette with potatoes, onions, and cheese, topped off by a drink of hot lemon. It doesn't take long on the trail to realise that the most avidly discussed topics amongst travellers are a) food and b) bowel movements - thankfully, so far I seemed to be doing pretty well on both counts! There were three Tibetans at the lodge that night: a man who spoke very good English, a woman, and a young boy who played a drum that was similar to an Irish 'Bodran' (a sideways drum like a giant tambourine that's hit with a stick). We laughed a lot together during the evening and went off to bed in high spirits.

I was up and off early the next morning, greeted by fantastic views enhanced by a fairly heavy snowfall the previous night. Later, I met up with Lise and we walked together for a while. It was good to be with someone who didn't feel obliged to chatter constantly and who was content to walk for much of the time in companionable silence. As the day went on, the scenery became more spectacular with towering peaks on every side. Frequently we came upon yaks, huge lumbering beasts covered in thick fur with gently tinkling bells around their necks. We passed a number of *Mani* Prayer walls, especially in the area around Langtang. These were constructed from carved stone tablets, many with the inscription *'Om Mani Padme Hum'* which, roughly translated, means 'Hail to the jewel in the lotus' the flower Buddhists see as a symbol of purity and beauty being able to emerge from mud. Most of the prayer walls were covered in carefully carved script, though some were decorated with intricate mandalas and Buddha-like figures. According to Buddhist doctrine, the walls should be passed from the left side in the clockwise direction of the revolution of the earth and the universe.

Trekkers returning to Dhunche reported that the lodge at Kyanchin was closed, but we carried on walking anyway and arrived at around five in the evening. Sheltering in one of the empty huts, we brewed up coffee and pitched the small dome tent that Lise and Alistair had hired. When darkness fell, we managed to get a good fire going and cooked a reasonable meal of noodles and soup before sitting around the campfire to talk for hours. It was difficult to sleep as we had all developed irritating coughs and at an altitude of about 5,000m it was difficult to breathe evenly. I was comfortable in my sleeping bag, but Lise and Alistair hardly slept because they were so cold; after all, it was minus10°C.

Early the next morning, we set off for Yala peak. We were awe-struck by the views, but it was hard going due to the steep terrain and high altitude. The snow cover was pretty thin, about 6 -10cm, but when we got to the cirque (an armchair shaped hollow at the head of the valley, formed by glacial erosion) about 500m below the peak, we got into a flattish boulder field with much deeper snow which made strenuous going and slowed us down. After sinking up to my waist several times, I soon announced that I wasn't suitably equipped as I only had lightweight fabric boots and no ice axe, so I turned back, especially as the weather also looked threatening. Doug and Lise were quick to agree and we started a speedy descent. Alistair, however, was determined to go on, despite our advice and the fact that we were far more experienced than he was. In my opinion, he was foolhardy to continue on his own with inadequate gear, bad weather, and no rescue services.

The rest of us got down in a couple of hours and huddled around a fire, drinking coffee and fixing something to eat. Alistair's decision had meant that there was no way we could leave and we had to wait for him to return. He came back three and a half hours later with a big grin asking 'Were you worried?' and claiming 'All's well that ends well'. These comments were met with a stony silence. While he was packing up his gear, Doug, Lise, and I made a speedy descent to Langtang where all the lodges were full. However, we managed to negotiate the use of a small shed for five Rupees (about 10p) a head. Before long, we had lit a fire and as we had previously bought food from one of the lodges, we were able to prepare a pretty good, albeit rather smoky, meal.

The next morning I decided that it was time to travel on my own again. I felt bad about leaving Lise alone with Alistair, Anbapu, and Jagind, but I felt I just had to get away. It was the right decision and for the first couple of hours I appreciated being alone while walking on virgin snow in a muffled silence only occasionally broken by the mellow music of yak bells. I stopped at a lodge below Ghore Tabela for a breakfast omelette and a few drinks of hot lemon. After a brief chat with three Spanish hippy types, I was off on my own again, down through the woods, melting snow plopping onto me from the branches above. The snow slowed me down quite a bit, especially when I got lower where it had turned to slush; my feet were soaked! It was incredible to see so many stark contrasts in the vegetation and scenery as I descended throughout the day. Before long, I had left the snow behind and was back amongst the cheese plants and ferns. Eventually, I reached Sybaru at around five, very tired, but happy after a hard, but satisfying day. Back at the *Yak Lodge* I had more joking with 'Wong-Wong' and chatted with a young Israeli couple while we dried out our boots by the hearth.

After breakfast, I was off again, dawdling along in the sunshine, enjoying the return journey as much as the climb. In Dunche I stayed at the *Hotel Langtang View*, where I met Lise, Alistair, Anbapu and Jagind again. We had a jovial evening. However, I felt ill during the night and went outside to throw up - it was like emptying a bucket! The next morning, I felt pretty queasy and couldn't face much breakfast. Thankfully, the bus journey back to Trisuli didn't take too long and although I didn't feel too ill, my stomach felt and sounded like a coffee percolator. The five-hour bus ride to Kathmandu was something to be endured, and wasn't made easier by a little brat tunelessly blowing into a harmonica for the whole trip. You can tell I was still feeling somewhat fragile, as normally I'd probably have found him cute. Back in Kathmandu, I managed to get the last room in the Tuckche Peak hotel and had a very good night's sleep - boy, did I need it!

The next morning I still felt rather weak, but managed a breakfast of muesli, fruit, and some delicious orange juice. Although I'd begun to feel a lot better in myself, I continued to suffer from the affliction that led to me spending more time than I would have liked in the confines of Nepalese toilets. However, this didn't stop me from enjoying a gentle walk in the Durbar Square area of Kathmandu. I got an enormous fright when Morden, the Norwegian I'd met days earlier on the trip to Dunche, sneaked up as I was dawdling along in a daydream and leapt out at me brandishing a large *Khukri* (Ghurka knife). Not a good idea, considering my condition at the time - he almost scared the shit out of me - or what was left! It was good to loiter in the Durbar Square watching tourists haggling and the locals enthusiastically playing a game which resembled a large-scale 'shove ha'penny'. In the evening, I went out to a restaurant with Lise, Doug, and Morden, but having been ill, I had no appetite. I didn't sleep too well, getting up every two or three hours and I still felt pretty feeble for the next two days. I didn't bother with anti-diarrhoea pills – I suspected they would just keep the bugs in me for longer. I drank a lot of bottled drinks and had a few 'Diarolyte' rehydration sachets. This seemed to do the trick. I got off pretty lightly really; in the next five months of travelling in India (a month) and Africa (four months) I only ever got traveller's diarrhoea again once, and that was for just twenty-four hours – too much information!

Once I had recovered, I spent a great day exploring the Patan district with Lise. We visited the Durbar Square again, bustling with street vendors selling everything from poles bristling with little wooden whistles to fierce-looking knives. In the afternoon, I bought a couple of attractive embroidered T-shirts which Lise kindly offered to take home for me. In the evening, I met John Edlin, later to be known as J.K. or Kiwi John. He 'd been in the army, but had had to leave after a bad accident on a 'flying fox', i.e. a zip wire. I was to join him and others for the next five months, travelling with the company *Encounter Overland,* a truck-based group which specialized in 'off the beaten track' travelling. We went out for a meal together and discovered that, luckily for both of us, we got along really well.

The next morning John and I met up with Lizzy, a girl who worked in the *Encounter Overland* offices back in London. We hired bikes and pedalled off to Bhaktapur, following dusty tracks lined with weeds, *Cannabis sativa* among them. It was hot and I was glad to have sunglasses to keep out the dust as much as the sun. After about an hour, we reached our destination and found a cafe where we quenched our thirst with Fantas - Lizzy had three in quick succession. There were more brick-built houses and paved roads there than in Kathmandu and it was cleaner too. The whole atmosphere seemed more relaxed and there were fewer tourists and beggars. In the afternoon we visited the Bodnanth Stupa which was adorned with hundreds of fluttering brightly-coloured prayer flags. Throughout the day, we had to dodge water bombs, part of another religious festival enjoyed by adults and children alike. John and I searched out *Nirvana's*, an American-style ice-cream parlour where we spoiled ourselves with two ice creams each. Thankfully, my stomach had now completely recovered, though I still had a pretty bad 'trekkers cough' from all those evenings in smoky huts.

After enjoying a huge breakfast at the *Kathmandu Guest House*, John and I boarded a truck with four others to go on an Encounter Overland white-water rafting trip with our Swedish guide Anders. The other four trekkers were an Austrian carpenter, living in Germany called Reinhart, a Swiss physiotherapist called Baerbel, and an Australian couple, Phil (a policeman) and his wife, Jo. After a veritable bombardment with water and dye bombs, we finally got the raft inflated and launched at Managhat. It was heavenly drifting down the Trisuli River in the warmth of the afternoon sun. This laid-back calm was interspersed from time to time with exhilarating, adrenalin-inducing rapids. The biggest of the day was *Tin-Davi*. When Anders yelled 'High side!' we all had to hurl ourselves at the topside of the raft to prevent it overturning in the swirling white water. The scenery was exquisite and we camped on a glistening beach of silvery white mica. The raft was set up as a lean-to and we also erected ingeniously designed tents which incorporated paddles as poles and had pockets for stones instead of using pegs.

By evening, we were ready for an excellent meal of steak in a spicy garlic and ginger sauce with boiled potatoes and steamed vegetables. Anders impressed us all by producing a gorgeous banana cake pudding, which really topped off the meal. Afterwards, we all got stuck into some good Khukri rum. Reinhardt, ever the comedian, when asked to help with the washing-up replied with 'I think I must make a telephone call to my mother'. Hmmm, we were in the middle of nowhere and many miles from the nearest telephone! An enormous, bright, full moon rose dramatically in the sky, a lone tree starkly silhouetted in front of it. We slowly became quiet and gazed at the silvery scene. Suddenly, a procession of locals came slowly down to the river carrying a body on a litter. It was burnt on a funeral pyre under the light of the full moon. Altogether, an other-worldly experience.

The next day, I was up by half past seven. The view from my sleeping bag was glorious. I had slept out under the boat lean-to rather than in a tent as I'd wanted to do some star-gazing. After a big breakfast, we eventually set off just before ten feeling happy and relaxed. However, the rapids on that day were far from relaxing. The best was called *Upset* and involved really good white-knuckle paddling. During the heat of the afternoon, it was simply great to be able to roll off the back of the raft and cool down in a splash. Our campsite was on a beach next to *Swimmers Rapid* which was a blast; you just held your legs up high and got whisked along in the middle of the white water. It was so much fun I did it twice.

A group of pretty little girls from a local village came down to the beach to play next to our camp. They had enormous brown eyes, wide pearly white grins, and endearing giggles - a joy to behold! Supper was a good stodgy cauliflower cheese and Anders put together a wicked Khukri rum punch again which led to a great evening of laughter and storytelling. Reinhardt, in particular, was a natural funster. Everywhere he went he just had to say 'I think here there may be snakes' and we were all in stitches. This became a sentence John and I adopted for the rest of the trip - the joke being, of course, that there are no snakes in Nepal.

We were all a bit sluggish the morning after the night before, thanks to the devastating effects of Anders's punch. However, we woke up once we got stuck into a few rapids. The biggest rapid on that day was the appropriately named *Motherf*cker*, which was especially good because the direction of the eddies meant that you could run it again and again. Our last rapid was *Pinball* which was also great fun. Finally we stopped at Mughling where we had to pack the raft into the *Encounter Overland* truck and say our goodbyes (though we'd be meeting up with Phil and Jo again later).

John and I were off on a five-day trek from Pokhara through Buhmdi, Panchase Lekh, Kaare, Sarngkot, and back to Pokhara. We took a bus to Chitwan. It was packed and although I eventually got a seat, I effectively ended up with three Nepalis sitting on my lap. We almost met with disaster when we got to the bus park as the driver tried to take the turn 10m too early and we nearly plunged down a 3m drop – scary!

On the campsite next to the lake we set up with another *Encounter Overland* group who were on a nine-week overland trip to Cairo. We had an evening of drinking, chat, and much hilarity thanks mainly to Reinhardt's antics. After the luxury of tea while still in our sleeping bags, John and I were up by six and set off on a five-day trek, accompanied by a porter, a cook, and a guide. We'd booked the trek as part of the rafting package, but didn't realise that there'd be just the two of us. If we'd known this, we'd rather have done a longer rafting trip or just gone trekking together without the porter, cook, and guide. However, the arrangements had been made and we enjoyed the benefit of not having to carry all our gear; neither did we have the hassle of arranging food and accommodation, so we accepted the situation and enjoyed it.

After a short boat ride across the lake, we made an easy climb up through woods to the terraced hillsides. It was pretty easy going. After a long and lazy lunch stop, we continued walking to our campsite near Bhumdi. While John and I sat in the shade of a tree, a couple of very timid small local girls came up and watched us. There was no 'One Rupee?' or 'One Pen?'. They were quiet and shy. I showed them the photos of my parents, brothers, and sister that I always take travelling with me. This proved to be a great success and aroused animated interest. A short while later, some older girls came along and I was soon submerged in a crowd all eager to see the pictures. I was really glad I'd brought them as they acted as a universal icebreaker. After night when sleep was interrupted by an incredible storm with hailstones the size of marbles (it was like being under fire and they hurt), it was well worth being up really early to enjoy the glorious view of Machhepuchre and the Annapurnas, enormous peaks standing proud, like islands above the early morning mist lingering in the valleys due to a temperature inversion. Our day was one of leisurely walking on narrow winding trails through rhododendrons heavy with seductive red blooms. We were enchanted by the melodious birdsong and it was great occasionally to come across happy smiling children shouting 'Hello, Bye, Bye' instead of begging.

After camping in the backyard of a house just below Panchase Lekh, we climbed to a view point at dawn to watch the sunrise over the Annapurnas – an unforgettable experience. It took a few hours to walk down to Kaare where we saw the first trekkers since leaving Pokhara. It was a sure sign that we'd chosen a good route. We slaked our thirst with a couple of cold Fantas after three days of smoky water. The houses in this village were different to the timber buildings roofed with wooden tiles weighed down with stones that I'd seen in the Langtang valley. Here, they were stone-built with slate-tiled roofs and there was a paved main street. Our campsite was enveloped in cloud when we got up the next morning, but luckily the tent had weathered the torrential downpour that had raged for most of the night. The day's walk along the ridge from Kaare to Sarangkot was leisurely, interrupted by the occasional doze in the sun and the odd Fanta stop.

The dawn view from Sarangkot was another belter - the mountains here really were something else! As we set off, a little group of tiny schoolgirls walked ahead of us, all wearing their school uniform, with their hair in bunches tied with cute little red bows. After following a steep track for a couple of hours to get back down to Pokhara, I had a much needed shower and general scrub up. John took great pleasure in a cut-throat razor shave and also got what he reckoned was an excellent shoulder and neck massage. A short walk led us to the discovery of a really good rooftop cafe with a mouth-watering collection of cakes which were very welcome after a few days of *dal bhat* a traditional Nepali meal consisting of steamed rice cooked lentil soup dal, and *pulgobi* (cauliflower) with far too much coriander for my digestion. I swear the cook's brother had a cauliflower and coriander farm! I haven't been able to tolerate much coriander since.

Finally, we left Pokhara and set off south to spend a couple of days in Chitwan National Park. On one early morning jungle walk, we were lucky enough to see eight white rhino - really big brutes, resplendent in their prehistoric armour. In the afternoon, I had the hilarious pleasure of helping to bathe a female elephant in the river. Her rough skin was coated in sun-dried mud and sprouted thick black hairs which felt like stiff wire. It was enormous fun riding her and then leaping off as she rolled over - there was no way I wanted to get squashed! At one point, she was carrying five of us as though we weren't even there. This colossal creature was a gentle playful giant, who delighted in squirting us with water sprayed accurately from her dextrous trunk.

Chapter 5 A ROUNDABOUT ROUTE TO BOMBAY

Nepal to Bombay overland

After an excellent month of trekking and white-water rafting, I headed south into India. I was surprised by how different India was to Nepal; I found it a much more intense experience altogether. The poverty was stark and the senses were constantly bombarded with unfamiliar and exotic sights, sounds, and smells.

Again, I was with an Encounter Overland group, travelling in a Bedford Blitz British army truck. Our driver was Chris, a Yorkshireman. John and I got on very well with him and ended up being his 'trailer packers'. Phil and Jo, the Australian couple with whom we'd been white-water rafting, rejoined us and there were two new Aussies – Fran and Sue. Quite a few Canadians had joined us as well - another Sue and her husband Rick, Diana who was a nurse, and Ted, a waiter.

Mercifully, the border crossing at Sanahli was not too slow, taking about two and a half hours during which we were entertained by the antics of a couple of persistent Nepali boys trying to sell us luke-warm Coca-Colas and Fantas. It was a long drive to Varanasi (known to many who have visited it as 'Verynasty'). The flat landscape was a sea of cornfields, often dotted with heads bobbing up and down as people weeded or cut the crop by hand. Even in the middle of nowhere, the road seemed to be intermittently lined with squatting peasants.

I got up at a quarter past five the next morning as the sun was rising – a visual treat. My plan was to visit the *Ghats* (steps leading down to the River Ganges). It was a wonderful experience to drift along in a boat, slipping through wispy clouds of mist, watching swimmers and people washing themselves as well as dhobi *wallahs* (laundrymen) washing clothes by slapping them onto the rocks. There were many beautiful old *dhows* (sailing boats) that could have come straight from a tale from the Arabian Nights. I watched with sad fascination as the body of a small child, wrapped in white cloth and weighted with a heavy stone, was carried down to a boat, ready to be floated out onto the sacred river. Further along the shore, small children played amongst the ashes of recent cremations - life and death are never far apart in India.

The Monkey Temple was interesting and its comical chattering furry occupants were captivating. The stallholders selling brightly-coloured flowers to visitors, provided a glorious subject for photography. Later in the day, a snake charmer visited the campsite and put on a pretty good display which included his wrapping an enormous python around my shoulders! In the early evening, I went to the Clark Hotel for a good relaxing dip in the pool, though the ultimate indulgence was the most incredible massage I have ever experienced. It only cost £1 but was worth many times that sum and I felt as though I had no bones left - I was helplessly relaxed, blissfully happy, and absolutely immobile.

From Varanasi we had a long drive to a bleak spot in the middle of the Panna wilderness on the Deccan Plateau. It was relaxing listening to Pink Floyd on my Walkman as the miles rolled by. When we stopped for lunch, we immediately drew a huge crowd. The people watched us intently, as though they'd never seen anyone eat before. Chris, our driver, crouched down and smiled at a little boy who promptly burst into tears! In the evening, it was good to enjoy a strong rum punch, though we sobered up pretty quickly when we found scorpions scurrying around, especially as we were only camping under flysheets.

A welcome break from the searing dry heat the next day was a stop at a waterfall at Pandama; though the waterfall was not much more than a trickle at that time of year, the deep pool below was excellent for swimming and provided us with an opportunity to try the traditional 'Dhobi Wallah' technique of washing clothes by wetting them and then beating them on the rocks.

Visiting the temples at Khajuraho was an enlightening experience for those used to the staid, reserved nature of most western religious practice. I didn't find the architecture particularly attractive, but the carvings that adorned them more than made up for that. They were simultaneously beautiful, interesting, and erotic. Our guide was unwittingly amusing, treating us to gems such as 'Here for your kind information we can see that sex is going on'. He was also good at pointing out small details we'd never have noticed without him. An example was the representation of a group of large serious-faced elephants standing on their victims' heads, with one elephant in the corner smiling while his victim escaped. It was not until you looked very closely that you could see why he was smiling - in the corner 'sex was going on'!

That night we set up camp next to the Haripura Dam. It had been a scorching day, up to 40°C, so we lay down under our mozzie nets and went to sleep counting shooting stars instead of sheep. The next day was a long drive to Agra. Our lunch stop was in the path of a flock of about a hundred goats that simply walked right on through our campsite as we ate. In the evening, one of our number, Canadian Sue, complained that she thought she had something in her eye. She certainly had; a mosquito had bitten her on the eyelid a couple of times and later Diane, a nurse, managed to extract eleven tiny larvae - not for the squeamish! I was amazed at the attitude of her boyfriend, whose main concern seemed to be the possibility of medical expenses, rather than any thought of the patient's discomfort or fear.

It was worth getting up before dawn to reach the Taj Mahal early enough to watch the sun rise. This was an experience that will stay with me forever. It was, without doubt, the most beautiful man-made structure I'd ever seen, the marble glowing with subtle hues as it was bathed by the golden sunlight - even the Pearly Gates of Heaven would have paled into insignificance after the magnificence of the Taj. After breakfast, we returned for an excellent guided tour. The noise inside the main dome was deafening and extraordinary; it felt almost as though I could have drowned in the sound as the tide of weird, distorted echoes washed over me. Later, we explored the 16th-century Agra fort. Built of red sandstone, it encompassed the imperial city of the Mughal rulers. It was interesting but not a patch on the Taj.

The following day, we visited Fatepuhr Sikri, a deserted sixteenth century Mughal city with few tourists. It was beautiful, especially the carved stone screens. I overheard a guide say 'This is where the king would expose himself to his peoples every morning' – Ahem!

The Observatory in Jaipur was our next stop. One couldn't help but marvel at the sophisticated astronomical and astrological calculations that were being made so long ago on impressive and beautifully simple stone instruments such as an 18th century sun clock which was accurate to within two seconds per day. The architecture of the City Museum was elegant, though some of the weapons in the armoury were gruesome in the extreme. The Jaipur Art Museum included some quite exquisite paintings of microscopic detail. All of the women portrayed seemed to have a rather hard stern expression, often with disproportionately large eyes, even though the remaining details of the paintings were fairly true to life. We hired pedal rickshaws to return to our campsite and the drivers raced each other until ours managed to go the wrong way - could this have been deliberate, so that he didn't have to keep up the effort? He was noticeably exhausted. In the evening, we all crammed into a couple of auto rickshaws and went to eat at the Rumbak Palace Hotel which was like a flash-back to the days of the British Empire.

To celebrate Ted's birthday (the Canadian waiter on the trip), John and I presented him with a novel gift, a black umbrella. In fact John and I had also bought one each for ourselves and it was a hoot to walk down the street together in style; the three stooges, comfortably shaded from the sun!

Visiting the Amber Palace involved a leisurely ride up the hill on a colourfully decorated elephant. It was sad to see that some of these noble beasts seemed to be pretty badly treated and I felt a bit of a hypocrite when I accepted the ride. In the palace, it was great to browse over the many carved stone panels, looking for the cleverly hidden pictures within pictures. The ceiling of the king's bedroom was a dome covered in thousands of little convex mirrors. The guide shut the door and we were all momentarily plunged into darkness before he lit a couple of candles which had a dramatic effect as the whole room appeared to be filled with flickering stars. Later we visited the sandy Jaipur golf course which failed to boast a single blade of grass.

In the evening, we gave Ted a birthday cake with a single fat candle, followed by rum punch . . . . By the end of the evening we had 'drunk ourselves indestructible' and, finding ourselves locked out, decided to climb back into the hotel complex. This involved leaping off a wall into the branches of a tree below. The next morning we looked at the crazy climb of the night before and were glad to be alive!

Pushkar was a beautiful, quiet place on the shores of a lake and less frantic than the other towns we'd visited so far. It was a Hindu pilgrimage site, the word 'pushkar' meaning lotus flower. In Hindu theology Brahma, the god of creation, is self-born in the lotus flower. We were told that, even though he is one of the Hindu holy trinity,

Pushkar is one of the few places in the world to have a temple dedicated to him.

Our accommodation was in an attractive old building with peacocks strutting through the grounds. I went for a few cups of tea in a nearby cafe where Pink Floyd and Led Zeppelin were blaring out over the *Ghats* (a flight of steps leading down to the river), and women in brightly-coloured saris did their washing.   The music seemed incongruous in the otherwise tranquil surroundings.

The long drive to Udaipur was made more bearable for John and me because we rode in the cab with Chris, listening to good, loud, driving music like ZZ Top and Bob Marley. In Udaipur, I spent an enjoyable day with Fran, an Australian member of the group, with whom I got on particularly well. At the City Palace, we had great views of the Lake Palace which is built on an island in the Pichola Lake, though it was fast becoming a mud palace rising, as it was, from a largely dried-out lake due to the drought. The City Palace had the best examples of Indian paintings I'd seen so far, including some gruesome depictions of severed heads. Later, we visited a fabric shop festooned with photos of its most famous customers, including Roger Moore who was there once when filming the James Bond movie *Octopussy*. Travelling around the city by auto rickshaw, it felt as though the drivers fancied themselves to be taking part in a Bond movie car chase. I feared for my life several times as they played 'chicken' with the big Tata trucks (Tata is the biggest automobile manufacturer in India) that were festooned with sparkling decorations.

Driving from Udaipur towards Mandu we passed quite a few road crews made up of fairly young women, dressed in bright, almost fluorescent saris. At one of our frequent *chai* (tea) stops the local blacksmith was at work and a small fire burned fiercely with the aid of a pair of goatskin bellows operated by a gnarled old woman. The blacksmith manipulated a glowing piece of metal with his tongs while two women wielded heavy lump hammers to temper the metal.

The next morning, we arrived in Mandu to find that there was a festival in full swing - there was even a manually turned ferris wheel which looked absolutely terrifying. It was good to find an inconspicuous spot and watch the frantic goings on around me. Amidst all this mayhem, I noticed a tree festooned with enormous fruit bats that were oblivious to the cacophony created by the cavalcade below.

It was great fun visiting the caves at Ajanta which go back as far as the second century BC. They contained some of the finest surviving examples of Indian art. They were filled with impressive statues of the Buddha carved out of the basalt – part of the huge ($500,000km^2$!) Deccan trap lava flows. The 6m long reclining Buddha was a stunning image of peace and serenity. The echoes made my skull resonate. Musical Ted boomed some brilliant musical scales, the last note in harmony with the echo. Later, we visited the caves at Ellora which weren't a patch on the splendours of Ajanta.

We had come to the end of March and Chris became the butt of what we thought would be a good April Fool joke. When he came to fetch his breakfast he opened a steaming pan to find his soft toy cat mascot 'Garfield' bubbling away. We had all thought it was about time that cat had a good wash! On our last day of driving in India we arrived in Bombay. We were unimpressed as it was hot, smelly, and far too hectic. Our accommodation was pretty good though, right next to the sea. For a short time, I escaped the frenzy of the city and stood, bathed in moonlight, in the surf of the Indian Ocean as the sand was sucked from beneath my feet by the undertow.

All too soon, we were flying out of Bombay. I could still hear the many voices of my time in India: 'Cold Limca', (lemonade); 'Bye bye' monkeys; 'One Rupee?'; 'Change money?'; 'Rickshaw?'; 'Yes! Yes! This I am not knowing!'; 'Top Quality!'; and the best – 'Luverley Jubberley!'. Many random but key memories flitted across my mind's eye: cows everywhere, the occasional waft of a gut-wrenching stench, almost overcomplicated intricate patterns in all forms of art and jewellery, roadside barbers giving cutthroat-razor shaves, cold showers, huge brass water pots, women in brightly-coloured saris, impossible burdens being carried on people's heads, mammoth loads teetering on *'Tata'* trucks, bullock carts, heads bobbing in cornfields as people harvested by hand, workers winnowing grain in shallow baskets, women with nose and toe rings, squeaky village water pumps, instant crowd formation, dazzling white smiles, *'Bidi'* cigarettes (thin cigarettes wrapped in a leaf and tied at one end with string), garish hand-painted cinema signs, people sleeping in unlikely places, markets buzzing with flies, the incongruity of old lifestyles cheek by jowl with the occasional modern convenience, a man with a Coca Cola bottle hanging from his turban, road-signs and menus using creative spelling, decrepit trucks, and endless potholes.

Wonderful!

Chapter 6 ICE ON THE EQUATOR AND GAME GALORE IN THE GARDEN OF EDEN

After India, I set off on a four month trip in Africa. Kiwi John (JK) resurfaced and he and I were first members of an Encounter Overland group to arrive in Nairobi. We both hit it off with Wayne, our new driver and leader, straight away. Once we'd sorted ourselves out, we went for a sandwich at the Thorn Tree Cafe, a place I'd visited when I'd spent a week on standby to go out to a drilling rig in Tanzania. Later, we went to see the movie *The Untouchables.* It felt odd to watch a film in a hot humid cinema with people talking and coming and going all the way through and with the audible frantic bustle of African city life humming along outside. Later, we met another Encounter Overland driver - the legendary Annie ('Annie the Animal') and three trekkers who'd just completed the trip we were about to begin. Inevitably, we spent that evening recounting previous adventures, fuelled by beer and laughter.

Our hotel was quite up-market by my standards as an independent traveller, but I certainly wasn't complaining, especially when I discovered the bath and endless supply of hot water - something of a rarity for me in India. It was good to relax and recharge my batteries. I was glad I'd brought my Walkman and a little pair of speakers to go with it. It was so much more sociable to share music, as long as the others felt the same way, than to cut oneself off by plugging into headphones. Admittedly though, there were occasions in the next four months when everyone needed to do just that. This group was larger than we'd experienced in Nepal or India. There were eleven New Zealanders, five Australians, one

Dutch girl, and yours truly, the only Brit. They promised to be an interesting bunch, some possessing useful skills. There was a carpenter, a plumber, a travel consultant, a medical technician, a hairdresser, an electrician, and three nurses. Most of us were in our early to mid-twenties and many were doing the African trip as part of a year or so of travelling.

Inevitably, we all had to stock up on quite a few bits and pieces and there were odd jobs to be done over the next day or two. It was good to collect my *Poste Restante* mail and this prompted a postcard-buying spree. I was impressed by the quality of the well-photographed scenes on sale and I spent some time in the more expensive shops where carvings were sold. They were real works of art, not tacky mass-produced 'tat for the tourists'. There was a lot of gorgeous jewellery too and if I'd had a girlfriend to go home to I'd no doubt have spent a fortune! The African jewellery was far more subtle and simple that the pieces I'd seen in India which had been too cluttered with fiddly detail for my liking.

We had a long pre-departure meeting which involved lots of form filling (visas etc.) and many tall stories from Wayne the driver; we were going to get used to them over the next few months! Afterwards, most of the group ate at the Millimani Hotel, though I joined John, Annie, and a couple of others at the Golden Candle restaurant for a good Indian meal. The beer we'd imbibed led to a rollicking attempt to hot-wire Wayne's truck whilst he was eating dinner. We'd hoped to give him the shock of his life when he left the restaurant to find his truck missing before the trip had even begun, but failed to achieve our goal, though we had a lot of fun trying.

At last, we left Nairobi on the road to Mombassa and drove about 130km before setting up camp by the roadside in the middle of nowhere. We cooked hefty steaks on an open fire for supper, but when it poured with rain in the evening, we retreated to the shelter of the 'cook tent' and proceeded to become somewhat convivial.

The next morning, we drove on to Mombassa where we stopped to shop, despite the horrendous stink of rotten cabbage that pervaded the market. In the afternoon, we arrived at Tiwi Beach, a glorious spot south of the crowded tourist honey-pot beaches near Mombassa. I felt the need for a bit of 'headspace' and found it while standing in the sea for a while, appreciating the sparkling warm water and the tickling sensation of the sand beneath my feet. The sound of the waves was mesmerising, especially when I stood with my back to the sea. The anticipation of an oncoming wave was wonderful. Happy hours of solitude were spent exploring rock-pools to find fist-sized cowries, wispy brittle stars, weird brightly-coloured bloated sea cucumbers, and sea urchins bristling with spines. At one particularly pleasant spot, I sat comfortably in a pool up to my neck in crystal clear warm water for an hour or so. Later, I slipped out of my marine reverie and went for a swim and a splash around in the sea with Beki, a lively New Zealander; we really hit it off. In the evening, we ate wonderful fresh fish, cooked over an open fire and after the meal, we sat around getting to know each other and sinking a few cold beers. The day ended with a skinny-dipping session in the surf under brilliant stars.

It took a long day of driving to get us from Mombassa back to Nairobi where we went to eat at a popular restaurant called

Carnivores in preparation for our Kilimanjaro Climb. This was, as you might expect, a meat-eater's paradise. I'd been a vegetarian, though not a very strict one, for years, but any thoughts of salads were thrown to the wind on that night as I sampled pork, chicken, cuckoo, rabbit, hartebeest, crocodile, and snake! The hartebeest was the most delicious, but the crocodile was almost impossibly chewy. There was no campsite, so some people slept in the truck, some under it, and JK and I slept in the trailer.

The next day was spent in the city buying plenty of chocolate to fuel the forthcoming climb. Eventually, we hit the road to and the following morning we reached our destination, the Kibo Hotel, near Kilimanjaro. There was a jovial atmosphere following quite a few sing-along sessions during the drive; the highlights having been *Mercedes Benz* by Janis Joplin and a very loose interpretation of *Old McDonald Had a Farm* with a wide variety of African wildlife as well as the more usual farm animals. In the evening, we all had a good laugh in the hotel bar playing Pass the Pigs, before a fantastic meal of duck cooked over an open fire. The open fire was to be our main method of cooking for the entire trip.

On the first day of our trek up Kilimanjaro we woke early and spent the morning getting kitted up as the porters arrived. There was raucous laughter as they decided who would carry what luggage. It was then a short drive to the Kilimanjaro Park Headquarters at the Marangu hut where there was a considerable amount of administration to be done which included paying the £68 fee for climbing the mountain.

Our trek started in a damp misty forest with straggling mosses hanging from the trees. After a while, the vegetation changed to a mixture of shrubs and ferns and increasingly open country. In less than three hours, we had reached the first hut, Mandara, where we found good bunkhouse-style accommodation complete with comfortable mattresses. The evening's entertainment included playing Pass the Pigs again and the card game Black Maria – all jovial noisy fun.

I woke slowly the next morning and ate an enormous, delicious avocado pear for breakfast. We set off through moss-festooned forest around half past seven. After a while, the scenery changed to fairly open moorland and the vegetation zones, which are usually associated with changing latitude, were noticeable as the altitude increased. Occasionally, the cloud cover broke and we were teased by glimpses of the towering majesty of the mighty Kilimanjaro. I walked with JK for most of the time and we were the first to arrive at the Horombo hut around eleven. I spent the rest of the day becoming acclimatized to the altitude, lazing around, reading, writing my diary, and generally feeling great.

In the morning as we looked out on the mountain we had come to refer to as 'Killi', we were treated to a fabulous rainbow. We walked out of the moorland and into high altitude desert which was like walking on the moon! When we got to the Kibo hut, I slipped away from the group and enjoyed an hour or so of excellent bouldering (climbing) on the craggy volcanic rocks. In the evening, our head guide, Siera, gave us a little 'Spiel' about the ascent. Apparently, he'd been on 700 Killi trips and many of the porters and guides seemed to live in fear of him. He only had to walk into the room and they would all go running. There were twenty-eight porters/guides accompanying us. This seemed rather over-the-top for a group of eighteen, but I got the impression that it was an aspect of park policy to provide a source of income for the local people.

Everyone went to bed early at around half past six, but we were up again at midnight to set off on the last leg. It was a steady relentless slog and before long, we began to feel the effects of altitude and started to slow down and take more frequent rests. Plodding wearily along in the dark, the group looked more like a funeral procession than a group of fit young trekkers! At last, we reached Gillman's Point at six in the morning, the summit where most of the group decided to call it a day.

JK and I were still feeling pretty good, so after a ten minute rest, we set off again accompanied by our guide Thomas, onwards and upwards towards Uhuru Peak, the highest of Mount Kilimanjaro's summits. It was quite hard going, mostly on steeply sloping dry snow. We followed one of the ridges that led up to the peak. It soon became extremely tough as the altitude began to take its toll. I felt pretty spaced-out, with poor co-ordination and I was seriously short of breath. Towards the top, I was staggering along like an old man and having to rest every twenty paces or so. If I'd been on my own I doubt if I'd have made it to the top, but Thomas gently coaxed us on and we arrived at Uhuru Peak (5,895m), the highest point in Africa, at around eight. It was a fantastic feeling and a spectacularly beautiful view across the snow and ice. JK seemed more affected by the altitude than I was and puked right on the summit. After a few essential 'me-me' photos, we began to descend. It was surprising how quickly the effects of altitude wore off. It was a tiring route march back to the Kibo hut; the zigzag path over wet scree was punishing for the ankles and knees. However, there were some long sections where I could make a controlled slide down the scree, using a ski pole as a brake; this was enormous fun. We got to the Kibo hut at about eleven, exhausted and hungry, but the only food available was black tea and dry bread with marmalade - not much replenishment after ten hours of walking! After half an hour we set off again at a stiff pace, getting to the Horombo hut and the rest of the team by two o'clock. It was good to have a bowl of hot soup on arrival and, needless to say, I spent most of the afternoon in a deep sleep. The next morning we were up early, setting off from the hut at half past six. After a chocolate stop at the Mandora hut we made the final descent to the Kibo Hotel. On such a glorious day it was good to watch the butterflies and spot the occasional monkey or two bounding from tree to tree. We got back to Marangu by mid-morning after our four days of trekking and after we had all had a good scrub we were ready to party through the night!

We left Kilimanjaro the next morning, partly due to torrential rain falling during the night which meant that a lot of damp kit had to be sorted and packed. However, one positive result of the weather was the treat of seeing the end of a rainbow bathing a hilltop in a halo of red light. The road surface was something of a challenge and warranted getting into four wheel drive before we continued through savannah and plantations of maize and coffee before arriving in Arusha around lunchtime. There, we were able to 'phone home and I was amazed by the good quality of the connection, though unfortunately, my folks were out and I only got to speak to my friend's father. After leaving Arusha, we spotted a number of Masai as we drove on through the savannah. Eventually, we set up camp in a disused stone quarry which was a pretty awful spot and the kind of campsite we were going to have to get used to. JK and I sorted out the trailer while the rest of the group went to visit a nearby Masai village.

The roads were pretty rough the next day too and it was a relief to take a break from bouncing along in the truck when we stopped at a little market at Mosquito Creek near Manyara Lake. I'm not usually a great collector of souvenirs, preferring to spend money on photography, but here, there were attractive examples of work by local craftsmen. I haggled like crazy and was well rewarded by my purchases - an intricate carving in ebony that depicts a family tree known as a *Makunde* and a fantastic batik portraying a group of dancers, it simply overflowed with energy; you could almost feel the drum-beat! I also bought a little musical instrument which I called *'plinker'* for want of a better word. It was actually a little thumb piano, about the size and shape of a hardback novel, with hammered wire keys attached to a wooden sound-box. The notes were haunting and clear. Our lunch stop was at the top of the scarp above Manyan Lake where we enjoyed a sublime view as we ate. Everyone had damp laundry and it wasn't long before the bushes surrounding the truck were festooned with drying clothes.

The next day, we drove from the Ngorongoro Crater campsite to the game park HQ. There, we attached chains to the back wheels. This was hard work leaving us all covered in mud. The clouds cleared and we enjoyed great weather for the rest of the day. With the top off the truck, we were able to climb up on the roof bars which gave us a great view. The sheer number of animals we saw was mind-blowing. There were legion zebra, gazelle, wildebeest, and hyena. The excitement level rose when we spotted lions. The experience of seeing these majestic beasts up close in the wild was completely different from seeing them in captivity or in a wildlife documentary film. By the end of the day, we'd seen nineteen lions including several couples, and two females together with their four cubs. We even saw a couple 'on the job'. It was a very quick affair and apparently during the height of the mating season they perform seventy times a day for a whole week! No wonder they looked so drained! We also stopped for a while to watch a magnificent male elephant feeding. He had enormous tusks and raggedy ears, no doubt a testament to tussles in his earlier life.

Lunchtime down by the hippo pool was spent watching numerous birds that sported intense blue and red plumage. During the afternoon, we saw a group of four rhino: two adults and their young. They were huge tank-like beasts. The young ones were play-fighting - tonnes of armour-skinned muscle slamming against each other like primeval rugby players. The ubiquitous hyenas looked mean, skulking, and devious. It's no wonder that advertisers have used them to symbolise car thieves. It was a truly fabulous day and everyone was on a real high with the beauty and excitement of it all. In the evening, we went to the Crater Lodge Rest House where we partook of a hearty meal of wildebeest – delicious! Unfortunately, we returned to our campsite to find that the cook tent had been raided; all our beer and the clothes that had been left out to dry had vanished. Bummer!

Heading towards the Serengeti National Park, I sat up at the front of the truck with Tracy, also known as 'Space', the Australian hairdresser; Greg, the technician; and Dave, the carpenter. We sat on the roof bars with feet on top of the cab. From that position we saw plenty of what was, by now, becoming familiar game, but with the added pleasure of seeing a few giraffe too. When we arrived at Olduvai Gorge at lunchtime we were met by a group of magnificent dignified Masai. We stopped off at the little archaeological museum dedicated to the remarkable early human remains of *Homo habilis* dated as being 1.9 million years old. Louis and Mary Leakey were the archaeologists responsible for most of the excavations and discoveries of the hominid fossils in this gorge during the middle of the twentieth century. Their discoveries convinced most scholars that humans originated in Africa and caused some revision of the understanding, current at the time, of human evolution. We were given an interesting talk by a speaker possessed of a (to us) richly comical accent. Out of respect, I had to stifle my laughter, the effort putting me at severe risk of internal injury.

As we travelled through the park we watched the astonishing landscape unfold. The scrubby bush opened out into the plains where we saw literally thousands of wildebeest, Thomson's gazelle, zebra and a large number of hyenas too. Occasionally, we'd spot small herds of goats shepherded by Masai boys. After a photo stop at the border between the Ngorongoro Conservation Area (NCA) and the Serengeti National Park, we drove back into the NCA for a couple of kilometres to camp. Our initial choice of camp was soon changed when someone spotted a lion! Eventually, we set up next to a *kopje*, a big pile of strangely weathered boulders similar to the granite tors of Dartmoor. Shortly after setting up, it started to rain heavily again, but we were undeterred as we tucked into the heavenly bread made by the cooks of the day. We went to sleep listening to the rumbling of lions and the cackling of hyenas - what a campsite!

When we woke the next morning, we were almost surrounded by huge numbers of wildebeest and zebra and as we drove off we spotted a pair of lions on a neighbouring *kopje*, less than 1km from where we had slept! Later, we were lucky enough to see a cheetah, an elegant animal, exuding both grace and power. The truck also passed close to a lioness that had dropped her small cub as we approached; she trotted off a few feet before hunkering down and mewling. Further on, at a fairly fresh wildebeest kill, five lionesses were leaving the carcass as the hyenas and vultures moved in to strip the steaming bones. It was mesmerizing to absorb the savage splendour of it all.

At the Naabi Gate, we encountered a 'jobsworth' official; this led to two hours of interminable wrangling and argument and ended with our having to pay $20 each for an 'extra day' in the park. It was worth all the bickering though, to see so much spectacular game. The following day, the most interesting spectacle was of a family group of ten giraffe. Camp was set up quite early that night as our driver, Wayne, needed to do some work on the truck. Some of us went off to explore a nearby village and were made to feel most welcome, the children bringing us low chairs to sit on and proudly showing us their toys - ingenious models of cars and trucks made from wire and old tin cans.

There was a 5:00 a.m. start the next morning in order to get to Mwanza in time to shop at the market. However, the fuel pump played up and we had a fairly lengthy stop while Wayne and Reggie, who worked as an assistant mechanic, fixed it. To relieve the boredom, Space, (the hairdresser) gave all the lads Mohican haircuts. We were always being stared at, so it seemed appropriate to look even more extraordinary! Finally, Wayne got a temporary repair sorted out and we limped on to the next stopping place where we were treated to one of nature's own *son et lumiere* spectacles, a prodigious lightshow. A huge electric storm lit up the sky with a phenomenal combination of sheet and forked lightning.

Luckily, the repairs held during the following day, though the badly potholed roads continued to take their toll and three of the leaves in the trailer's suspension had snapped. We managed to stagger into Mwanza in time for lunch. After a really good meal at the New Mwanza Hotel, we set off on the aimless, but usually rewarding wanderings that had become the norm on arrival in a new place. I bought a huge two-pint enamelled mug for Pete's birthday. He was a New Zealand plumber, very energetic and pro-active. He was newly married to Andrea, another Kiwi, who was a medical technician. While Wayne and Reggie were working on the truck, Beki and I gave each other much-needed hair washes under the garage tap (no pride these travellers!). In the evening, we camped at the old showground, a few kilometres out of Mwanza. Pete managed to 'skull' the huge mug full of beer which prompted the start of a somewhat intoxicated birthday celebration.

The next day, Beki tried to get her camera, a Pentax zoom 70, fixed, but with no success. She gave me all her film and we agreed to share my cameras, an Olympus OM-10 SLR and an Olympus AF-1 35mm compact and then get double sets of all the prints. In the evening, we met another truckload of overlanders who were with the company Guerba. They seemed a subdued bunch and I felt that I'd made the right decision when I chose to travel with Encounter Overland. Later Beki and I joined Reggie and went to a local pub where we ended up dancing with the locals who found our antics side-splitting.

Before we left Mwanza the next morning, I bought a charming rough clay bowl. I also bought a wooden box to house it, in the hope that I would get it home in one piece - it did! Just before we left, I blew my last few Tanzanian Schillings at the Blue Cafe. I savoured quality ice cream as I admired the huge expanse of Lake Victoria dotted with ancient-looking sailing boats. After that, the road to Busisi was a bit of a come-down as it was practically corrugated – an uncomfortable ride indeed!

After an early afternoon ferry crossing at Busisi, the roads continued to deteriorate even more and we broke another leaf of the truck suspension before the day was over. That night, I went to sleep listening to the sound of drumming and singing drifting over from a nearby village. The truck got well and truly stuck in the mud when we tried to leave our campsite the next morning and it took about an hour and a half to get her back on the road using a four-wheel drive, mud-mats, and brute force. A small crowd gathered and helped us get unstuck. Meanwhile, children had dug up our rubbish pit and were having heated arguments about who would keep which empty tin or bottle.

Somehow Wayne managed to overshoot our next campsite by half an hour and it was a minor miracle that he eventually found it in the dark. In the morning, we forged on; the roads were as bumpy as ever which resulted in the back seat of the truck being christened the 'jump seat' for obvious reasons. Sometimes, whoever was sitting in it would bounce 30cm up in the air, so it was just as well that there was a handle to cling onto on the tail gate. At last, we reached the roadside gravel pit which was to be our home for the night and the heavens opened within minutes of our having pitched our tents. The site was instantly flooded. I dug a drainage ditch and built a rampart which seemed moderately effective, though I still had to sponge half a bowl of water out of my tent. The next morning, after a couple of hours driving, we came to the first bit of surfaced road we had encountered for days. It was lined with huts in little groves of banana trees and children came running out to wave to us and then continued to run along behind the truck until, out of breath, they collapsed with uncontrollable laughter.

Chapter 7 THE MOUNTAINS OF THE MOON AND A DOUBLE HELPING OF GORILLAS

Passing through Rwanda, climbing in the Ruwenzoris, and paying homage to the silverback gorillas in Zaire.

There was a marked change once we had crossed into Rwanda from Tanzania at Rusamo Falls, almost like being transported suddenly from Africa to Europe. There were good roads, modern vehicles and houses, and the whole feel of the place was more affluent. It was astonishing to see the town lights as night fell after so many nights out in the bush sleeping beneath a velvety black sky pricked with glittering stars. Kigali was set in a beautiful valley surrounded by fertile green hills. We set up camp at the Presbyterian Mission and then ate at a good restaurant called *Le Petite Kigali* where we enjoyed the local beer, Primus, which was only about 50 pence for a 72cl bottle. Again, my fractured French proved to be useful, thanks to my long-suffering teacher at the City of Norwich School.

Our first day started with a disappointing anticlimax as the post office, with its long-awaited Poste Restante, was closed. However, there was plenty to see and the markets stimulated the senses. Stallholders sang the praises of their goods and there were bright colours and wonderful (and not so wonderful) smells. The markets were generally a lot cleaner and better stocked than those we had seen so far in Africa. There was only one stall on the main market selling anything remotely like a souvenir. It was a toy stall and I fell in love with a simple hand-carved wooden model of a VW Beetle which cost about £1. This remains one of my favourite mementos to this day and was the first of many hand-crafted VW Beetle car models I have since collected from around the world. Later, I found a shop aimed wholeheartedly at tourists, full of delightful wares, but without the charm of the more rough and ready things one stumbles on out of the blue. However, I did buy a few unusual cards made from thin strips of dried banana leaves which depicted typical local scenes.

As we roamed around town we got bemused and amused looks thanks to our Mohican haircuts! We fell into conversation with a few people too, which was, as always, interesting and fun. One of them was wearing an almost fluorescent suit – a remarkable sight. After a day of wandering the streets, it was great to get back to the mission and the rare luxury of hot showers and real beds. The next day, we were relieved to find the post office open, but amazed to find a pretty hopeless *Poste Restante* service in what was an otherwise modern and, in some ways, westernised town. The alphabetical sorting wasn't anywhere near alphabetical, but eventually I found my name and was pleased to find a pile of mail which motivated me to continue my steady stream of cards to friends and the weekly cards I was sending to my family. I learned later that some of them took weeks to get home.

I'd experienced some toothache after crunching on a stone that had been cunningly disguised as a grain of rice, so I took my life in my hands and went in search of a dentist. I found one and spent forty-five minutes in the waiting-room reading my mail as a steady stream of people filed past, many clutching their jaws. When my turn finally came, I could have been anywhere in Europe. The surgery was up-to-date and the dentist spoke good English, and was keen to have a chat. He examined my teeth, took an X-ray, and gave me some painkillers and a hydrogen peroxide mouthwash. I returned next morning and as the X-ray didn't reveal any problems, he said that no treatment was necessary. When I got back to Britain, my dentist found a tiny hairline crack in one of my molars which needed a filling.

After a couple of days resting and recuperating we set off again. We were met by crowds of waving children wherever we went. Everyone was friendly; one very fit chap even managed to pace the truck up a fairly steep hill on his bike, occasionally getting a sly tow from the trailer. The scenery was magical. The hills, many of them volcanoes, poked above the morning mist. Just outside Rwhengeri, we stopped to visit a cave. It had one big passage about 10m high that was filled with thousands of bats. This must have been a major roost and there were huge piles of extremely smelly guano to match. When I shone my Petzl head torch up to the roof, thousands of tiny red eyes gleamed back at me out of the darkness and the noise level, already high, rose to fever pitch.

The border crossing into Zaire, as it was then known, (since 1997, known by its former name - the Democratic Republic of Congo), went surprisingly smoothly considering some of the horror stories we'd heard, and before long we were on the road to Goma, a one-street town with a well-supplied supermarket and very little else. On arrival, we got the shopping done and then all succumbed to the temptation of a patisserie selling delectable pastries and croissants.

Our campsite was at the Circle Sports Centre which had showers, alas only cold. After a day of faffing about in Goma, we headed off to camp in the Virunga Park, amid the spectacular Ruwenzori Mountains, referred to in guide books as The Mountains of the Moon. On the way, we saw another stunning rainbow. I know I mentioned earlier that I'd seen the best ever, but this one really did cap even that! On the road, we spotted a few country people carrying huge bundles of sugar cane on ingenious wooden scooters, complete with front suspension made from old truck inner-tubes. These were to become a common sight in Zaire as the children were always 'hanging out' with their scooters, the African equivalent of the Raleigh 'Chopper' bikes that were all the rage in the 1970s.

About half an hour after we set up camp, another Encounter Overland Truck pulled up and naturally a party ensued. They were on a southbound trip and conversation was lively over a few crates of Primus and a couple of bowls of a wicked punch concocted by Louise and Space. The Kiwi boys did admirable renditions of their favourite *hakas*, (traditional ancestral Maori dances which were used to lay down a challenge). The lads performed modern-day versions such as *Warriors* and the *Keys* to the *Zephyr*. We were impressed. Wayne managed to get completely trashed or 'raging' as the Kiwis say. He was spotted drinking rum punch out of one of his wellies! Towards the end of the evening Eddie, the other Encounter Overland driver, was held down while Space gave him a very rough Mohican haircut!

We got up at six o'clock the next morning and set off to climb the active Nyiragongo volcano (3,470m) which had erupted at least thirty-four times since 1882. All of us were sweating beer as we climbed and I swear you could smell it pouring out of us. It was a pretty hard three and a half hour slog to get to the summit. Unfortunately, the top was in thick cloud, though occasionally it cleared enough for us to peer down into the bottom of the crater hundreds of metres below. On the way down we had spectacular views of the parasitic cones that clung to the lower slopes of the main cone. The heavens opened and the tramp down the steep trails through the thick vegetation seemed interminable. Eventually, we arrived at the truck and after a four-hour drive were forced to stop a kilometre or so short of our intended campsite. There was a primitive bridge made from four thick logs that was too broken down to be fixed effectively, so we back-tracked and managed to set up in a rather cramped clearing by the roadside.

The 6:00 a.m. start the next morning heralded one of the most enduring and memorable days of the African experience. We went tracking Silverback Mountain Gorillas in the Virunga National Park. After a suitably fortifying breakfast of porridge, we walked up to the Jimbo Guide's hut and spent forty-five minutes going through the usual bother. If anything varied even a hair's breadth from 'the book' you could bet your life an official would spot it and be as obstreperous as possible about it. Our group (John, Louise, Kirsty, Ann, Greg, and I) finally set off with two guides at about half past eight. It wasn't long before we were making our way through thick jungle, the guides hacking a trail through the dense undergrowth with their keenly sharpened machetes. It was easy to imagine that we were the first people ever to enter this primeval tangle of vegetation. Two hours of damp, determined battle with the jungle led to a steady build-up of excited anticipation. We were not to be disappointed.

Suddenly, we came across the gorillas. It was a heart-stopping moment. I felt exultant! Here was the Rugendo family group made up of one huge silverback male, four adult females, and four infants. One of the infants was very young, perhaps only a few months old, while the others were between two and three years old. They were surprisingly relaxed. The baby of the group just couldn't stop yawning. They all farted like crazy too. There was much lazy rolling around and stretching, or lying down with both hands behind their heads.

It was uncanny to watch the behaviour of the gorillas as it seemed so typically human; so did their features, hands, feet, and huge deep, dark brown eyes. They observed us in a contemplative way - calm and serene. Their faces and expressions were as different as those in any group of nine people, each displaying his or her own character and mannerisms. We were very close, literally at arm's length. We were careful not to venture any closer to the enormous bulk of the silverback. His head was massive and his forearm thicker than an adult rugby player's thigh. He was 1.6m tall and probably not far off 1.6m around the chest too. What a monster! It was easy to see how such magnificent creatures have gained an almost mythical status regarding their intelligence and strength. On this day, they were all very docile and the silverback tolerated the youngsters who delighted in clambering over him, pausing occasionally to pick off a few ants. The ants were horrendous - huge creatures measuring 1.5cm in length that gave really painful nips and were quite hard to get off once they had sunk their jaws into one's legs and ankles; it was a mercy they didn't sting. It was a thrilling photo opportunity. We had plenty of time just to sit and watch, silenced and awestruck by the majestic beauty of the magnificent creatures. It was obvious that gorillas are very tactile animals, always close to each other and constantly cuddling and grooming. We spent a wonderful hour or so with them before heading back. Goodness knows how the guides managed to retrace their steps to the hut, but they did, and in only an hour.

After a rest back at camp I went shopping with Beki and Space in the market in the small village nearby. We fooled around with the local children; their sense of fun is universal - laughter is truly the best international language. A local man kindly took us to a nearby village off the main road where we bought a few pumpkins. On our return, we were, of course, accompanied by the usual cheerful entourage of inquisitive youngsters. Back at camp, I relaxed for a while listening to a tape of Ladysmith Black Mombazo on the Walkman. Their soft harmonies seemed appropriate. I was becoming more and more hooked by African music.

The next morning, there were two free places on the day's trip to visit the gorillas and John and I jumped at the opportunity to get a second chance to see them - even at $40 the experience would be far more valuable than any souvenir. This time, our group consisted of Beki, who soon became my girlfriend as the trip progressed; Space, the fun-loving hairdresser; Darlene, an Australian nurse; and Ermin, a quiet Dutch clerk. The weather was a lot better and it only took forty-five minutes of tracking to find the gorillas, even though they were in a much denser jungle thicket than the group we had seen the day before. After watching for half an hour, the family moved off and we followed them for fifteen minutes before they settled down to a serious bamboo-munching session. While they were eating, we enjoyed observing them for another hour. The silverback in this group was another giant; he was accompanied by a large passive female and eight youngsters. They were eating for almost all of the time we were with them and it was a surprisingly different experience to the previous day.

The youngsters were enormously entertaining, clowning around and, at times, it was almost as though they were putting on a show specifically for us. They seemed to be posing for photographs. One of them crept up to the guide and tugged at his trousers before losing his cool and scampering off, occasionally pausing to clap his hands and shake his head as he went. They ate like machines, ramming bamboo into their mouths. They seemed to choose a comfortable spot, sit down, and munch on everything within an arm's length before moving on, leaving a devastated patch behind them. When the father silverback stopped eating, he dozed off with one youngster sleeping on his chest, his tiny arms around Dad's neck. The rest of the youngsters continued to frolic, often climbing on branches which bent and broke and when they occasionally fell on the 'Old Man', he didn't even flinch!

After a while, a female arrived with a baby riding on her back. The silverback woke and they had a little cuddle before he set about grooming her with profound gentleness and dexterity for such a ponderous animal. One of the juveniles made a mock charge at

Dad, who gave him a hefty box in the ear before turning his attention back to Mum. The chastised youngster whimpered a lot and sought sympathy from his siblings. We were so close to the family that we experienced an intimacy so special that it brought tears to my eyes.

At times, the youngsters approached us and even reached out to us. Maybe this was why the silverback made a short mock charge and then leaned over and pushed the guide on the shoulder, as if to say 'Don't mess with us'. Needless to say we almost collapsed at this point! However, having asserted his authority, the Old Man just sat down again and continued to stuff his face with bamboo as if nothing had happened. One of the smaller juveniles climbed a flimsy tree and sat about 8m above us. We were all so engrossed in watching the gorillas on the ground that we forgot about him, until he had a piss, right onto my head - Hmmm. . . . I guess not many people can say they've been pissed on by a mountain gorilla! Some of the others got splashed too and for about ten minutes we practically suffocated trying to stifle our laughter.

A few minutes after we had left the gorillas, the heavens opened yet again. The rain was so heavy we actually heard it approaching; everyone was thoroughly drenched. On our way back to camp we were frequently greeted with '*Jambo*' and '*Bonjour*' as we walked in a happy daze, smiling until our cheeks ached as we continued to bask in the glow of an ecstatic experience.

Chapter 8 MUD, SWEAT, AND BEERS!

Crossing Zaire and the Central African Republic in the rainy season

We struck our camp near the Jimbo Guides Hut and set off along the usual dirt road. It was lined with maize fields and banana trees and we were treated to views of the Virunga volcanoes. At the edge of Virunga Game Park we encountered a truck stuck in the mud. This was the first of many, as it turned out. It was getting dark, so we had to camp where we were, even though it was a marshy area. We took off the trailer and pitched the cook tent on the road between trailer and truck. I helped Beki prepare supper, it took ages to strip every last scrap of meat from a scrawny goat, but we were proud of the finished meal.

In the middle of the night screaming led me to a scene from an Alfred Hitchcock movie. Ann, an Aussie student had woken up in the cook tent with ants almost 2cm long in her hair. There were thousands of the biting bastards everywhere! We had asked for it though, as the bucket of scraps from the previous night's meal had been left out – lesson learned!

We set off at around seven and rolled the top of the truck down so that we could soak up the sun on what was a real scorcher of a day at about 38°C. I spotted a number of woven nests made by bright yellow birds and we saw thousands of colourful butterflies, some with wings as much as 10cm across. There were many baboons too. They always looked as though they were 'cruisin' for a bruisin''. Once we'd got onto the transit road through the park we also saw hippos and stopped for a while to watch one wallowing in a small pool. We were greatly impressed by the size of his enormous behind as he ambled off. There were many impala as well, some accompanied by their young and, at one point, an extremely ugly warthog appeared sporting mean-looking tusks.

We spent an hour or so wandering around Kanyabayonga, a fairly big town of mud huts, many of them thatched. I passed the time of day with a local lad who let me try out his wooden trike, much to the amusement of his mates. I also found a Primus T-shirt for sale and couldn't resist buying it as a novel souvenir of the many companionable occasions when Primus was the drink of choice (about 30p a litre). After a short drive out of town, we stopped for lunch. Within a few minutes a crowd had gathered. Wayne counted 180 spectators while we were eating. One little boy was transfixed, watching every movement of Pete's fork. However, although the people here were poor, they seemed to have enough to eat and apparently, there was good medical care too; they certainly looked fit.

After lunch, the settlement seemed to follow the road for miles. There was one brief market stop where we were lucky enough to find strawberries. Shortly afterwards, a soldier told us that the road ahead was blocked by a landslide and we spent a good while walking down to investigate the situation. It had been cleared, but there were about twenty trucks waiting to get through. This chaos forced us to camp on the road about half a kilometre away in what was not a very good site, but it was some consolation to have the first decent camp-fire for what had seemed like ages.

The following morning, we were up early and were greeted by misty views as we travelled through hilly areas that were more heavily cultivated. The numerous villages looked more prosperous and neat and tidy than many we'd seen before and some gardens even had flowers. In one village, we passed a beggar woman with what I took to be a huge goitre swelling on her neck. It prompted a comment from Tracey about the fact that in western society we tend not to tolerate beggars, while in Zaire begging seemed to be an accepted form of earning one's living. The local people gave money to beggars in what seemed to be, in effect, their version of welfare.

Having crossed the Equator at 9:30 a.m. and stopping for the usual team photos we stopped for lunch in Butembo. Wayne went off with a few local people and came back very pleased with himself as he had bought us a freshly butchered goat for supper. The goat was christened Blair, after one of the guys on the trip! In the afternoon, we met a long-wheel-base Land Rover with a British driver, Jack, who was accompanied by three amiable Kiwis and two Brits. They had bad news about the road ahead and told us that two large trucks had tried to cross a bridge at the same time, thus causing its collapse. However, they'd worked out an alternative route, so we did a quick U-turn and joined them to camp in the middle of another small village. The next morning Blair (the man, not the goat) was throwing up. He didn't get any sympathy from anyone, as he'd got thoroughly pissed, loud, and obnoxious the previous night.

In Beni (my town!), we saw the first tarmac-surfaced road for days. I spotted an amusing barber's shop sign with illustrations of the styles on offer and was pleased when the proprietor was keen to have his photo taken standing in the doorway. We then took the detour that Jack had recommended. In the scattered settlements strung out along the road, the huts were no longer predominantly thatched. Many had roofs covered with dried banana leaves or wooden tiles, a simple but effective building style that had probably remained unchanged for hundreds, if not thousands, of years. Many women walking along the road carried huge heavy bundles of branches and logs on their heads. As the day progressed, we drove along much narrower roads through increasingly dense jungle where we could have been forgiven for expecting to see Tarzan swinging by. The trees were massive, surrounded by dense undergrowth and draped in vines and creepers. There was a huge variety of brightly-coloured butterflies, especially at the point where we had a pee stop. Mineral salts attracted them, apparently. Soon after that, the road surface deteriorated to such a degree that we stopped to fit chains to the tyres. This was just in time, as minutes later we came across a small truck which had been coming the other way and got stuck on a tree stump.

From then on, the road went from bad to worse and became increasingly muddy. We managed to power through in our four-wheel drive with the chains biting well most of the time, but there were increasingly frequent stops to dig or pull the truck out of holes which were up to 1.5m deep. It took ten of us hauling on the rope together to free it from the glutinous mud. Once the knot gave way and five of us landed flat on our backs in the mire, laughing helplessly. When, finally, we arrived at the mission in Mambasa around nine at night, Wayne said it had been one of the toughest days of driving he'd experienced since he'd worked for Encounter Overland. But worse was to come as we passed through Zaire in the wet season. Mud, mud, and more mud awaited us!

The campsite at the Mambassa mission was good with cold showers to scrub away the grime of several days on the road. There was an aged female chimp cooped up in a cage about 2m by 3m on the site. It seemed criminal for her to be so cruelly confined. She had beautiful hands which felt tough yet soft when poignantly, she held hands with me!

That night, there was a cracking thunderstorm. It was deeply relaxing to lie in the tent and meditate on the torrential rain. The next morning, I helped Wayne get the chains off the truck as we didn't think we'd need them for a while. We stopped in Mambasa town where Beki and I found a lady making little sweet buns fried in oil which were particularly delicious. Soon after, we spotted a pretty young woman with an amazing spiky hairdo pounding grain with a big mortar and pestle. She was very jolly and full of smiles when she noticed us watching and came over to say 'hello' and shake hands. She invited us into her tiny courtyard and we were introduced to her father who was as drunk as a skunk on the local firewater. He chatted affably for a while in a mixture of French and Swahili, but our good mood was to be brought down when, on the way back, we saw a young man carrying two freshly killed monkeys slung over his shoulder. It was a disturbing sight; they looked so human it seemed almost cannibalistic.

Our next destination was Epulu where we struck camp beside a fast-flowing river. We visited the Okapi Breeding and Research

Station. A girl from the station showed us the Okapi they'd caught and intended to export to zoos in the States. The little known weird-looking critters are a cross between a zebra and a giraffe. We were also introduced to the resident pet monkey who clambered all over everybody, prompting a flurry of happy snaps.

The jungle was beautiful with golden sunlight filtering in skinny beams through the dense foliage. We were taken to visit a Bambuti settlement. Pygmies are usually wandering hunter-gatherers but this tribe has elected to stay put. The Bambuti are the shortest group of pygmies in Africa, averaging under 140cm. They have a different blood type from other pygmy groups and probably inhabited the area as long as 4,500 years ago. They welcomed tourist groups and were paid a nominal fee by the wildlife station. The station also paid for the children to attend primary school, though our guide commented cynically that this was partly because they were so maddened by the children hanging around the station all day.

Visiting the pygmies was one of the tackiest things I've ever done on my travels. I felt there was something shameful in putting them 'on show' as it were. They sat around outside their 'National Geographic" photo worthy leaf covered huts smoking dope in metre long pipes made from the stems of banana tree leaves, their proud traditions abandoned for the tourist dollar. It had also saddened me in Kenya and Tanzania to see that many of the Masai seemed to have become totally reliant on tourism even though they had had a long tradition of semi-nomadic life in which they had farmed desert and scrubland.

On the way back to our campsite, we met a woman from the station with a young chimp clinging tightly to her back. Though the word 'cute' is not a word I'd normally use, I have to admit that 'cute' is exactly what this little fellow was, with his incredibly soft hands, tiny ears and his soulful eyes. He didn't seem very happy which wasn't surprising as we learned that he'd been bought by tourists who'd then found they couldn't get him out of the country, so he'd been given to the wildlife station. He was an orphan whose mother had been killed so that her young could be captured and sold before they'd learned anything about life in the jungle. It was now too late for him to return to the wild and his future life would be as a pet, always dependent on humans.

After a reviving night's sleep we left the wildlife station shortly after seven. It started to rain which made the road slippery, causing us to slide around in an alarming way. We were held up by an articulated truck that had got stuck in the mud and spent half an hour helping to drag, push, and pull it free so that we could get past. It was a tight fit and we only just squeezed through with centimetres to spare. We slogged onward through the seemingly endless, dense jungle, occasionally succumbing to the fate of the articulated truck and having to dig our way out of the mud by putting logs in the ruts. The mud wasn't so much deep and sticky as liquid and slithery and I began to wonder if the local lorry drivers had as many words for mud as Eskimos are reputed to have for snow.

While we ate lunch in a small roadside quarry, a group of six pygmies walked past, stoned out of their minds. Throughout the day, we passed many pygmy villages, including one where we were able to watch a tribal dance, accompanied by mesmerising drumming and chanting. The men danced in tall conical hats and masks, while the women shimmied around the edge wearing grass skirts. They spotted us and came over. The lead dancer, wearing a black and white striped mask was utterly and completely blitzed. As we were beginning to move off, he jumped onto the trailer, swayed around, tried to get into the truck, and fell. Luckily, he wasn't hurt, but the crowd was not pleased and pelted us with any missiles they could lay their hands on – bamboo and wood for the most part – as we drew away. I felt they couldn't be blamed. How would we feel if a group of tourists were to roll up to stare and photograph us when we were taking part in a significant ceremony? I felt uneasy. There's a fine line between gratuitous gawping and respectful observation.

In the late afternoon, we set up camp in a stone quarry where a couple of other overland trucks joined us in the evening. They were from two other companies called Hobo and Economic, not a very cheerful bunch. They had only a two-wheel drive, no chains, and no mud mats, so they were likely to have an 'interesting' time getting through the bogs we had braved. We pushed on and experienced a long day on bad roads, though this was made bearable by the fact that Beki and I were able to travel in the cab with Wayne. It was her birthday and we listened to ZZ Top, B52's and The The. Wayne also introduced us to Dave Warner on a couple of fantastic tracks - *It's a Mug's Game* and *Car Park*. I bought Beki a huge bunch of about a hundred small, deliciously sweet "Ladies' fingers" bananas for one hundred Zaire schillings in a tiny village. Much of the drive was like going through a tunnel of bamboo. Drive, drive, drive to

Kisangani or bust. Ultimately, as we approached the city we hit 20km of surfaced road, the first we'd seen for days, so we really burned it up for the last few kilometres.

We arrived at the Olympia Hotel and after a good shower and sort-out, celebrated Beki's birthday with a splendid meal in the hotel's open-air restaurant, during which she was forced to wear a ridiculous birthday hat. Later, we walked into town and then got a lift in the back of a Land Rover from a Portuguese chap, who took us to the *Manekin-pis* disco. It seemed incongruous to be dancing to loud pop chart music under festoons of fairy lights after days on end in the jungle. It was good to share a hotel room rather than a tent to celebrate Beki's birthday.

Food shopping in Kisangani market was strange; it was like a ghost town might have been a year or two after war had ripped through it. Space and Beki made fools of themselves by assuming that onions were ten Zaire schillings a pile, when they turned out to be ten Zaire schillings *each*! This got half the market howling with laughter at the dumb "*Mzungus*", which is what the locals call white folks, literally translated from the Swahili *Mzungu* meaning 'aimless wanderers' – they had a point! We bought loads of scrummy baby tomatoes wrapped in young banana leaves tied at the top with vines to keep them fresh. We also eyed some huge land snails about 15cm long for sale, along with dried fish, which were long and thin, but coiled back on themselves and skewered into blocks; they looked semi-fossilized and boy, did they stink! I don't know why, but a crazy woman pursued us all around the market trying to sell the girls an enormous and particularly ghastly bra! We weren't tempted by the fish or the bra.

After taking the shopping bags back to camp, we found about a dozen barbers doing al-fresco haircuts in the shade of a clump of bamboo. This was obviously a regular event, as the ground was covered with cuttings of African hair which looked for all the world like Velcro. Later, we stumbled across a cake shop where we enjoyed a few samosas and ice creams. One of the guys who worked there, Richard, spoke pretty good English and was keen to practise on us, so we hung around. When we got back to camp we dozed as the fan rotated sluggishly above us, half-heartedly stirring the thick muggy air and in the evening, we walked to the yacht club. We were impressed when a Mercedes stopped to give us a lift. However, this being Zaire, we had to be dropped off 100m before the club, due to a huge puddle in the road. The restaurant was right on the banks of the Congo with a great atmosphere and wonderful food.

Visiting the Livingstone Falls was a grand day out. A ten-minute walk took us down to the Congo (Zaire) River where a dugout, about 50cm wide, was waiting for us. We were crammed into it and crossed a small tributary before changing to a much larger dugout, 1m wide and about 10m long. This enormous canoe was carved from a single log and was able to carry all nineteen of us plus four strong men who used long wooden paddles with streamlined leaf-shaped blades. It nosed upstream to the first section of white water where fish traps were set, apparently one for each local village.

The traps were ingeniously woven from bamboo and suspended from wooden frames. They were enormous conical structures about 3-4m long and 2m wide at the mouth, tapering to 15cm at the end where the fish were trapped. The rapids were full-on, but the fishermen were undeterred as they clambered around on the scaffolding and waded through the swirling torrent below to check their catches. They positively rippled with muscles developed by a life of swimming in the formidably strong current. There were also people fishing in pairs from slender 7m long dugout canoes. They threw circular cast nets in graceful arcs and as they pulled them in, weights around the bottom closed the nets to trap the fish.

After a while on the river, we stopped at a little village. The children were quiet and shy, but all of them wanted to hold our hands. The chief of the village turned up in an outfit obviously put on for the tourists. He wore a leopard skin hat, blue towelling shorts and a big rag around his waist. He played the village drum for us, a hollow log about 1.5m long and 60cm thick with a 1cm slot cut in the top. It gave a really gutsy, booming sound. I was offered a try and I enjoyed beating out a funky rhythm. The heat and humidity sucked the energy out of us all. We'd heard that a few days travelling down the Congo on one of the big ferries was a real 'must' for travellers. However, unfortunately, all of the ferries were leaving too late for us so this was an experience we had to miss.

After relishing the pleasure of what would probably be the last shower for several days, we left the Olympia Hotel. On the way out of Kisangani we stopped off at a roadside tailor's where many of us had ordered shorts and shirts made from flour sacks. They weren't ready, which got some people rather wound up, though I felt pretty relaxed and calm about the whole stupid business. Apparently, the delay at the tailor's was due to a huge order of trousers made with a fabric covered in pictures of the president to celebrate his birthday that week – fair enough! Eventually, we left Kisangani three hours later than had been planned.

It was a bumpy ride; we were back to unsurfaced roads within a few kilometres out of the town. Each small village we passed had a huge log drum as a centrepiece. At one point, we were waiting to cross a river by ferry when I spotted one of the neat little chairs that are ubiquitous in Zaire. Each chair is made from a simple but ingenious design of two boards neatly slotted together to give a low seat with a sloping backrest. I was invited to sit down on it and found it really comfortable, so I asked the owner if I could buy it. After a bit of haggling, I got it for 2,000 Zaire schillings (about £5). I was chuffed to bits with the chair which remains one of my favourite and most used items brought home from my many travels. It's a genuine souvenir, polished by years of use, rather than a bit of tat made for gullible tourists. After crossing the river, we drove through thick jungle for a few hours, not stopping until dark when we set up camp in a small clearing by the roadside.

I had a memorable twenty-fourth birthday, much of which was spent digging the truck out of mud bogs. The day started early; I was up with Beki at 4.45 a.m.! We drove through a seemingly endless tunnel of dense foliage for kilometre after kilometre. The small clusters of thatched mud houses we passed along the road usually had a few palms nearby from which the villagers picked bright orange fruit to make cooking oil.

There was a major delay when we came across a small truck stuck up to its axles in a deep mud bog. We tried to drive around it, but ended up getting stuck ourselves - very stuck! It took two hours of digging, mud-matting, and even jacking the truck up to get the mud-mats into more effective positions. It was all hard work. While we were trying to get free a wealthy-looking Italian bloke pulled up in a Toyota Land Cruiser. It transpired that he was the president of the Afrikannonball Rally and was sussing out the route prior to the event which was due to take place in July. It was to be from Tunis to Botswana and contestants would aim to complete it in just twenty days - incredible! For the time being, however, he just had to wait. We eventually managed to get the truck moving again by all of us making superhuman efforts as we pulled on a rope. However, before the Italian chap, who had been waiting patiently for over an hour, could drive through, a minibus arrived and pushed in to the queue of vehicles; of course it promptly got stuck too. This was despite not only our having told its driver not to come through, but also the people in the original stuck truck had made it clear that he should wait his turn. We proceeded to pull the minibus out to help the Italian guy get past. What a bunch of fools the minibus crew and passengers were! They just stood around and watched, even when a soldier ordered them to help. This surprised us as most people in Zaire seemed to fear the military. Once the minibus was free, our Italian friend powered through without any problem; his four by four Toyota Landcruiser was so light with only him in it, he said he hardly ever found himself in difficulties.

Our lunch stop was literally in the middle of the road, surrounded by thick jungle teeming with butterflies. An old friend of mine had sent me some balloons for my birthday which I had collected from *Poste Restante* in Rwanda and I provided much entertainment by blowing them up and letting them fly amongst an energetic bunch of children who piled on top of each other in their efforts to grab the balloons; the balloons, of course, had a tendency to burst which provoked shrieks of laughter. I even managed to make one of those silly balloon dogs, much to the wonder of the assembled throng. When we stopped in Buta we discovered that it was not only *my* birthday, but also that of president Mobutu, so there was a public holiday. Apparently, this public holiday was not one for parties, but for people to stay at home to discuss the politics of Zaire. This can't have taken long as I spotted one big hoarding that proclaimed 'One people, One country, One party, One leader' - so not much to discuss there!

In the afternoon, we came to a bridge made from four 70cm thick logs with a few 3cm boards laid across them. We carefully re-arranged them, put mud-mats down and took off the trailer. Wayne drove over the bridge *'pole, pole'* (slowly, slowly in Swahili), keeping a close eye on the wheels. For a moment, it looked as though one of the back wheels was going to slip off one of the thick logs, but we just managed to make it across. It took a team effort to manhandle the trailer over the bridge. Blair almost got run over as Wayne reversed back to reconnect the trailer. Later in the day, just as it was getting dark, we had to rebuild yet another bridge and as this took so long, we decided to set up camp five minutes later, hacking ourselves a clearing with a machete, rather than driving on in the dark. My birthday meal was rehydrated mince - I can think of better celebration dinners!

The next morning after only an hour of driving, we came across another broken bridge which occasioned yet another major rebuilding project. It took an hour and a half and left us all sweating profusely in the oppressive, humid heat that we never quite grew used to. When we stopped for a late lunch by a fast flowing stream, Beki and I slipped off and had a skinny-dip surrounded by butterflies. It was good to have a much-needed wash as the brightly coloured creatures flitted around us.

While we were eating our supper we heard drumming from a nearby village. Later, I went to investigate, accompanied by Beki, Darlene, Kirsty (an Australian nurse), and Kerry (a rather quiet teacher from New Zealand). There was some apprehension as we approached the village as we didn't want to create a situation like the one a few days before when the pygmy dancer had jumped onto the back of the truck. We needn't have worried. There were about fifty people dancing around a couple of drums that were being played with great enthusiasm. They created an infectious rhythm and we simply couldn't help being drawn in. We stood watching and listening for a while until they noticed us, stopped their drumming, and came over. I immediately approached them with my hand held out and there followed a lot of handshaking "*Bon soirs*" and beaming smiles. It was a warm welcome and a great evening. Some of the children ran off and reappeared moments later with seats for us. The party started again; the men and boys played the metre high drums which gave a really meaty, bass sound. There was a great deal of singing too. Combined with the drumming, a wall of sound was produced that Phil Spector would have been proud of. I sat there and revelled in this very special experience, smiling from ear to ear until my cheeks 'fair ached with grinnin', as a very old great uncle of mine was wont to say.

The women moved in sassy style, wiggling their bums in time with the beat, some dancing with their babies wrapped up on their backs in brightly coloured cloth papooses. The adults shuffled around in a circle and were soon joined by the older children. They beckoned for us to join in, so we all got up and became part of the ring. It was wonderful to join the villagers in a genuine Saturday night party. They were laughing with us as well as at us and we were made to feel part of it all. The singing almost became a chant. One or two guys shouted a line which the rest of us repeated. This was certainly one of the highlights of the trip. It was a situation where producing a camera would have been inappropriate. However, my mental picture of the evening will always be spectacularly clear. After about an hour, we decided to leave, not wanting to overstay our welcome. We shook hands with everyone amidst a chorus of "*Bon soir*", "*Merci beaucoup*", and "*Tres bon*". Walking back to camp in the moonlight, surrounded by the multitudinous sounds of the jungle, was a fitting end to a marvellous day.

The next day we were up at 4.30 a.m. We got to Bomba around lunchtime and went down to the river which must have been a kilometre wide. It was big, slow, and powerful, thick with floating vegetation and logs. It didn't take us long to find a bar and relax with a few cold beers before hitting the road again around two. The jungle seemed to be thinning out somewhat and in the afternoon we passed termite mounds about 4m high. There was a beautiful red sunset and it looked as if the sky were on fire. It didn't last long though, as night really does fall quite suddenly near the Equator.

Our campsite was around 30km from Lisala and we had to fight the mozzies as we pitched our tents. The next day of driving was punctuated by repairs to the broken leaves of the truck and trailer springs. The suspension had taken a real hammering. When we stopped for lunch, hordes of children appeared from nowhere. We had unwittingly stopped just outside a primary school and were surrounded instantly. The roads provided different problems in the afternoon and we had a few delays waiting for trucks that had got stuck in sand. The *'Piq Niq'* campsite next to the Mongala river in Businga was an excellent quiet spot and it wasn't long before we were tucking into delicious sweet and sour pork - one of the best meals we'd had for a while.

It was good to be able to have a lie-in the next morning, though eventually we had to get up because it was so hot in the tent. It must have been around 30°C by nine and as much as 38°C later in the day. Beki and I went down to a secluded spot by the river and had a good wash and laundry session. Later, we rigged up a rope to swing out over the river and leap into the water. The local children were keen to join us in this frivolity and a good time was had by all. In the afternoon, we took our camp beds down to a shady spot by the river and relaxed, listening to music on the Walkman. I managed to rewire the headphones to make a double set which saved on batteries and made listening more sociable. The children liked it too!

Unfortunately, our relaxed interlude was short-lived and the next morning we discovered that the cover of the trailer had been slashed and three packs were missing, one belonging to Beki, another to Greg, and the third to Tracey (an Australian therapist). Beki was understandably distraught as her diary and all of her exposed film had gone. Wayne informed the police and it wasn't long before Beki was filling in a report form to document all that had been taken. Greg was worst off as he had not only lost his pack, but his money-belt (including his passport) as well. Speaking of money-belts, later Beki and I went down to our favourite spot by the river for a swim and I managed to dive in while still wearing mine - my passport would never be the same again!

When we went back to camp for lunch, the owner of 'Piq Niq' told us that he'd been to see a local photographer to see if anyone had tried to sell any film. It was a long shot, but it paid off as someone had, indeed, tried to sell a used roll of film, so at least we had one lead to follow up. The campsite owner was obviously going out of his way to help us and quite rightly too, as there had been, supposedly, two guards posted on the site the previous night.

We heard later that one rucksack had been recovered, so a group of us went over to the police station. When we arrived, we found that the police had four young suspects aged from about sixteen to eighteen who were tied together and lying face down on the floor. The commander questioned them between sessions of beating by a couple of soldiers brandishing thin whippy sticks. They really laid into the accused, hitting their backs, behind their knees, and the soles of their feet. If they tried to roll over as they writhed around, the soldiers pinned down their heads with a hefty boot. The supposed thieves howled and whimpered and a few sticks got broken. Beki said she would have liked to be doing the beating and I was alarmed to find myself watching with morbid fascination as the police inflicted pain on bound human beings. After only seconds, however, I turned away, disgusted with myself and feeling helpless in the face of cruel, but locally accepted police methods. I suppose it was the norm in that particular culture and, in fact, quite a large crowd had gathered to watch. I was disturbed and ashamed to find that I felt strangely detached. Maybe it's true that too many violent films and TV shows have raised our tolerance to violence - a frightening thought.

We moved away and waited beneath a shady tree. Later, one of the soldiers produced Beki's little photo album and a few toiletries turned up too. There were groups of children around us on the grass, most of them having boisterous play fights. A couple of lads entertained us and each other by both getting inside a tattered blue jersey, each with an arm through a one of the sleeves. Another teenager strutted around wearing a pair of sunglasses with no lenses. He obviously considered himself to be the ultimate cool dude. One of the younger children, about four years old, who'd been scrapping and tumbling with the others, held onto my arm and hugged my leg as we left to go to another police station where an additional rucksack had been recovered. When we arrived, we found a further pack, though it was disappointingly empty. Later Wayne, Beki, and I returned to the first police station where the soldiers were still torturing their suspects. This time, they were weaving sticks between the fingers of the thieves' hands with palms together and fingers spread and then, with a soldier on each side, squeezing the sticks together, crushing their knuckles. It all looked excruciatingly painful. The torture continued. It was unbearable to watch and we left.

That night we were woken by Space who was shouting that the thatched hut next to our tent had erupted in flames. One of the two German blokes in it had kicked over a kerosene lamp! The hut burned to the ground in a matter of minutes. This was not a good week for the campsite owner.

Beki and I went back to the police station the next morning to be told that, although the finger torture had been kept up for most of the night, the suspects hadn't talked. The police had recovered a few more odds and ends, though nothing of great importance.

I spent most of that day in and out of the water, the only way to cool down and calm down. The locals at the riverside drummed the water with cupped hands - a great sound which helped with the calming process. In the afternoon, Wayne decided that we should leave, though poor old Greg and Anne had to stay for another couple of days to wait and see whether anything more would turn up. If not, they would have to go to Kinchasa and get a new passport for Greg from the British Embassy which could take two or three weeks. Wayne gave them a list of times and places where they should be able to rendezvous with us and wishing them well, we said our goodbyes.

Eventually, we hit the road around two in the afternoon. The camp was in a quarry 10km from Gbadolite, a luxurious town planned by Mr Mobutu to become the 'Versailles of the Jungle'. It was weird to see modern brick-built buildings with glass windows, a flashy airport, and well-stocked stores after so many days of mud bogs and rural Africa. It felt peculiar to be able to pop into an urban supermarket that could have been anywhere in Europe and splash out on chocolate and apples - delicious!

The roads were good and had both street and traffic lights. We saw a few chauffeur-driven Mercedes too, presumably for President Mobutu's henchmen. We had to stop in the middle of the road at one point while the Zaire flag was raised. Everything had to come to a halt and everyone had to stop whatever he or she was doing and wait, presumably out of respect. However, out of the corner of my eye, I spied a group of guys who were playing an improvised game of pinball by flicking a marble with a piece of wood causing it to roll across and down the sloping board which was festooned with traps made from thread looped around nails. The rules seemed to have been that if the marble got caught in a trap they won the number of Zaire schillings indicated for that trap.

The Immigration office seemed to have every available space covered with pictures of President Mobutu wearing his leopard-skin hat. We got held up for half an hour while the officials matched our faces to our passport photos and recorded all of our visa numbers. They seemed to be unnecessarily pedantic and Wayne warned us that this kind of practice would get a lot worse in the next few countries. While we were away from the truck, someone stole the water-hose from behind the cab. It was a pity; all of these thefts tended to make us distrust everyone, occasionally to a degree almost verging on paranoia. Luckily, the vast majority of the time, the situation was far more positive and most of the people we met were delightful, trustworthy, and welcoming. I was glad not to be travelling alone though, as I felt that I would have had to spend so much time watching my gear that I'd have hardly taken in my surroundings.

It was a refreshingly speedy drive from Gbadolite to the border between Zaire and the Central African Republic (CAR). We sat around outside and while our passports were being checked, I gave my last birthday balloon to a devastatingly cute little four-year-old girl and was rewarded with her bright toothy grin. Unfortunately, it was election day in the CAR so there was no ferry. The temperature was 41°C in the back of the truck. We could do no more than sit around drinking litres of water and reflecting on our African travel experiences. Being constantly on the move, we acknowledged that it was easy for too much to happen too quickly. We agreed that we had all reached a sightseeing saturation point where the brain refuses to continue to respond to new stimuli in a fresh way and although we were gathering experiences which would, no doubt, influence us for the rest of our lives and which we'd relate with enthusiasm and pleasure when we got home, we'd reached a point when, arriving at a 'tourist attraction', the main 'attraction' became, not the spectacle, but good food, washing facilities, and best of all - a clean, flushing toilet!

Later, we drove down to the ferry and set up camp before cooling down in the river. Due to the recent thefts, we decided to have a guard rota. Beki and I were on watch from ten to twelve that night, sitting out under an almost full moon. The next day, we were packed and ready to go by seven, but the expected ferry didn't materialise. Finally, we crossed at nine, having found the devout captain of the ferry in the local church. The ferry was almost out of fuel and we had to siphon some diesel out of the truck to get across!

Once in the Central African Republic, there was a delay at the immigration post, so we made for the market. A cow was being slaughtered as we passed a butcher's stall; the blood from its throat spurted about 2m through the air - a gruesome spectacle that made Beki run for cover. Back at the immigration post, the official had apparently said to Wayne 'I don't have to let you through today because it is Sunday, but I might if you give me a present . . .' Wayne gave him a Phil Collins cassette which seemed to do the trick. As a consequence, by mid-morning we were through customs and back on the road.

This was to be one of our longest drives, but we were resigned to it as we had to get to Bangui before the weekend in order to get our Nigerian and Cameroon visas. When we had a lunch stop, a Kiwi guy and his German girlfriend pulled up on huge trails motorbikes and stopped for a chat. Travelling by motorbike has a lot of appeal, though I imagine that security must be a constant worry. They told us that they had had their passports stolen in Bangui and then had had to buy them back. Later in the day, we met a Guerba overland truck with a group of thirteen people who were mostly a lot older than we were; they had two drivers and a Kenyan cook. They told us yet more horror stories about Bangui, including the fact that four tents had been cut open one night . . . .

Drive, drive, drive - the truck kicked up a cloud of orange dust as we gunned along. Wayne caught sight of a woman walking by the roadside with two full crates of Primus beer on her head and pronounced that he had found the perfect wife - a woman who could carry all the booze to parties and then carry him home on her head at the end of the evening! We stopped to cook another dehydrated meal at about six and then crashed out for a couple of hours before driving on into the night - Bangui or bust!

Around three in the early hours, everything ground to a halt and we had to fix a flat tyre. Then, later, in the pouring rain, we had to stop and sort out an electrical problem too. It was half past eight before we eventually we made it to the police check post just outside town. We were lucky to get through in ten minutes and managed to keep possession of our passports. Apparently, nearly all people who had passed through recently had had their passports held for a couple of days. Soon after, it was off to find the only campsite in town and get settled in. Later, eight of us crammed into a taxi and went to the Nigerian embassy. The official there was most friendly and helpful, very softly and quietly spoken, a really likeable chap. Everyone, except Wayne, proceeded to fill in the two three-page forms required for each passport. This took at least a couple of hours. Beki and Dave (the carpenter) went to the post office to collect our *Poste Restante* mail, which we eagerly awaited, and I was gratified to get a good stack, the first for over a month. A letter from my brother Joe made me smile. He'd been working as a volunteer in a Mexican orphanage for three months and was now travelling around that country, Guatemala, Belize, and Costa Rica. Reading about his adventures was an inspiration and I started planning how I might go there myself someday.

I was woken up at six o'clock the next morning by a rooster which sounded as though it was perched on top of the tent. We wandered into town and sorted out some local currency before visiting the artisan's market, a thinly disguised tourist trap where Beki shopped until she dropped. I bought a few trinkets myself, including a couple of small 3cm long bronze cats. The air was too thick, hot, and muggy to allow any haste, but on the way back I was just about able to summon up the strength to help a local girl lift a massive metal bowl of fruit onto her head and was thanked by yet another truly radiant African smile.

After a few more evening meals of dehydrated food on the road, the temptation to eat out was irresistible. *Le Quatre Saisons* Pizzeria in Bangui had excellent fare - great salad and delicious pizzas. Beki and I ate slowly and savoured every mouthful. Eventually, we took a taxi to a local market. Our first impression wasn't good as there were many revolting piles of cattle horns and fly-blown meat being chopped up with an axe. As we explored further though, we found Muslim traders selling brightly-coloured clothes and fabrics in the maze of alleyways between the stalls.

On the way back to camp, we met Pete the Plumber and Andrea the Medical Technician who had just bought an ornately-carved wooden chair similar in construction to the one I had bought a week earlier, though theirs had obviously been made specifically for the tourist market. I found the hut of the craftsman who had made it and despite my reservations about buying touristy articles, my resolution buckled and I bought another chair, this one covered in carvings of fish and fishermen.

After supper, Wayne had us all in stitches as he read us a copy of a letter of complaint that had been forwarded to him from the Encounter Overland office in London. It was from an American girl who must have been an unbearable travelling companion. Amongst her list of complaints was the charge that she had been given a burnt scone, because, she alleged, she was one of the 'outcast group'. Wayne said that there had been thirteen people on that particular trip who were fine, but four who were utterly awful. Soon, a Kamuka overland truck parked next to us and an entertaining evening followed. Wayne set fire to our knackered tyre and added a couple of aerosol cans which exploded noisily. The evening calmed down as time went on. Beki and I had to stay up for the duration as we were on the two to four o'clock guard duty. Around three, the wind picked up suddenly and we had to drag everything under the cover of the cook tent before pegging it down firmly, just in time for a biblical downpour.

It was a tonic to spend a couple of days hanging loose in Bangui while we waited for our visas to be processed. One evening, eleven of us squeezed into a taxi and went to Le Bistro restaurant, which was okay but not outstanding. We met a German guy travelling on his own in a VW camper van. He'd been on the road for six months and was heading for South Africa, having funded the trip by busking back home in Germany. I guessed he would have to wait until the end of the wet season though, if he were to have any chance of getting through the mud bogs of Zaire. A second overladen taxi took us back to camp for our mid-trip party which became a mozzie-net party as opposed to the toga party made legendary by the National Lampoon film *Animal House*.

After a few days our passports and visas were sorted out and we were off to Boali Falls. Our camp was quite close to the falls and we were made welcome by the local people. A couple of sweet little girls delighted in plaiting first Beki's hair and then mine. We were easily persuaded to buy some cute little balsa models of boats that were cleverly designed so that when we pulled a string the rowers rowed! The Falls were spectacular, though apparently, displayed only a shadow of their former glory owing to a hydroelectric power scheme up river. Apparently, they used to be considered second only to the Victoria Falls.

The next day, there were frequent *"Barriers du Pluie"* where barriers go down across the roads if it rains and all vehicles have to wait until it's dry enough to move on. This must be very frustrating for travellers in the short term, but it certainly appeared to be effective, judging by the good condition of most of the roads. When we struck camp, I rigged up a sort of mozzie net 'door' to our tent in an attempt to keep the little beasties out, while allowing us to have the tent door open to keep cool. I was pleased to find that this worked very well.

The cooks for the last day before making for the Republic of Cameroon were disappointed in the market in Berberati where all that was on offer was smelly dried fish and ghastly charred monkey. They made the best of it, however, and we had lunch down by the river in no-man's land before tackling the next leg of our journey.

Chapter 9 WARM WATER, WAITING, AND WRANGLING

Cameroon and Nigeria

Having crossed the border by mid afternoon, we drove for a couple of hours before setting up camp next to some deserted huts. The next day was a long one, made more trying by nine military checkpoints, each of which took twenty minutes or so to get through. Each time, we thought 'after this, we can really get going', but no chance. There were three checkpoints in Batouri, one of which involved a military policeman trying to fine Wayne for parking with the trailer not quite straight. As if that weren't enough, at the next checkpoint we had to wait for an hour while the chap in authority decided to have his lunch before checking our passports. Relentlessly, each military person asked the same questions, sometimes only five minutes apart. Later, to cap it all, we had over an hour's delay when we had to get the mud-mats out again as we struggled through a 100m section where an articulated truck had become engulfed in the deep, slimy muck.

We provided great amusement for the local population once we were through. I dashed to be the first at a tap to clean up and a kindly elderly lady kept it flowing for me so that I could have a long final rinse. For some reason, this caused great glee amongst her friends and when I turned round to give them an exaggerated bow of thanks, they were rendered helpless with hoots of laughter.

The next day, we had more muddy problems. We came across a spot where a truck had skidded across the road blocking the route for thirteen more trucks waiting to get past. There was a detour around the sticky spot, mostly following a route that had been cleared for an overhead power line. However, this was still tenaciously gluey, so we attached the four-wheel drive shaft again and ended up mud-matting for three hours to cover one kilometre! About five minutes up the road, we met a road maintenance truck. It stopped and the driver leapt out and ranted at Wayne as he wanted to fine us 150,00CFA (about £300) for passing a *"Barrier du Pluie"* which was on the section of road we had missed because we had taken the detour. Wayne was understandably unhappy and ended up being told he was to be taken to the police station by the maintenance man. However, in the nearby town of Minta, where the fine was to be processed, he was told to get out and wait. We stopped there for lunch and after a couple of hours hanging around, as there was still no sign of anyone from the authorities, Wayne decided to 'do a runner' and we set off.

After yet another quarry campsite we were up and on the road before dawn the next day. This felt like one early start too many to me. There were fewer delays at military checkpoints this time, however, because a soldier hopped up into the cab early on and travelled with us for a while; this undoubtedly facilitated our swifter passage through later checkpoints.

Yaounde, the capital of Cameroon, founded in 1880 by German traders, it was the most westernised town I'd visited in Africa. Many buildings wouldn't have looked out of place in a modern American or European city and plenty were downright luxurious. After so many days, during which we'd only passed a handful of vehicles, it was a shock to encounter so much traffic, even to the extent of being stuck in jams rather than mud. Wandering around town later, Beki and I explored a five-storey spiral building that housed a large market. We steered clear of a loud argument between several guys involved in a street card gambling game and made for calmer waters where Beki got her sandals fixed by a roadside cobbler whose workshop was the shade of his umbrella. This was a better atmosphere and we chatted and joked with him for ages.

On arriving back at camp, we were given an impromptu cabaret by JK and Blair who had drunk a little too much in town and consequently, had had some difficulty in pitching their tent. We found it hilarious and were all in good spirits as we feasted on catfish and fresh veggies - a real treat after so much dehydrated stuff. We were rejoined by Greg and Anne. Unfortunately, Greg's passport hadn't turned up and they had had to get a temporary one from the British Embassy in Kinchasa. Needless to say, they were glad to be back with the rest of the group. In the light of the troubles we'd had with passports, Wayne asked me if I'd be willing, when the time came, to fly ahead from Kano to Lagos to sort out our Algerian visas; I accepted the job.

The next day, we made it to the Atlantic coast. Neither the east nor west coast of Africa had been on the official itinerary, so this was a generous bonus thanks to Wayne's spontaneous nature and willingness to go along with what the group wanted. It was fantastic to go for a swim in the ocean. After a brief shop in Kiribi we drove down a dirt track to the beach on the south side of the river and started to set up camp. A handful of cheerful local inhabitants gathered and made themselves at home, but then an irate individual approached, ranting and raving in French. It transpired, once Wayne had calmed him down, that he was the village chief and was angry because we hadn't asked his permission to camp in that place and he wanted 5000 CFA (Central African francs) for the privilege. It wasn't very much really, but Wayne could see potential trouble and decided to leave. It took forty-five minutes of mud and sand-matting to make our way off the beach and pull the truck back up a slippery slope.

When we reached the top, a young local chap invited us to camp next to his village on the other side of the river and Wayne had to squeeze the truck down a narrow lane to get to it. It was a much better site altogether within sight of the beautiful Kiribi Falls, locally referred to as the Lobe Chutes. The next day was glorious and we watched the sun slowly illuminate the Falls as it rose in the sky. A haze of fine spray hung over the water and occasionally pale rainbows appeared. Beki and I did a heap of washing and enjoyed bathing too. It was invigorating to sit in the middle of the rapids and feel the force of the water, even if it did almost pull my shorts off!

Beki, Pete, Darlene, and I went for a canoe trip upstream from Kiribi Falls. Our paddler was a young lad of about fifteen called Peter. He was the one who'd told us where to camp. The *pirogue* (canoe) was about 5m long and narrow, but comfortable enough. The river flowed big, brown, warm, and quietly powerful – mirror-flat, but with the rumble of the rapids in the distance to remind us of the cataract downstream. It was a pleasureable experience - quiet, peaceful, and relaxing. The only sounds were the birds, the dull booming of the falls, and the occasional splash of Peter's single leaf-bladed paddle. I spotted a mongoose trying to steal from a pile of the ubiquitous wickerwork fish and prawn traps stacked on the riverbank. He looked mischievous and rather quaint. The jungle towered above us as we followed the river, trees rose up to 30m high right next to the bank and were festooned with swinging vines - real Tarzan country! Being just the five of us and Peter, it was a different experience to our dug-out trip in Kisangani. It was good to be in a small group for a change.

After an hour on the river we went to a nearby bar for a cold drink. We were greeted by a local character who must have been about fifty years old. He jigged around and talked in a voice like Donald Duck, much to the amusement of the villagers as well as to us, but I left them all to have an exhilarating run in the surf to cool down before returning to the truck and moving on to a campsite just past Edea, a town bustling and busy with nightlife.

We were dead tired on the following day when we drove to Limbe and we dozed in the truck, heads bobbing up and down like puppets. It was horrendously uncomfortable, yet somehow, we all managed to catch up on deep sleep – God knows how Wayne coped with so little sleep! After a brief stop in Limbe, we drove to Six Mile Beach, a gently curving shore about 1km long with dark grey, almost black sand containing the mineral, *specular haematite*. There were about 150 very white tourists there when we arrived, but they had all left by early evening. It was supposedly illegal to camp there, but Wayne bribed the guards, so we had the beach to ourselves. Wayne was working on the truck, adjusting the clutch rod when it snapped in his hands. This unleashed a torrent of colourful language - understandable, for it has to be said, that vehicle had been giving us repeated problems. Eventually, he managed a bodged job that was good enough to get us into town. He was gratified when we were all obviously impressed by his ingenuity. We got a wonderful blaze going on the beach when it got dark and later, lying on a camp-bed looking up through a canopy of green, I listened to the wonderfully comforting sound of the surf.

I started the next day with a solitary skinny-dip. After breakfast, I bought a few postcards in town and treated myself to a delicious doughnut before we left Limbe. Many of the villages we passed through were like something out of a movie of the old Wild West with just a single main street and houses made from wooden boards. After bedding down at our next camp, we were woken by the incredibly loud croaking of thousands of frogs and toads.

After crossing into Nigeria, we were stopped by police five times within the first half hour. However, they were much friendlier than those in Cameroon and they helped us out with directions and joked about our dirty truck. Our first Nigerian campsite was an old garage and we arrived just in time, as a storm was approaching. The wind was so strong that a couple of the tents actually got blown over. Once the wind had abated, the heavens opened. Eventually, we went to bed, lulled to sleep by the music of the rain drumming on canvas of our tent.

The drive the next day was through jungle and plantations and was reminiscent of an almost primeval environment. As we drove along, I caught sight of a tiny bright green tree frog clinging to one of the bars of the truck and watched it for at least fifteen minutes as it struggled desperately to find sanctuary in the furled canopy. It settled there and rode with us safely all the way to our next destination, Calabar. There, JK and I were on guard duty for so long that when we finally got to the bank to change our money, they only had small denomination notes left. I changed £40 and got 152 notes which made a wad of about 3cm thick. With this in my pocket, I met up with Terry (the travel consultant), Russell (the technician) and Pete and Dave, whom you've already met. We found a good bar and got rid of some of the notes on quite a few cold beers before returning to the truck. I wrote my diary in the cook tent with occasional interruptions from a huge 8cm long lime-green praying mantis. There was quite a lot of heated discussion around the campfire that evening as several people were beginning to look forward to getting away from the group after over two months. However, there had been surprisingly little dissent so far, especially when one considers how much we had been through – both good and bad.

The next day the jungle thinned and the trees gradually became smaller as we continued. Many of the huts we passed were circular with conical thatched roofs. Passing through one small town, I was amused to see the traffic police standing on little islands, directing the traffic with what looked to me like ping-pong bats with 'Stop' and 'Go' on them.

At our next campsite, I found some enormous toads that looked like semi-deflated footballs. They were probably the same toads that had made such a racket a few nights before - a really loud and weirdly synchronised chorus. Hundreds would sing for a while, only to stop as suddenly as they had started. Later in the day, when we stopped at Jos, I noticed that many people, especially women, had decorative geometrical scars on their faces. I also saw quite a few with varying degrees of deformity. I'd seen a lot of disease and deformity throughout Africa, mostly, I think, as a result of leprosy, elephantitus, rickets, malnutrition, and polio. Many of those suffering were beggars. I felt grateful that in the UK we could take advantage of the opportunity to make monthly donations from a pay cheque and be sure that the money would go to reputable charities through Gift Aid.

At a lunch stop outside Jos, JK, and I went over to talk to a couple of men working in a neighbouring field and had a go at helping them dig a furrow for potatoes using a mattock. This helped me appreciate even more just how difficult and physically demanding it is for the subsistence farmer.

Over lunch, there was a discussion about going to Lagos for visas and the need for a 1,000km detour to get a Moroccan visa for Irmin, the Dutch girl. She'd failed to arrange this before the trip and hadn't recognised how it would impact on the rest of the group. Many of us were singularly unimpressed and made our feelings known. An expression of remorse might have made it easier to bear.

When we entered the Yankari Game Reserve in the late afternoon, having followed a dirt track through dense savannah, we came across a herd of elephants. We marvelled at these impressive creatures. There were about forty, including quite a few young. When we stopped, they backed away from the road and held their trunks up high. A couple of bulls made mock charges towards us, extending their ears and kicking up clouds of dust whilst the others in the herd trumpeted loudly. It was a dramatic and exciting display. Then we realised what all the fuss was about; by stopping we had divided the herd. When the other half appeared, the trumpeting, squealing, and grunting really sounded as though the separated elephants were having a conversation. It was a special experience to watch and listen to them. However, we knew it was distressing for them to be divided, so we drove on to our campsite at Wikki Warm Springs.

It was a heavenly spot where we could sit up to our necks in crystal clear water at a constant comfortable temperature of 31°C. It was so good to wake up the next morning knowing that we didn't have to rush off anywhere and a swim in the springs was a refreshing start to the day. There were bands of marauding baboons all around the site. One of them managed to make a lightning raid on the cab of the truck and got away with some of Wayne's biscuits. He chased the culprit, cursing, and brandishing a spade.

A small group of us went for a drive in the Game Reserve bus and soon met a herd of about fifteen elephants. We stopped to watch them for a while as they threw dust over themselves in an effort to cool down. There were quite a few bushbuck and waterbuck too, but they were difficult to see because it was the wet season and the vegetation was dense. However, brilliantly coloured birds were abundant. When we stopped to have a look at a warm, bubbling spring, I noticed a two-foot long Nile monitor lizard which looked convincingly prehistoric. There were too many tsetse flies, however, and boy, did they hurt when they bit!

Back at the bar, we had a few beers as we watched the tiny blue and yellow lizards which looked comical as they dashed to and fro. Later, I washed my sleeping bag which had become rather smelly after nearly five months of travel around Nepal, India, and Africa! Luckily, it was so hot that it was bone dry by bedtime. I also had a good time climbing a crag above the point where the water resurged from a 150m long underground river. This was great fun because I could make really desperate moves and fall off, simply making a colossal splash in the pool below.

We had to leave slightly earlier than planned the next day because the President was visiting Wikki Warm Springs; we actually passed his limousine later in the day. As we drove on, we encountered much drier savannah country and it felt good to be into new scenery after so long in the jungle. There were quite a few kopjes topped with trees which appeared to sprout directly from the rocks. Unfortunately, the truck had a blow-out but, but no worries, Greg and I managed to do a speedy wheel change which only took about fifteen minutes.

In the late afternoon, we set up camp in the middle of thorny scrub. Once we were established, Beki and I 'chatted' wordlessly with laughs, smiles, and signs to three lads who had appeared from nowhere and had watched us quietly as we pitched our tent. In the evening, about half of our group had the gruesome task of digging '*chiggers*' (the larvae of parasitic mites which live in the mud bogs) out of their feet. They bite their host and cause intense irritation and wheals, entering the soles of the feet through pores in the skin. Only JK and I had been lucky enough not to be affected, probably because rather than flip-flops, we had been wearing the footwear of the future - wellies! While on the subject of creepy-crawlies, when I took the tent down the next morning, I found a mean looking sand-coloured scorpion under the groundsheet!

As we journeyed on, the savannah became increasingly dry and dotted with occasional extraordinary Baobab trees, the source of many traditional remedies and folklore. They can grow for thousands of years and are among the oldest living things on earth. They store water in their trunks during the rainy season and produce fruit later in the year when everything else is barren. For obvious reasons, it's also known as 'The Tree of Life'.

The truck had another big blowout which made everyone jump out of their seats and their skins and which left the rear left tyre absolutely shredded. While Wayne was fixing the wheel, I strolled over to the nearest village and watched a diminutive old woman with a pestle pounding grain in a large mortar. Later, we had yet another blowout on the same wheel; we were only 8km from Kano, our destination. Wayne, Pete, and Dave hitched a lift into town to get a new tyre and, fortunately, they were back within an hour.

We drew up at the official Kano State Tourist Camp and found another Encounter Overland truck there. It was sparkling clean with a thief-proof hard-top trailer for the rucksacks. These had apparently become standard issue by the time they'd set out, though that was little consolation for Beki, Tracey, and Greg who were still suffering from losing their kit in Zaire. There were seven Americans, six Brits, and a couple of others on the other truck. I chatted with a guy from Erpingham, near Cromer, a thirty minute drive from Norwich, where I grew up – small world!

Later, Beki and I took a taxi to the market, accompanied by a 'guide' who had chosen to adopt us. Alharji Bara was friendly and informative and spoke reasonable English. It was definitely worth having him along to help us explore. We were immediately struck by a *potpourri* of aromas - incense, garlic, herbs, and gum Arabic with its singular musky smell. Alharji was great, explaining many interesting details with genuine enthusiasm. One stall was selling balls of pigment which were ground down and mixed with water to produce the ink for writing with a split cane pen. Many stalls were selling *Kohl*, the mineral galena (lead ore), which is ground up and kept in small vials to be used as eye shadow by many of the local women - can't be too healthy! There was also potash (potassium) for sale to be used as a medicinal cure-all. Many stalls had high piles of intriguing bowls full of sweet-smelling grasses, dried herbs, and bark fragments. One pot of dried herbs was apparently mixed with water and rubbed onto the bodies of children to encourage 'sweating out' malaria; a sort of herbal 'Deep Heat'.

Numerous stalls were selling 100 per cent cotton hand-woven rugs and fabrics, many with distinctive, original designs. I bought some striking blue and white tie-dye fabric. Other stalls were selling a wide variety of leather goods, including awful handbags made from the skin of young alligators with the head still intact. On the way back to camp, we stopped to visit the dye pits. These were circular shafts about a metre across and 1-3m deep, full of foul-smelling dye; apparently, urine is used to fix it. The process is completed in one day. The fabric is then hung out to dry or draped over bushes in the afternoon sun.

I was up at half past five to find that Mohammed, the resident 'fixer' of the Kano State Tourist Camp, had sorted out our transport to the airport in preparation for the journey to the Algerian embassy to sort our visas. A chap called John from the other Encounter Overland truck, joined me. After dodging the persistent ticket touts, buying my own, paying airport tax, and checking in, I couldn't resist the improbable offer of having my leather sandals polished - for the princely sum of one Nigerian naira – a bargain!

Once in Lagos, we took a taxi to the British High Commission. John stopped there while the taxi driver spent half an hour aimlessly wandering in search of the Algerian embassy for me; nobody seemed to know where it was. When we finally found it, the driver wanted more money than he had previously estimated because of the long drive. I told him that if he'd agreed to take me to a destination he didn't know, then the consequence was his problem and, to give him his due, he accepted the situation. When, finally, I arrived at the embassy, I got a calm and friendly reception. I explained my requirements and asked how long it would take. I swallowed hard when I was told ten days, then I went into persuasive mode – it seemed to work; the official went off to talk to one of his superiors and came back half an hour later with a thick wad of visa applications, saying that the visas might even be ready the next day! It took me three solid hours to fill in the forms and to get a serious dose of writer's cramp.

Once I'd finished and left the embassy, I checked out the Federal Palace Hotel where I was served by waiters smartly dressed in black trousers with distinctly exaggerated flairs. Near the hotel, I noticed the office of a company called Petrologging, a similar outfit to Exploration Logging, the company I'd worked for previously on oil rigs and I had an interesting chat with the guys working there.

The next day, I returned to the embassy. Again, the trip took quite a while as I got another taxi driver who hadn't a clue where he was going. He kicked up a fuss when we finally arrived and I told him that, after such an unnecessarily roundabout journey, I would pay twenty Naira and no more; he could take it or leave it. He took it. Thereafter, it took almost an hour to get all the visas and passports sorted out, but that was a distinct improvement on ten days.

When I left, and despite my earlier experiences with Lagos taxi drivers, I risked asking my next driver, Moshundi, to show me around the city. He was a genial fellow, but the tour wasn't really a good idea as Lagos was a big, noisy, smelly, modern city that could have been almost anywhere in the world. The roads were wide, but clogged with traffic and many of the buildings were high-rise and featureless. There appeared not to be an old town district as there is usually in most developing world cities. I ended up in a large bookshop where I enjoyed a long browse and bought a couple of paperbacks by Nigerian authors. The girl at the till found my small silver frog earring very amusing and we laughed about it together. Later, I stopped for some street food including some delicious spicy chicken. When I'd finished, a young man aged about nineteen came up to me beaming with delight and told me that he had felt compelled to write to me while I was sitting eating my lunch. He handed me a note which said 'Jesus loves You'. I was touched. He didn't say another word. He just gave me a happy wave, turned, and walked away - a rather charming experience before my last Lagos taxi driver wiped the smile off my face! He behaved as his predecessors had done; he didn't even know the way to the airport!

That night, I got back to Kano at tennish and went straight to the Central Hotel bar to meet Lou (a nurse), Terry, Russell, and Space. We left at two in the morning and were promptly arrested by a couple of policemen with machine guns and an attitude to match. It seems we had broken a curfew we hadn't even known existed. We tried to talk our way out of it, but they weren't impressed. By now, I'd been appointed 'spokesperson' for the group and despite my protestations, when we were addressed by the most senior officer, he insisted that we should be taken to the police station. At this moment, a police car pulled up and I turned on what I hoped was charm to turbo capacity and, chancing my arm, talked about football. To everyone's relief, amusement, and surprise, including mine, this got us off the hook. It was a crazy charade – I'm not even that fond of football, but it worked. Back at the camp, we entertained the rest of the group with the story of our arrest. We rather gilded the lily, but there you go – travellers' tales!

The next evening we met Patrick, a friendly local man, and a few of his friends, and went to a nightclub called Woodlands. It was flashy by African standards with over-amplified music and disco lights. However, there were only eight people there. During the long wait for dinner we talked to Patrick and his friends about politics, including the North-South conflict in Nigeria and the various plights of Christians, Muslims, and 'Chrislims' (adherents to both Christianity and Islam). It was an interesting and stimulating conversation and good to hear many different views. The meal we had ordered never materialised and it was, by now, so late that we couldn't find another place open. We went home hungry.

The next day, Irmin, the rather timid Dutch girl who'd caused problems earlier by not having secured her Moroccan visa before the trip, returned from the doctor with confirmation that she had malaria. Poor soul really seemed to have a tendency to be unfortunate.

On that day, it fell to Beki and me to do the food shopping. It turned out to be a particularly arduous task. It was, of course, hot, and it took ages to find what we wanted as we had to battle through dense crowds and occasional potash-laden donkeys, to get it. Tired out and a little grumpy after our endeavours, we took a taxi back to camp and were disarmed when the friendly local guy who had shared part of the ride, insisted on paying our fare, even though he'd only been in the taxi with us for a few minutes. Most of the Nigerians we met were genuinely friendly and extremely generous.

The next day dawned in spectacular fashion with a glowering brown sky, thunder, lightning, and torrential rain. After a cleansing 'shower' under the spouts of water that channelled off the roof of the camp buildings, I took time out just to stand and stare at the big fat raindrops tumbling over each other to reach the ground. Puddles formed quickly and soon became a battlefield of tiny explosions as the hissing rain bubbled and spat on impact. Every bubble was a perfect hemisphere for a brief moment. But perfection is short-lived when it's raining. Rills became streams and streams became small rivers in no time, but in that part of the world, almost as abruptly, the situation was reversed and only dry empty channels and a few muddy puddles remained. While they existed, however, every stream was fast and bright; glistening crystal bubbles chasing one another along all available edges and ledges. Then they tumbled off in procession. Falling to a pool, they burst on the surface to form a tiny spout of water and maybe a further bubble. Then they lost their identity and became part of the body of water as the force of their impact spread perfect rings that seemed to oscillate and expand forever. Everything shone, but eventually, it all turned to dull mud – a bit like life sometimes!

The next evening we had a big party with the group on the Guerba truck. Many yarns were spun; the events recounted became increasingly more highly coloured, improbable, and exaggerated. There was a lot of fooling around with Dave, Terry, and Pete jumping over burning tyres, for example. Not surprisingly, our group, party animals to a man and woman, totally out-boogied the Guerba crew. By half past three, there were ten of us still going strong and only one 'Goobie' left. Amazingly, we were all up by seven to watch a dance troupe from Niger that was staying at the camp. They were dressed in full regalia with swords and beautiful leather gear. The drumming was stupendous too - I couldn't help wiggling as I watched.

Chapter 10 SO HOT YOU DON'T SWEAT

Crossing the Sahara in the dry season

When we finally left our Nigerian base in Kano after our ten-day stay, the floor of the truck was loaded two-deep with 850 cans of soft drinks to slake our thirst in the Sahara. JK and I were gratified to find that our canvas water bags definitely provided the coolest water on the truck. Happily, we got across the Nigeria-Niger border in forty-five minutes, but the other side proved to be a pain as JK and I had to unload the entire contents of the trailer twice within 100m; once was for the police and once for customs. When we had got through, we had only driven 30km before the police stopped us yet again. Luckily for JK and me, Wayne managed to talk them out of a third search.

There was a marked change in scenery as we drove north; the land dried out and the vegetation thinned from trees to scrub. We were in fairly open savannah by the end of the day. In many of the villages, the huts were encircled by mud walls covered in hand prints where the wet dirt had been slapped on. There was usually one hut outside the perimeter wall which we supposed must have been for guards, guests, quarantine, or ritual isolation. We never did find out which. There were also grain stores - barrel-shaped huts with woven walls and thatched roofs. They were on stilts to keep the grain dry and to reduce attack by vermin. Throughout the day, several Harmattan winds hit; hot, dry winds that blow from the northeast or east in the western Sahara. They carry large amounts of red desert dust hundreds of kilometres out over the Atlantic Ocean, which occasionally covers the bonnets of cars on the south coast of the U.K. when the wind blows from the south.

We were up at dawn and headed off to Zinder at seven the next morning. We passed through an increasingly flat and arid landscape dotted with thorny acacia bushes. There was so much dust in the air that it created a ghostly haze first thing in the morning. Donkeys were the local form of transport and we passed many piled high with impossibly large and often improbable loads including water pots, animal fodder, flour sacks, and even bunches of live chickens trussed up by their feet.

In Zinder, we had to get our passports stamped. This was something we were to get used to in every Niger town. It wasn't all bad news, as whilst we were waiting we had time to do other things. Beki and I made friends with a woman who invited us into her home. Her grandmother lived next door and looked about one hundred years old. The house was a typical of the region, constructed from mud bricks with thick walls and plain, sparsely furnished, cool rooms. Later, we rambled around the market, which was rather smelly, to a large extent because many stalls were selling vulture's claws and beaks as well as sheep's heads with their eyes lolling out.

Then, it was off towards Agadez amidst a chorus of children shouting "*Donnez moi un cadeau!*" - A pity to be hearing that kind of thing again. The temperature reached 40°C even when the truck was moving. As the scrub merged into desert and the roads became increasingly sandy and potholed, it was almost as though we were on another planet. The semi-desert was dotted with the nomads' dome-shaped tents, made from tarpaulins stretched over frameworks of bowed branches.

Towards the end of the day it was good to have a beer. I found that wrapping a wet bandanna around the bottle and hanging it over the side of the truck cooled it to a drinkable temperature. The setting sun was a perfect white disc. I went to sleep in the open, under a star-lit sky, something I was going to miss when I got back to the UK. It was chilly around five in the morning, but by half past six, it was already 28°C and not long after, it reached a searing 40°C. We forged ahead, passing a few small camel trains led by stately Tuareg (Berber people with a traditionally nomadic lifestyle), dressed in navy blue robes with black turbans and carrying long, leather-sheathed swords.

Agadez, a centre of trade since before the fourteenth century, was a busy town known for its camel market, silver artefacts, and leatherwork. It was also a centre for the transportation of uranium mined in the surrounding area. Beki and I met a young Fulani man who took us to his silver-smithing workshop where he showed us the jewellery he'd made out of low-grade silver, characteristic of the region with most of the designs based on a cross. Later, a few of us enjoyed a few beers in a friendly local bar. Just as we got back to the truck, a fierce storm blew up and the sky turned yellow, orange, red, and ultimately, dark brown. It was suddenly as though night had fallen, even though the sun had been blazing down only minutes before. Visibility was practically nil, so we had to wait for fifteen minutes or so with scarves over our heads to keep out the dust. Nevertheless, we soon found a good campsite and enjoyed a meal of camel meat that tasted a helluva lot better than that I'd eaten when I was working on oil rigs in Syria. I went to sleep counting shooting stars – bliss!

The next day, we continued our journey; the desert opened out to endless horizons; the land and sky merging in the dusty haze. We made for Arlit, an industrial town founded in 1969 following the discovery of uranium. It had grown up around the mining industry which was developed by the French government. All sorts of rubbish, including old tyres and bits of wood, held down tin roofs of many rather dismal buildings. The school was a flimsy roadside shack made from sticks supporting woven matting. It seemed incongruous that most of the primitive mud-walled huts had both power and telephone lines.

Our 'road' had been reduced to tyre tracks across the stony ground, though it was generally firm enough to allow us to make pretty good progress at between 40 to 50kmph. We followed the simple markers that were placed every kilometre, usually made of sand-filled oil drums with a post sticking out of the top. In the heat of the day, we stopped to give food and water to a woman and her five children who were sitting out in the open beside the track in the middle of the desert. I found it difficult to understand how anyone could scrape any kind of existence in this area.

The truck got stuck a few times, so we had to do some rescue work. The sand was so hot we couldn't stand on it with bare feet. We only saw a couple of other trucks on the road, though there were quite a few abandoned vehicles. These had been totally stripped of anything useful and only the sandblasted body remained. We had a photo stop when we found an old VW Combi with "Kiwis" spray-painted on the side and an arrow pointing the way they had probably gone. The heat was relentless and the desert became sandier with a few crescent shaped barchan dunes.

In the evening, we camped in the lee of a 20m high ridge. I went for a pretty long walk into the desert and gloried in the isolation. Everyone was pissed off though when, a few hours later, five trucks pulled up and set up camp a couple of hundred metres away. It was hard to believe that with all that space in the middle of the desert, they felt compelled to settle close to us, thus ruining our solitude.

I slept on my own, a few hundred metres away from the truck. It was marvellous to wake up out of sight of the others, completely alone and at peace as I watched the silver sun rise over the flat gravelly desert. A lone butterfly fluttered around my head. I was amazed that it had migrated through such an inhospitable region. After the peace of early morning, I was equally happy to listen to *Dark side of the Moon* blasting out on the Walkman as we roared on our way.

We crossed the Niger border into Algeria. There were just a few mud huts, a clump of trees, and a huddle of makeshift camps, plus the inevitable camels and donkeys. Some of the camel herders were equipped with *guerbas*, traditional goatskin bags used to keep water cool. Others had similar containers made from old car inner tubes. There was also a huge stockpile of cans of white paint; the mind boggles as to what it was doing there! Luckily, there was somewhat sulphurous water available, so we all took advantage of the opportunity to have a good wash.

It was supposed to be half an hour's drive to the Algerian border post, so after two and a half hours of following a maze of tracks in the sand, repeatedly getting stuck, and having to sand-mat our way out, we finally decided to turn back and follow our own tracks back to the Niger border post. It took us over an hour and a half to find it. Would you believe that we had no compass? Enough said and a lesson learned!

Eventually, we reached the Algerian border post in the early afternoon and found it was quite literally that - a post stuck in the sand surrounded by a cluster of portacabins. It was 47°C. When we got out of the truck, we were struck by a dry blast of heat such as occurs when an oven door is opened to take out the Sunday roast! It was so hot that we weren't even aware of sweating because of instant evaporation. As we drove north, the desert continued to change in character. I loved the fact that throughout the expedition there had been a continuous unfolding of contrasting landscapes each, it seemed, better than the last. Our camp that night was among a collection of bizarrely shaped mesa-like rock formations (tall, with steep sides and a relatively flat top) - a really beautiful spot.

Driving off through the mist next morning, the contorted shapes of the mesas loomed out of the gloom revealing a spectral landscape. It was at times like these that having studied geology really added to my enjoyment, as well as providing me with plenty of real-life examples that I'd use as a teacher in the future. Following a braided miscellany of tyre tracks, we passed more abandoned vehicles, all reduced to bare metal frames where no speck of paint had been able to cling in the face of the frequent sandstorms – truly efficient sand-blasting. I was glad of the chance to ride in the cab with Beki and Wayne, boogying around to loud music including Hunters and Collectors, George Thorogood and the Destroyers, Paul Kelly, ZZ Top, and INXS.

Lunch was in the skimpy shade of a solitary wizened tree, the last resting place of a desiccated camel that lay nearby. The track markers had become more widely-spaced, sometimes ten kilometres or more apart, and we were lost for an hour or so which was a serious worry. We wouldn't be travelling without a compass again – the shame of it!

At last, we found the trail again and came across the crumbling remains of short sections of tar-sealed road which gradually evolved into good new road. We stopped to increase the tyre pressures so that we could speed up and really start to eat up the kilometres. There were some classic geological formations with intrusive discordant dykes and concordant sills and spectacular volcanic plugs with superb columnar jointing that made them look like some sort of alien landing pad - echoes of the film *Encounters of the Third Kind*.

Tamanrasset was the first settlement we'd seen in 400km; it was a complete contrast to the African towns we'd visited up until then. The inhabitants were Arabic and there were no women to be seen. It was a real pain to be impelled by law to cash £100, which was effectively an Algerian tourist tax, when there really wasn't anything one would want to buy. I'd bought a few, I hope, well chosen traditional artefacts since we began our trip, but I've never been an avid collector of souvenirs and prefer to spend my money on photography, both for my own pleasure and as a way of sharing at least a glimpse of my travels with family and friends. A few weather-beaten men rode through town on camels, dusty from long travels in the desert. They looked out of keeping gliding along between cars and streetlights. Each animal wore a small (7cm square and 1cm thick) silver box around its neck as a charm to bring it good health and good luck. Many of the people wore a collection of leather charm bags too.

The trip to Assakrem hermitage was made in Land Cruisers. It was a three-hour drive through scenery that looked Tolkeinesque, thanks to the volcanic origin of the landscape. We walked up to the hermitage - a gathering of a few stone huts; one was a little church with goatskins on the floor, a small stone slab table, and a small altar. Behind a beautiful heavy blanket, there was a 'library' which housed French Bibles. I didn't feel comfortable being in such a special place with so many people, so I went outside and contemplated the quiet majesty of the mountains. I found a good viewpoint, a comfortable rock to sit on, and soaked it all up for an hour - the cold breeze tugged at my hair as I watched in awe as falcons played in the thermals. At times, it felt almost as though the wind was blowing right through me, rather than around me. It was a good time to think about people I knew, my future career, ambitions, plans for further travels, and also to take time to reflect on past experiences. My head was really buzzing. I stayed on my little perch, my eyrie, until everyone else had gone back down the mountain to the hut where we were to spend the night. There, we had a meal of spicy noodle soup followed by mutton stew with couscous, the local staple diet.

I was up at six the next morning and steamed back up to the hermitage on my own to sit on 'my rock' again for sunrise, solitude, and introspection. Some of the group attended a service in the hermitage, it seemed to me with the attitude of visiting a tourist attraction rather than to worship; I decided not to go as I felt that such a service should be respected as a serious religious event.

I still had a load of Dinars to spend and ended up buying a local outfit consisting of a pair of baggy white trousers, a long white shirt, and a turban to complete the look. An expensive fancy dress outfit at £36, but there really wasn't anything else I had an inclination to buy. It would be fun to use it once I was back in the UK. Pete and I were hungry, so we spent our last currency on a whole roast chicken which we quickly demolished between us.

After a visit to a doctor, Irmin had decided to abandon the trip because she was still suffering from malaria. It must have been a great disappointment for her, but also, I would think, a real relief. After saying our goodbyes, we set off on a good tar-sealed road and, as the afternoon progressed, we passed quite a few picture-book oases with splashes of verdant vegetation among the bleached browns of the desert. I wore my turban and was amazed at how effective it was at keeping my head cool. Wayne made a brief diversion to visit a cluster of white buildings called Marabout Moulay Hassan. Apparently, a priest had died there on his way to Mecca and it's now considered good luck for travellers to circle the chapel three times in thoughtful silence. A burnt out VW nearby had not, it seemed, kept to this tradition!

We travelled on roads of variable quality through flat desert dotted with impressive kopjes. There was a dramatic gorge as we left Arak which was, maybe, 100m deep. Eventually, we entered a region that was stereotypically desert, with massive classic dunes called seif dunes. Their flowing curves cast subtle shadows that created delicate colourscapes in shades of orange and yellow. Some reminded me of a reclining nude sculpted by Henry Moore.

The following day, we passed through In Salah, with a temperature of more than 50°C; it's known as the hottest place in the Sahara and was once an important stop on the trans-Saharan caravan route. As usual, Beki and I went for a quick look around the market before doing our guard duty on the truck and splurged on a honeydew melon, cold drinks, chocolate . . . . and ice cream! Darlene went to the doctor and came back with the grim news that she had hepatitis, so she flew to Algiers to rest for a week before meeting us again in Morocco.

The next day we passed through Reggane and discovered that we'd be driving on tar-sealed roads all the way to London – time for me to take off the four-wheel drive shaft! We all managed to get a much-needed wash, "showering" under a tap 1.5m off the ground. Dave and I bought a huge watermelon and chomped and slurped our way through the succulent flesh and in the afternoon, we found a large covered well, about 4m across and 2m deep, with a 4m drop down to the water. In the 50°C heat it was just too tempting and we took turns jumping in and hauling ourselves out using a knotted rope. Camping amongst the dunes was heavenly.

However, the next morning we found we were stuck and had to sand-mat and pull the truck back onto the road. At a lunch stop about 18km out of Taghit, we had a look at the *Gravures rupastres*, prehistoric rock carvings of animals. They had a simple graceful beauty. The most interesting carvings were outlines of hands and feet, possibly those of the artist or artists. It was an almost spiritual experience to gaze on marks made by people so long ago, wondering how they'd felt at the time, what their family circumstances were, what human concerns we might still share in common.

Ever onward! We encountered numerous dust devils (small whirlwinds) during the rest of the day's drive. We even drove straight through one with its marvellous swirling patterns writhing across the road. As we left the desert behind, the way was often strewn with bundles of barbed wire that blew around like some kind of metallic tumbleweed in a post-apocalyptic Western film.

Many of the Algerian towns seemed to be deserted. Even when the truck stopped, the usual swarms of children we'd become used to failed to appear. We'd almost come to expect crowds of inquisitive onlookers to materialize whenever we came to a halt. At last, we felt a cool breeze as we approached the Mediterranean coast and there were cheers of delight from everyone when we first saw the sea. Beni Sef, however, was a rather tacky little resort with a European feel to it. Many of the houses were whitewashed and they had bright blue shutters. Some of the people looked more Spanish than Algerian.

The next day, I went off on my own and enjoyed a leisurely few hours exploring the craggy coastline and clambering down to an isolated cove to go skinny-dipping in emerald-green water. Later, I went back into town and splurged on ice creams again! The next morning, I was rudely awoken at half past four by the bloodcurdling screams of a hyrax (a small thick-set furry animal like a cross between a rabbit and a rat) and a pre-dawn chorus of barking dogs. The nightmarish clamour only lasted for about five minutes, but it had banished sleep for me. Not to worry, I lay awake thinking about our next stop – Morocco.

Chapter 11 GORGEOUS GORGES AND MEDINA MAZES

Morocco

We passed through the border crossing into Morocco quickly and smoothly.   This was a relief as Wayne had said it had taken ten hours on his last trip.   Once there, we passed through Oujda, a place significantly more westernised and affluent than anywhere we'd been for months, though there were still donkey carts mingling with Mercedes in the streets.   There were also more women in evidence than in Algeria where I don't think I saw more than a hundred in the whole country; most of them had been dressed in modest clothing to comply with Muslim custom.

A couple of hours' journey beyond Oujda, it was noticeably cooler.   We camped in a plantation of tall thin trees where, for the first time in weeks, many of us felt the need to don sweatshirts during the day.   The next day, we started to climb zigzag roads into the mountains where we had spectacular views over the plains below.   There were many gypsies living in tarpaulin benders, shepherding flocks of sheep and goats on the dusty scrub.

The geology was a textbook example of intensely folded rocks having contorted into fantastic shapes when the African continent collided with Europe more than 50 million years ago.   There were a few mud-walled lookout towers and forts as well as villages which looked like scenes from the Bible. At the beginning of the Ziz Gorge, we stopped off at a roadside cafe where I noticed incongruous western posters advertising bands including the Scorpions, and Van

Halen. Wayne was in a playful mood and we drove in to the tunnel at the beginning of the gorge with the horn going full blast which gave rise to an overwhelmingly deafening noise. Our camp that night was a few kilometres from Errichidia.

The next morning I woke with sand in every orifice, but thankfully I hadn't had any nocturnal encounters with the giant scorpions we found around the campsite before we left. Towering cliffs, 150m high, dwarfed the truck as we drove along the bottom of the spectacular Todra Gorge, situated on the east side of the High Atlas Mountains. The road was only 15m wide in places. The whole place simply cried out to the rock-climber in me. Friendly people waved, many wearing baggy tops with hoods and bright yellow pointed slippers which brought back to mind childhood picture books of Aladin and Ali Baba. The truck was given a long overdue wash in the stream at the bottom of the gorge and, for the umpteenth time, we managed to get stuck. Wayne and Dave had to lie down in the water to put the four by four drive-shaft on again, much to the amusement of the villagers. After that, a lazy evening was spent lounging around under a colourful marquee-type tent where a chap was playing some really good rhythms on ceramic-bodied, bongo-style drums.

The next day I walked up one of the gullies branching off the main gorge. I saw a couple of Berber shepherds with their goats and dogs, but once I'd left them behind I was completely alone. The silence was golden, broken only by the occasional bleating goat, the sound echoing around the gorge. I did some bouldering, giving me a tiny, but tantalising taste of the fantastic potential of the area.

Shortly after we left the dramatic gorge, we drove through a town in high spirits, squirting any children we passed, and each other, with water pistols. We decided that every traveller should have one! As we crossed the Atlas Mountains there were many small terraced fields bordered by dry stone walls, and I spotted the first 'walking bushes' I had seen since Nepal - children carrying huge bundles of animal fodder.

We set up camp just past the Tizi-In-Tichka Pass which proved to be pretty chilly as night fell. The next morning, we descended, negotiating countless tortuous hairpin bends made even more hazardous by the many over-laden donkeys and their owners who were teetering down the winding roads. Passing through villages, I noticed that rather than carrying water jugs on their heads, as is the style in most of Africa, here women carried them slung over one shoulder. Further on, it was also interesting to see how the fruit of the prickly pear cactus was harvested. A long pole was used; it had a split at the end with a bit of string attached in such a way that when it was pulled the "jaws" opened and then closed around the fruit - clever huh?

It was something of a culture shock to enter the hustle and bustle of Marrakesh, a city which had been founded in 1062. The stout red sandstone twelfth century fortifications gave rise to the popular name, the 'Red City'. We found our campsite which we shared with hundreds of others. It was a far cry from the secluded sites we'd become accustomed to. The 'exotic adventure' element of the trip definitely ended here. Nevertheless, there was still much to do and see. I made a symbolic gesture to this change by buying a copy of The Times and reading it at a street cafe whilst sipping delicious freshly-squeezed orange juice as modern traffic, donkey carts, sheep, goats, and cows trundled by. I'd never seen so many mopeds in my life, many of them carrying two men with a live (or dead) sheep or goat awkwardly sandwiched between them!

Of course it didn't take Beki (with me in tow) long to find the way to the *medina* (the old market) where we were quickly adopted by one of the many opportunists who pounced on anyone foreigners, in order to make a coin or two. Mustafa was friendly and not too pushy, so we let him show us around, communicating in a mixture of French and English. Before long, we were deep in the heart of the souk, a tangle of twisting narrow alleys where there was every kind of delight to discover. There were piles of brightly-coloured, pungent spices and apothecaries sold strange, unidentifiable, dried medicinal roots and herbs which hung in bunches from the ceiling. Later, we drifted back to the more touristy section of the market. There, we found stalls selling beautifully crafted wooden boxes made from a type of cedar wood that smelt gorgeous. While Beki haggled for one of these, I loitered outside and was offered 3 kg of Kif (marijuana) by a shady character. I quickly escaped, not wishing to star in a sequel to the *Midnight Express* film! We moved on to the leather section, where I haggled like a veteran, using every trick in the book to get good deals on presents for my family.

Later, we passed the time by watching the many street performers busking in the square. There were clowns, acrobats, snake charmers, quacks, and even dentists. It was interesting to notice that most of those watching were locals. The tourists seemed to prefer to frequent western-style shops and the few large 'souvenir supermarkets' that catered mainly for foreign sightseers.

The square was almost completely surrounded by a line of stalls selling delicious orange juice, true 'liquid sunshine'. There were also countless Moroccan fast food stalls which included fish and chips as well as traditional Moroccan fare. Sellers wandered around dressed in fancy red traditional costumes, serving water in shiny brass cups filled from a goatskin *guerba*. As dusk fell, Beki and I went to a cafe that had a balcony overlooking the square where we enjoyed delicious omelettes. Below, feverishly dancing dervishes were accompanied by the mesmeric rhythm of finger cymbals.

The next day, we returned to the *medina* where I have to admit to having become increasingly short-tempered with the pushy salesmen, especially the ones who physically grabbed prospective customers and refused to let go, even when it was blindingly obvious that there was not to be a sale. Many of them seemed to have a rich vocabulary of particularly offensive English swear words and we were often subjected to a vivid torrent of abuse for walking away – a far cry from the many friendly encounters we'd had on our earlier journeys. In the evening, we ate at the unfortunately named *Foucal* restaurant.

After a great breakfast of fruit salad and croissants the next morning, we left Marrakesh and headed for Fez, 476km away. We passed through avenues of trees between mud-banked fields. As I watched children playing in the irrigation channels, I thought about how soon I'd be leaving Africa, though in my heart, I think, I left

Africa when we left Nigeria. Everyone was disappointed to find the Fez post office closed and no prospect of mail for several days. It was, on the surface at least, a modern, almost European city complete with fashionable street cafes though we learned that its history went back as far as the eighth century. JK, Blair, and I went food shopping which was rendered excruciating due to the persistence of more over-zealous vendors pressing their wares on us from every side. Maybe it was because we'd all been on the road too long that we were becoming intolerant, but I certainly hadn't felt so menaced anywhere else in the world.

In the afternoon, several of us went for a Turkish bath and massage. It was so hot and steamy that we could almost feel a stream of dirt being flushed out of each pore. The massage was not the ultimate relaxation that I'd experienced in India; this was more of a wrestling match - feet behind the ears and all!

On a tour of Fez the next day, our guide, Gali, gave us a good introductory talk which helped to put the city into some sort of context before we went off on our own. He told us that Its history went as far back as the eighth century and we visited the fourteenth century King's Palace in the Jewish quarter, which had been restored by King Hassan II in 1968. The gardens were stunning and the colossal bronze doors were mighty, though apparently, they were never opened. The whole population was busy preparing for the festival of Abraham which involved a bloody sheep sacrifice from every family.

Many of the buildings resembled those I'd seen in Andalusia a year or two before, a part of the world which had been heavily influenced by early Muslim architecture. We were fascinated to see that many constructions had holes in the walls to allow the swallows through because they were considered holy. The fourteenth century hospital was next to a cemetery - easy come, easy go, I suppose! The *Medina* in Fez is the largest and oldest in Africa and about 20,000 people a week come from all over Morocco to visit. Thirty five per cent of the local population make an informal living from handicrafts. Gali the Guide kept reeling off statistics saying 'It is the largest in the total world!'

In the depths of the Medina the air was alive with smells, both good and bad. There were spices, perfumes, mint, cedar wood, bread, dye pits, the tannery, and donkeys which clip-clopped along through the narrow alleys, scattering people to right and left. The gaudy stalls were piled so high that the stallholder was often completely hidden by his wares. The only respite from the cacophony of noise was to be found in the mosques. The buzz of extreme activity was partly due to the fact that the Medina was to be closed for a week for the Abraham sheep festival and associated holiday. At lunchtime, I escaped the bustle by finding a little cafe where I could sit upstairs and watch the life of the streets below. Children were selling snacks of boiled potatoes with salt and spice and old men sold water in large, brown, spotty, clay mugs.

In the afternoon, we visited the fourteenth century Koranic School where we saw the cedar and marble fountain used for the customary thrice-daily ablutions. Gali gave us an interesting short lecture on the Muslim faith and I was left pondering why so many people seem to live their lives following their own particular religion without ever questioning it. Later, we went to the government carpet emporium.   This was a co-operative of 1,300 women carpet-weavers who sold their goods through a shop which was situated in the Bahir Palace, a fourteenth century residence. After a talk about carpets, some of the group capitulated before the salesmen's wiles and bought rugs, many of which cost several hundreds of pounds. Meanwhile, underwhelmed by the whole business, I fell asleep! In the evening, we went out for a group meal which was accompanied by belly dancers, acrobats, and a few of our number getting dressed up in traditional local clothes to the amusement of all.

The next couple of days were spent taking it easy, loafing about on the campsite and sitting in street cafes. After picking up our mail from the *Poste Restante*, we left Fez and headed into the Rif Mountains where the main cash crop seemed to be marijuana with huge fields of 2m high plants. We camped next to the beach about 20km from Cueta and after a hurried dash arrived at the ferry terminal with minutes to spare. Wayne wasn't amused when he had to pay extra because the trailer was 10cms too high. This made us miss the crossing after all and delayed us for two hours.

It was time for our last goodbye to Africa. Once in Spain, the truck did a screeching emergency stop at McDonalds and we all gorged on the first junk food we'd had for four months. It still tasted bland - give me traditional, slow-cooked local fare any day of the week! Torremelinos was tourist hell and I'm sorry to say that some of the Brits on the loose there were embarrassing to say the least. But then, one has to be fair, and I wondered how others might have judged us, from time to time, on our travels.

After staying at a huge crowded campsite on the edge of town, the next couple of days were just drive, drive, and drive. Finally, we had the humiliating experience of having to use the mud mats for the last time to get us out of a campsite before the last long haul to Calais, the ferry back to 'Blighty' and the end of almost six months of fantastic adventure travel.

12 SPELEOMASOCHISM

Cave digging in Agen Allwed, Wales

Caving in Wales was certainly a change from travelling through India, Nepal, and Africa, but no less exciting. After I'd left the oil industry, taken time out for the above travels, and then trained as a teacher, I took a job at Monmouth Comprehensive School, where I worked for twenty years teaching Geology and Geography. Beautiful, but very flat Norfolk had been my base since childhood, but now I was in climbing and caving country. I soon developed a fascination for underground exploration. It didn't take long to become well and truly hooked and I found myself agreeing to the ultimate challenge for the speleomasochists amongst us (those who are drawn to what many regard as the extreme activity of caving) – an Aggy Dig.

'9 a.m. at Whitewalls then?'

'Okay'

Why do I do it? Why do I always seem to find myself saying 'Yes' when people ask me to follow backbreaking, dirty, uncomfortable pursuits? 'Filthy' is one of the more polite of the many adjectives I've heard used to describe the now legendary Aggy Digs. I was invited along to the first of many when I met Martyn Farr, the internationally renowned cave diver, photographer, and writer, while working at the Trefil Mountain Centre in May 1991. I was excited. He was, after all, particularly celebrated in the UK for, among many other discoveries and explorations, his completion of the first traverse of Llangattock Mountain in 1986, the longest and deepest caving through trip in the British Isles at the time. The mountains of Wales were now my home patch and I wasn't going to miss out on such an opportunity.

I spent much of my free time that summer with Martyn (and others he had persuaded to take part), in digging the nether regions of Ogof Agen Allwedd (Welsh for Keyhole Cave), the longest cave system (about 32 ½ km) on the Llangattock escarpment. The endeavour was to connect it with Daren Cilau (Rock of Refuge) a neighbouring cave with a formidable reputation where I have had many adventures. The arduous entrance series has been described as being like crawling through an inside out cheese grater and leads to 28km of passages including some of the most spectacular and remote caving in the U.K.

On one such trip in July of the same year, the weather was wonderful above ground as we trudged along the old tram road towards Agen Allwed or Aggy as it was known to the caving community. It prompted thoughts of other less gruelling pastimes we could have chosen to follow in the sunshine, but these were soon banished when, after a struggle with the gate (since then, replaced, thank goodness), we entered the entrance series, which starts with a pleasant rifty passage with requires a few entertaining bridging and thrutching moves to negotiate. The passage soon deteriorates to follow a small stream and leads to the first boulder choke, where a roof collapse that blocked the passage was first penetrated by diggers from the Hereford Caving Club in 1957. We got through the entrance series in about twenty minutes. By the time we'd made it through the first boulder choke to reach Baron's

Chamber, the enormous chamber at the start of the 1200m long Main Passage, any traces of the previous night's beer had been sweated out. About half way along Main Passage we headed into the 1600m Southern Streamway, a tortuous series of hands and knees crawls, boulder thruthces and seemingly endless sinuous passages that require adopting a sideways 'crab walk'. It was a relief to reach the first little stream inlet as we all needed to rehydrate by this stage. At Waterfall Chamber we descended the 2m knotted rope and re-filled our drink bottles, knowing how parched we'd be by the time we reached the dig camp. Things started to slow down when we got out of the streamway and into the sandy crawls where I ended up getting a face-full in at least one of the tighter flat-out squeezes. This was where the sweat really began to flow and I began, once more, to question my sanity.

By the time we arrived at the dig camp (two hours and forty minutes of hard caving from the entrance), Martyn Farr had sped ahead and got a brew on. We had some tea and a bite to eat before the real suffering started as we got stuck in. In the three months preceding this trip, we'd progressed the sandy dig by about fifteen to twenty metres. The sand was generally soft, but getting the spoil out to a spot where it could be dumped required a determined and well-organised team. The sandy dig was in a low, often almost flat-out crawl, so no job was easy and all tasks were awkward. At the business end, digging had become ever more unpleasant. There was very little draught and the passage was now so long that with a team of four or five, the oxygen was quickly used up; we were down to less than an hour's worth in a single trip.

The next step was to install a bellows system to suck out the bad air, thereby causing fresh(er) air to be sucked in to replace it. Dragging digging trays was not much fun, especially as there was a one metre step up into the passage that made the long haul to the spoil heap even harder than it would have been on a flat surface. On every dig we hoped to break through, if not into the neighbouring cave system of Daren Cilau, at least into some open draughting passage with enough space to dump spoil and make our task a little easier. Each trip I'd been on had made one or two metres of passage after four to six hours of digging. Estimates vary, but most agreed that we were now about thirty metres from Daren. However, digging could only realistically continue if the bad air problem was sorted out.

After digging for a few hours, we had another brew before heading out. At this point, Tony (a blacksmith who worked in the Tower Pit colliery who was an incredibly strong mountain of a man and our cave digging team's secret weapon) let rip with some bang (explosive) in the Mother of all Battles Choke. The explosives we used on cave digging trips were usually Ajax, which are like the sticks of dynamite shown in cartoons, or Semtex, a plastic explosive that packs far more punch. We also employed Cordtex, a cord impregnated with explosives used for splitting boulders. The Mother of all Battles Choke was a long-term project which we had been wrestling with for some time. There was a good draught, suggesting bigger, open passage beyond the passage blocked by the choke but it was a dig for the desperate, with far too much 'hanging death' (huge boulders that have no visible means of support) for my liking.

The trip out was a hell-for-leather sprint that broke down into sandy crawls, streamway, main passage, and entrance series. Having done it so many times we all knew every stoop and wriggle and could judge the best way to negotiate every constriction with the minimum of effort and impact, making it possible to move fast without ending up covered in bruises. The end of each section was a relief, especially getting out of the sandy crawls! From dig camp back to the entrance took about two hours and twenty minutes. Then came the slog along the Llangattock escarpment, following the old tramroad back to Whitewalls to change. We were utterly exhausted and drove home like zombies. I've never been good at cleaning my caving gear immediately after trips, and I certainly haven't ever attempted it after an Aggy dig. The only thing on my mind on the journey home was a long soak in a hot bath followed by a few beers. Funny, how you get a second wind after excessive exercise though - I once partied until two thirty in the morning after an eleven-hour Aggy dig.

So, that's what such an expedition is like; as I said at the beginning - the ultimate in speleomasochism. But let's face it, even when the connection is finally made, how many people will be mad enough to embark on what will probably be a twelve-hour through trip?

The simple answer is that I would!

Some time later, recovering from the excesses of a boisterous New Year celebration, I had another call inviting me, this time, to hold the flash unit for Martyn on a cave photography trip. I'd been cajoled and coerced into many such ventures before, but this time I didn't need any persuasion. This trip would involve a cave dive, something I hadn't tried before and was keen to experience under such expert leadership and tuition.

I met Martyn, and his long-standing diving partner Nick Geh, in the car park of the Drum and Monkey pub in the Clydach Gorge, near Blackwood in South Wales. Once kitted up, I felt decidedly ungainly, laden with lead weights and with a small air bottle slung on my right thigh so that I'd still be able to get through the narrower sections of passage.

We entered Ogof Capel around midday and Martyn dived first, steady as ever. I'd seen him prepare for dives many times before when I'd been enveigled into 'portering' his diving bottles for hours through some of the most squalid caves I'd ever visited. I was always struck by his focused calm as he went methodically through his routines with considered precision; it was almost like watching a religious ritual.

Martyn had briefed me thoroughly and I felt confident as I entered the water, remembering that the main thing was to 'Go steady'. The hardest part was getting into the water - it was so incredibly cold that when I felt a lump in my throat I thought it might well be my bollocks! After the literally breathtaking cold shock of my first duck under the water, I positioned my mouthpiece and steadied my breathing before submerging into the inky blackness of the sump, the flooded section of the cave. Enveloped by the icy temperature and gripped by acute excitement and a sense of isolation, I dived into a wider passage, pinching my nose to equalize the pressure as I went. Knowing that most British cave dives are done in conditions where you can barely see the end of your arm through the murk, I was surprised by how good the visibility was as I pushed forward through a wide low passage and up a boulder slope, finally emerging into an air bell (an air pocket in the roof of what is an otherwise completely flooded passage) after about 12m. This might not sound much, but believe me, for a cave-diving virgin, it might as well have been 120m.

Martyn was waiting for me and suggested that I should dive the next sump first. This meant I had even better visibility and as I'd gained confidence from the first dive, I really enjoyed the shorter (6m) second sump, slowly and steadily pulling myself hand over hand along the rope. The exhilaration of the other-worldly environment and the sound of the periodic bursts of bubbles from my sub-aqua gear made it easy to understand why a dedicated few become addicted to this extreme form of cave exploration.

Once all three of us had passed the sumps, we spent a few hours photographing the beautiful formations, particularly the pure white 'straws' (stalactites which are very thin - about 5mm thick and typically made of calcite), some of which were up to 2m long. Later, we went and poked at a couple of digs at the end of Slalom Passage. Martyn tackled a choke where fallen rock had blocked the way and had later been cemented by calcite. In order to break his way through, he had to use a lump hammer and chisel. Meanwhile, Nick and I made about 8m of progress, digging out sand where the roof was so low that we had to lie flat – difficult! After seven hours underground, I relished the dives on the way out of the cave. What a perfect way to start the year!

Chapter 13 SWANSONG IN PARADISE

Backpacking from Bangkok to Bali

My work on exploration oil rigs was punctuated by working for as an outdoor pursuits instructor for S.E.A.L. Guides, based at Edale Youth Hostel. This is where I met Ali, a beautiful actress, in 1987. It was pretty well love at first sight, though it was a while before we got together. We had been together for three years and had shared many caving., climbing, mountain biking and mountaineering adventures together. I had already been on my 'big trip' and Ali wanted to do one too. We planned to travel together for six weeks, then Ali would continue and we hoped to meet up again the following summer in Australia.

We flew out of London the day after my last day of term and arrived in Bangkok twenty-seven hours later, having had a seven-hour stopover in Moscow and a couple of hours in Dubai. So far, so good! The only problem was that, on arrival, we found the Russian airline, Aeroflot, had lost my luggage. The powers that be reckoned it would be three days before I got it back - in fact, although I didn't know it at the time, I wasn't to get it back for six weeks. So there I was, not realising that I had forty-odd days of travel ahead and nothing more than the clothes I stood up in, my diary, and my cameras. Actually, this was nowhere near as bad as it sounds and, in many ways, it was a blessing to travel even lighter than usual, though it was taking minimalism a bit far!

We took a taxi to the Banglangpoo area of Bangkok. It was strange to be speeding along a five-lane highway peopled by manic drivers who seldom used indicators and motorbikes, some with passengers riding side-saddle, all roaring along at about 75kmph. We had to find accommodation and after looking at a couple of dreadful rooms we found the Nith Charoen Hotel where a friendly girl on the front desk showed us to a clean cool room with an effective fan (very important!), mozzi- meshed windows, and an *en-suite* shower and loo. It wasn't bad for 150 baht (about £3) each.

It didn't take long to unpack and after settling in and showering, we set off along the Khaosan Road, a Mecca for backpackers, and found the Sitdhi restaurant where we satisfied our ravenous hunger with vegetables, prawns, and rice for the equivalent of about 50p. Later, we browsed through some of the nearby touristy shops that stayed open until all hours, eventually stopping at a cafe to enjoy an absolutely divine Papaya shake while the film *'E.T.'* played on a video above the bar. Exhausted by our marathon journey, we returned to the hotel to sleep under a welcome humming fan, glad to have arrived, and with six weeks of fun and frolics ahead of us.

We were soon in sight-seeing mode and started with a tuk-tuk (auto rickshaw) ride to the Giant Swing, a religious structure which was originally constructed in 1794, but had undergone repair and rebuilding since then. Only the frame remained. It consisted of two colossal pillars standing over 20m high with an elaborately carved cross bar. We learned that the Swing Ceremony was a Brahmin new year's observance that carried on for ten days and was last performed in 1935. It was at the entrance of Wat Suthat, one of the most important temples in Bangkok, so we visited that too. The construction of the temple had begun in 1807 and took forty years to complete. It housed an impressive eight metre high bronze Buddha, which was about eight hundred years old and had been reclaimed from an abandoned temple. We also admired the magnificent murals which depicted stories of previous incarnations of the Buddha.

It wasn't long before we moved on to another temple, Wat Traimit, where there was an amazing 4m high solid gold Buddha weighing over five tonnes. We waited for a large crowd of Japanese visitors to leave before taking a few photos ourselves; then we went to Chinatown where we felt we'd finally 'arrived'. Other tourists had been left behind and we explored the narrow shady street market with an olfactory overdose of smells that defied identification. There was a truly amazing selection of fruits, vegetables, meat, fish, and even sharks' fins.

After stepping back in time in Chinatown, we stepped forward again by visiting the Siam Centre. This was a spotless, sparkling, modern shopping centre with a McDonalds and an American-style ice-cream parlour where we splashed out on the lychee flavoured special. In the blistering afternoon sun, we walked on to the Erawan Shrine; by then the sweat was tracing rivulets down our backs. This shrine was dedicated to the Hindu god Brahma and his elephant Erawan and was frequently used as the venue for traditional Thai dancing. Sadly, we weren't able to witness a performance, so we travelled on to visit Jim Thompson's house where our interesting guided tour was unfortunately marred by a group of Americans who provided a competing, non-stop, very loud commentary. However, we were able to learn that Jim Thompson had been an American entrepreneur who'd started the Thai silk industry after World War II. He'd built himself a magnificent home from the collected parts of six traditional historic Thai houses to accommodate a magnificent collection of South Asian art. He'd become something of a legend in Thailand for his contribution to the country's economy, for his undoubted love of his adopted home, and for his mysterious disappearance in 1967 whilst on holiday with friends in Malaysia. He simply went for a walk one day and never returned.

Later, we took a short bus ride to the temple of Wat Pho where we marvelled at the enormous forty-five metre-long reclining Buddha modelled out of plaster around a brick core and finished in gold leaf. Even the soles of his feet were wonderfully decorated in mother of pearl. I wished, however, that the crowds could have shown a little more respect by not taking pictures of believers at prayer. The surrounding buildings were also interesting with tall spires covered in multicoloured ceramic tiles. It took quite a while to take it all in and we were about to leave as the temple was closing, when we got talking with a Buddhist monk called Sompong. He was keen to practise his English and we chatted happily for over an hour before his teacher, Chai, turned up and offered to take us to watch Thai dancing at the Temple of Dawn. We weren't disappointed. Ali was especially delighted to witness the grace, symbolism, and the rich variety of movement of Thai dancing. Afterwards, Chai took us back to visit Sompong's room, a simple 3m square with Spartan facilities where we were made to feel hugely welcome. Eventually, we took a bus home just before midnight, exhausted after a marathon day of exploring Thai culture.

After a few days in Bangkok we were getting itchy feet, wanting to escape to less busy destinations, but there was still no sign of my rucksack, so we ended up hanging around for longer than we'd originally intended. After a fruitless trip to the airport, I bought a few clothes and resigned myself to saying goodbye to my gear for a while – bummer!

Our last day in Bangkok was spent on a minibus tour which we shared with a British couple who had spent ten months touring Australia; their stories fired Ali's enthusiasm for her planned trip and led me to daydream about our being reunited the following summer and perhaps spending a week on one of the uninhabited Whitsunday Islands.

We stopped briefly at a colourful orchid and butterfly farm where there was also a 'factory' making coconut sugar that tasted just like fudge. However, things went downhill from there. Despite our efforts to get to the floating market as early as possible in order to avoid the crowds, we were dismayed to find the place already boiling with overheated humanity. The skinny 'longtail' boats proved to be rather unstable; Ali's face was a picture of *Angst* every time the boat rocked. Unfortunately, the touts in the main market area were unusually pushy and aggressive, even for a tourist site. At one point, a guy draped a huge snake around my shoulders from behind, heckling hard for money for a photo. I walked on, ignoring him for several minutes before he realised he might lose his reptile, so he retrieved it and backed off. Unfortunately, there was no improvement when our little band moved on to a snake farm which was ghastly.

We were glad to get back to the relative calm of our hotel in the evening, especially as we'd managed to arrange transport to the island of Koh Samoi for the following day. In the evening, we were back on the Kohsan Road; Ali had resisted the temptation to buy an entire new wardrobe so far, but she finally succumbed to some gorgeous baggy silk trousers and a white cotton shirt. I bought another shirt too - after all, Aeroflot still had all my clothes.

Eventually, we arrived at the bus stop and waited - and waited. At last, we left an hour later than advertised. The bus was cramped and crudely air-conditioned, but sometimes one has to be grateful for small mercies. Ali seemed to get a fair amount of sleep, lying with her head in my lap. Unfortunately, I just couldn't get comfortable and by the end of our twelve-hour journey to Surat Thani my feet had swollen quite alarmingly. Oh, the joys of exotic travel! Luckily they rapidly returned to normal.

The ferry took a couple of hours to transport us over to Koh Samui. We hired a beach bungalow from one of the many, thankfully not too pushy, touts on the boat. When we landed, five of us were hustled on to a *bemo* (a kind of mini-bus) that took us to a pickup truck. We clambered into the back and set off for Mae Nam Villa with the wind in our hair. As we bounced along, we chatted with Mark, a Londoner, who aimed to complete a round-the-world trip in just eight weeks, and a Danish couple, Steve and Nina, who were both teachers. They were genuinely appalled when I told them how little I earned as a teacher in Britain.

At last, we arrived, tired and dusty, to be wholeheartedly impressed by the tropical idyll of Mae Nam, fringed with palm trees and with a beach of pure white coral sand. Our bungalow was only 50m from the beach; we could see the sea from the veranda and the lapping of the waves lulled us to sleep each night. It was a simple but clean room with what can loosely be described as an *en-suite* shower and all this for 80 baht (about 80p) each per night! Even the food was great, with fresh fried fish and vegetables and incredibly potent chillies for 35 baht (about 40p). In the evening, we went for a truly romantic walk along the beach - this was more like it! What a relief, after the hectic chaos of Bangkok. We needed a rest; we needed to slow down.

Ali, always a stickler for money management (she recorded every penny we spent), reckoned we should be slowing down our spending too. I agreed, though I didn't want to spoil my holiday by worrying unduly about prices that only differed by a few pence when everything was several orders of magnitude cheaper than in the UK. It's too easy to get hung up about cost. You can travel very cheaply without being obsessive about accounting.

It was heavenly to wake up to the gentle sound of waves and to spend a lazy day strolling along the shore. Ali bought a beautiful blue sarong from a chap on the beach; she looked absolutely gorgeous. Later, we took a taxi into town. Koh Samui seemed to be a rapidly growing tourist destination and we felt we'd been lucky to find Mae Nam Villa which was a little off the beaten track. That evening we had one of the best meals of the whole trip - a Thai shark curry in coconut milk – delicious! The atmosphere was literally electric, with a spectacular lightning storm over the sea providing the backdrop to our open sided restaurant meal next to the beach. Ali's '*Maglite*' torch, a leaving present from our friends in Chepstow, proved to be invaluable as we stumbled through the palm trees to the main road at five o'clock the next morning to meet our coach which, this time, had good air-conditioning, comfortable seats, and even a TV showing Thai boxing. I hadn't been used to such luxury on my previous expeditions and reminisced about the mixed pleasures and challenges of crossing Africa in a Bedford Blitz British army truck. The coach crossed back to the mainland on a huge ferry (we'd arrived on a very small boat); then it was endless driving through a string of scruffy little towns almost all the way to Hat Yai.

Within half an hour of arriving, we managed to arrange onward travel by minibus to the border town of Sungai Golok for only 130 baht (about £5 each). This three and a half hour drive was through more pleasant scenery, though Sungat Golok proved to be a shabby town where all we could find was a grubby room in what was laughingly called the '*Savoy Hotel'*!. In the evening, we went for a meal at a place where nobody could speak any English. We communicated through gestures and smiles and were rewarded with a fragrant mixture of fried vegetables, including crunchy asparagus and prawns in a hot sauce, for less than 100 baht (about £4.00 each), including drinks, so it wasn't all bad news.

Our first impression of Sugai Golok as not being a tourist-oriented town proved to be correct as we traipsed around for twenty minutes or so the next morning in search of a taxi. In desperation, we eventually risked life and limb by taking a couple of motorbike 'taxis' to the border for 10 baht each (practically nothing); Ali held on for dear life with her unwieldy rucksack, and I held my breath with my little holdall under one arm. We arrived unscathed and laughing and had an easy border crossing, despite the large sign declaring that 'hippies' were not welcome. This was accompanied by a hilarious list of 'how to identify a hippy'. Admittedly, we could have been accused of matching a couple of the criteria, but were allowed through without any trouble.

NOTICE

By virtue of section 16 of the Immigration act 1979 The Minister of Interior issues the following order to identify an alien with 'Hippy Characteristics'.

1 A person who wears just a singlet or waistcoat without inner wear.

2 A person who wears shorts which are not respectable.

3 A person who wears any type of slipper or wooden sandals, except when part of a national costume.

4 A person who wears silk pants that do not look respectable.

5 A person who has long hair that appears untidy or dirty.

6 A person who is dressed in an impolite or dirty looking manner.

Once over the border in Runtau Panjang we could tell we had arrived in Malaysia by the immediately obvious Muslim presence. A bus ride took us to Kata Bahru for just over two Malaysian dollars (about 50p) each. A rather mean and heavy-looking policeman armed with a formidable machine gun came onto the bus and harassed a couple of women for about ten minutes with no reason that we could divine; maybe they had too much hand-luggage.

Kota Bahru proved to be bigger than we'd expected and was consequently, rather a disappointment. We took a cycle rickshaw to look for accommodation and settled for 'Mummy's'. It was scruffy, but for ten Malaysian dollars, not bad value. It had a laid-back atmosphere and the undeniable attraction was 'Mummy' herself; a large laughing Taiwanese lady who spoke reasonable English and was constantly entertaining. It was here that we met Leo, a friendly Welshman and total 'space cadet'. It seems he'd travelled the hippy trail in 1978 and had spent most of the last fourteen years living in Thailand.

As always, we were drawn to the market where we sampled a crazy variety of street food including a whole chilli-stuffed barbecued fish on a stick, satay chicken, boiled sweet corn, and blue rice followed by banana pancakes and some almost fluorescent sweets. We stuffed ourselves.

At five o'clock the next morning, we left 'Mummy's' to take the jungle railway, third class, to Jerantut. Being the only tourists on the train made a welcome change, though to be honest, there hadn't been many in Kata Bahru either. Our carriage was shared with a few folk, large quantities of fruit, vegetables, and many chickens (both dead and alive), and yet we still managed to sleep for the first few hours of the very long journey.

We drove through impressive dense jungle with a classic closed canopy layer at about 30m interrupted by towering emergent up to 50m high. There were some implausible limestone outcrops which were chock full of caves with huge potential as far as climbing was concerned. Leo had recommended sorting out a trek from Kuala Lipis. However, the tourist information centre in Kota Bahru suggested getting off at Jerantut and, as Leo, entertaining though he was, seemed to be something of a maverick, it seemed prudent to follow the advice given by the information centre. The main advantage of travelling independently was the opportunity to be spontaneous and act on any whim or fancy.

No sooner had we left Kuala Lipis, than we got talking to the effervescent and improbably named 'Thong', a fellow passenger who lived locally, and by the time we'd reached Jerantut, he'd convinced us that trekking in Taman Rimba Kenong, starting from Kuala Lipis, was a much better option than the heavily visited and expensive Taman Negra. So . . . we stopped in Jerantut for a couple of hours, had a meal, treated ourselves to an ice lolly for pudding, and then returned to the station to catch a train back to Kuala Lipis! Thong found us again and talked enthusiastically, non-stop, all the way. We began to wonder whether we could stand four days of trekking with such a chatterbox for company.

Kuala Lipis was a small town and it didn't take long to meet fellow travellers who were also in search of a trek. Ben was an accountant and Nettie, a nurse. They were a Dutch couple; Rob was a post graduate economist and his mate Grant had recently graduated as a Mechanical Engineer. Rob and Grant had already done some research and we went along to check the trekking deal. In the end, we all booked a four-day trek which included a guide,

Abdul. It cost 120 Malaysian dollars each (about £50), including boat transport which seemed to be a pretty good deal.

Our jungle trekking trip started with just over an hour's ride up the river in a boat rather like a motorised punt. As we travelled further, the sea of green foliage was interrupted by flashes of brightly coloured kingfishers and legion other exotic birds. After picking up Abdul, our cheerful guide, we arrived at our destination where we clambered up a slippery wooden landing stage and walked a few hundred metres to a little wooden hut. It was the local grocery store where we bought basic provisions and divided the load between us.

Once we'd started walking, it wasn't long before we were in dense vegetation The track we followed was only 30cm wide and didn't appear to be much used. Abdul told us that tourists had only been visiting the area for a few years, but that the nearby region of Taman Negra had been a popular site for some time. He was right; we didn't see anyone all day. It was dark at ground level due to the dense canopy overhead; only two per cent of sunlight made it to the forest floor, evidently, the noise made by the insects was deafening and it was difficult to work out what type of creature was making each sound; some of the smallest insects seem to be blessed with the loudest voices. Occasionally, there would be a sudden racket above as a troop of monkeys crashed past overhead; in general, we heard a lot more wildlife than we saw.

To begin with, everyone talked excitedly, but before long we became quiet, absorbing the sounds of the jungle and trying to concentrate on where to put our feet as we crossed countless streams and a few rivers, wading through the shallower ones and gingerly balancing on precarious fallen log bridges to cross others. Some of the bridges were wet and slippery and although no one actually fell in, we each had moments when we thought we might. After a couple of hours of walking at a pretty brisk pace, we stopped to rest. All of us were soaked with sweat and glad of a cool drink, while some of us had to remove leeches from our legs. The leeches attach to the skin in warm wet places using their front suckers and then use a combination of mucus and suction to stay attached and secrete an anticoagulant enzyme. Once attached a leech will feed until it is full, which may take anything from twenty minutes to two hours. All sorts of techniques have been cited for leech removal, including using a cigarette lighter, salt and alcohol, all of which detach the leech quickly but have the gruesome and undesired effect of causing the leech to regurgitate its stomach contents into the wound. I found that the best method was to use a fingernail to break the seal of the front sucker, then the back sucker, before flicking the pesky critter away. The anticoagulant means the wound bleeds for ages, so it is important to keep it clean until it has properly clotted.

The trekking was hard work and we were glad to arrive at our campsite in the early evening. Everyone was knackered and very grateful when Abdul made us each a cup of tea. This was followed by a tasty meal consisting of vegetables, chicken, and rice, all cooked over an open fire. Our campsite was in the mouth of a cave, and as a speleologist (caver), I couldn't resist the temptation to slip off and explore the big dry passages. I came across loads of large nasty-looking spiders (some as big as my hand), along with many bats, and established that this would be a good place for further exploration the next day. In the evening, the conversations were diverse and covered topics about anything from world, British, Malaysian, and Dutch politics to the British Royal Family, the Olympics, and our various jobs. Bed was a groundsheet on the floor of the cave and thankfully, there were not too many biting insects, though some, as always, found Ali! Poor Ali really couldn't resist scratching her bites and still has the scars to prove it. Incredibly bright glow-worms pin-pricked the darkness and it was never quiet at night.

It was surprisingly cold at five in the morning, but human nature dictated that we should cling to the last vestiges of sleep for another few hours. We eventually got up around half past eight and all tucked into a hearty breakfast before lazily packing our gear and setting off through the jungle to experience a forty-five minute caving trip. I was armed only with a weedy hand torch, thanks to Aeroflot having lost my rucksack which had contained my Petzl Zoom head torch. Abdul couldn't tell us the name of the cave, only that the Malaysian for cave is 'Gua' and that there were at least fifty caves in the White Mountain area where we were trekking. Most of them had been explored to some extent, though I felt that the whole area promised further exciting research. However, Abdul told us that any budding cave-baggers would need to carry a gun, as many of the entrances were occupied by wild cats, tigers, tapirs, and even elephants. This brought a whole new meaning to the concept of 'access problems'!

Just before we arrived at the cave entrance, Abdul chose a long straight stick and sharpened it to a cruel point 'In case of cave snakes' . . . . We entered a couple of large chambers, maybe 10m across and some 30m high, with large ancient algae-covered calcite cave formations. About 40m into the cave, our guide pointed out a bat snake nesting in a crevice. It was about 40cm long and 1.5cm fat. Not surprisingly, bat snakes eat bats, so they're very fast, their backward pointing scales making it possible for them to glide effortlessly up apparently sheer rock faces – they're also poisonous to humans. After hearing this we proceeded with extra caution!

The floors of the passages were covered with mud and guano and the passages were just high enough to allow us to walk upright. They were mostly fossil vadose canyon passages with no scalloping or evidence of roof falls. At one short easy squeeze, I thought I could detect a hint of urgency in Abdul's voice as I followed him through. I could soon see why, but chose not to tell the rest of the group until they'd all got through. It was then that we all looked back to see two 1.5m long bat snakes 3m directly above the squeeze! One of them had only just caught a bat and we watched in morbid fascination as it swallowed it whole.

The next few chambers were packed with thousands more bats. In some places there were so many that we couldn't see the roof. As we passed, hundreds of them left their roosts and flew around us in a dense swarm that reminded me of the Alfred Hitchcock film '*The Birds*'. When we emerged, after a tricky little traverse across extremely slippery guano, there were more bats flying around the entrance, even though it was a bright day. It was a short, but exciting through trip.

Quite a hard day of trekking followed, though not as strenuous as the first, for we'd gained some altitude and the vegetation was not quite so dense. Most of the day was spent following and crossing (countless times) the Sungai Kenong River. Abdul assured us it was clean and we all drank from it greedily. In the early evening, we set up camp next to the river. We swung out Tarzan style over the water on a sturdy liana (a woody climbing plant) and plunged into the water to wash away the sweat that had poured out of us all day. After a good chat around the fire, we retired to bed under a simple tarp tent at about ten o'clock – completely bushed!

On the morning of our third day in the jungle, we had a wonderfully lazy time playing about in some nearby waterfalls and fishing. Using bamboo poles as rods, we caught loads of small fish, rather like the dace we have in the UK. Fried and eaten whole they tasted good - like bacon, strangely enough. After lunch, we set off again and it wasn't long before the trails became noticeably well-trodden. We were getting into an area much visited by people on shorter treks. True enough, we met another band of explorers, one of whom had managed to fall off one of the log bridges and was concerned about drying out his passport and cash. Ten minutes before we set up camp under a large overhanging crag festooned with greenery, we spotted some large footprints. They were as big as my hand and Abdul identified them as two-hour-old tiger tracks! There was a lot of crashing about in the jungle that night - too clumsy for tigers; Abdul reckoned it was elephants.

On the fourth morning, we went on another short caving trip. More large dry vadose fossil passage with very little roof collapse and lots of extremely rotten calcite flowstone deposits coating the walls. There were a few awkward climbs that had to be tackled holding my torch in my mouth. Once out of the cave, we scrambled up over jagged weathered limestone scattered with potholes and prickly vegetation; a fall here would have been very nasty. After a while, we burst out of the undergrowth almost half way up an escarpment into blazing sunshine with a magnificent view over the steaming jungle.

Later, we clambered back down to the main trail and made our way through small rubber tree plantations to arrive back at the little grocery store. There was plenty to see along the way: exquisitely coloured butterflies, 12cm long bright green crickets, a couple of flying lizards, and a nightjar-like bird sitting on one of its chicks. Back at the grocery hut, we cooked some vegetables and noodles spiced with some tiny, but very strong chillies that we'd been given by the woman who lived next door.

After the customary group photos, we set off for the boat. On the way down, we passed a little pet monkey on a chain. When we first spotted him he was hugging a chicken (!) who seemed quite happy with her companion, but he soon clambered up onto Rob's shoulder, leading to more photos. On the boat back to Kuala Lipis, it was a relief to feel a cool breeze after the humidity of the jungle and good to reminisce about the past few days of experiences destined to become dearly treasured. It was also the first time in four days that the shirt on my back was dried by the sun - glorious!

The adventure was not over though. On the way back we spotted a huge (1m long) red and black iguana lumbering out of the river, as well as a couple of chimpanzees, and another electric blue kingfisher. It was interesting to observe the variety of local fishing methods too. There were plenty of fixed lines, some traps, some nets tied out, and a few energetic fishermen were casting out circular throw nets, fringed with weights to make them draw closed as they were retrieved.

The following morning, after a delicious breakfast of pancakes with freshly squeezed lime juice, Ali and I set off by bus to Kuala Lumpur. Wow, what a journey – I've never been on a road with so many hairpin bends – terrifying! Towards the end, we were both feeling a touch queasy; partly our own fault for sitting at the back. It was impossible to doze, let alone sleep, as we had to hold on tightly to prevent ourselves sliding off the seats as we slewed around the bends at speed. At one brief pit stop for drinks and a snack, we bought some prawn crackers as big as our heads.

Arriving in Kuala Lumpur at around lunchtime, the contrast of dropping into the intense environment of a big city after the remoteness of our jungle trek was a shock. The Traveller's Moon Lodge, which had been recommended by the woman who ran the Gin Loke Hotel, was full, so we booked into the Traveller's Moon Home, run by the same family, a few doors down the street. It was here that we managed to get our repulsively pungent laundry done for six Malaysian dollars (about £1.50) and we cleaned ourselves up too. I tried, in vain, to phone Aeroflot – no success – what a drag.

After spending several hours relaxing in the city, we eventually ended up in a camera shop where we spent ages quizzing the knowledgeable assistant. Then, over lunch, we proceeded to talk one another into spending money we couldn't afford on photographic equipment. When we returned to the shop, I succumbed, after ten years of using my trusty Olympus OM-10, to the temptation of 'going automatic' and bought a Canon EOS-1000F with a Sigma 35-135 autofocus zoom (£236, duty free). Ali bought a clever little Olympus AF1-Twin for £108; a weatherproof number with the advantage of a 35mmm and a 70mm lens. Needless to say, as supposedly low-budget travellers, when we got back to the hotel we couldn't believe what we'd done.

Aeroflot continued to disappoint and after two weeks I was still no nearer to retrieving my lost luggage. KL airport had no record of it, though Aeroflot had promised to forward the details. I became resigned to the fact that my rucksack had been lost and consoled myself with the fact that, at least, I was insured and that travelling light is always best. I bought a small holdall in Chinatown to carry the few items of clothing I had picked up along the way.

Visiting the KL butterfly and bird parks provided a good opportunity to practise using our new state-of-the-art cameras before going for a doze in a nearby park. We gambled on taking a bus back into town, not knowing exactly where it was going, but luckily it ended up taking us exactly where we wanted to be. Ali and I were both hot, tired, and hungry when we got back to the guesthouse and after almost an hour spent looking for somewhere to eat, our already ragged tempers became somewhat frayed.

We were both glad to leave Kuala Lumpur, even if it did mean arriving at Butterworth bus station at 4.45 a.m. I slept on a bench for a while as Ali browsed through the guidebook, planning our next move. As the sun was rising at around seven o'clock, we were already on board the ferry to Penang and then took the four-hour catamaran ferry to Sumatra. It wasn't until we'd boarded that Ali confessed to suffering from seasickness; this proved to be all too true and before long, the poor girl was as grey as cold porridge and had had to dash off to throw up.

When we arrived at Bulawan in the afternoon, we were frustrated to find the boat going round in circles - literally - for half an hour before we were allowed to dock. Luckily, it didn't take long to find a bank where we could change money and we emerged with a huge wad of notes; half a million Rupiah (about £150). After a quick bus ride to Medan, we had an intense half an hour in a melee of ticket touts and confused tourists. This eventually led to us joining six others on a bus to Lake Toba. However, it wasn't as simple and straightforward as it might sound as the minibus taking us to the bus station got lost and, yet again, we were going round in circles - what a navigationally-challenged introduction to Sumatra!

We flagged down a rickety old bus which we shared with a noisy collection of live ducks and chickens crammed under the seats and spilling into the aisle. It stopped every few minutes to pick up increasingly improbable packages and impossibly large numbers of passengers. Boy, were we glad to reach the shores of Lake Toba four and a half hours later! After a 26-hour travelling marathon from Kuala Lumpur we were too tired to bargain and booked into the overpriced Marina Inn, close to the ferry terminal.

Our choice of accommodation proved to be less than perfect when the next morning, Ali spotted a pervy eye at the keyhole while she was getting dressed. I opened the door with a jolt, told the startled teenager to piss off and unceremoniously kicked him up the arse. He howled and fled at speed! Luckily, we'd already paid the night before, so we were able to scarper pretty niftily ourselves.

It took a lazy half hour on the Lake Toba ferry to get us to Samosir Island and a ten minute walk to get to Tuk-Tuk Timbul, a guesthouse recommended by the guidebook as being quiet and serving excellent food. This proved to be the case. Our accommodation was one of a group of Batak style traditional huts next to the lake, each room with a truly breathtaking view for less than £1.50 a night in English money. The long journey had left us exhausted and we spent the afternoon relaxing on our veranda, relieved at the prospect of a few days in one place.

The following day, we hired a couple of beaten-up old pushbikes and headed off towards Tomok, a village just south of the Tuk-Tuk peninsula. Poor old Ali; after twenty minutes, it was obvious that she was feeling really ill. We stopped for a drink and then decided it would be best to head back and to add insult to injury, I got a flat tyre on the way.

Back at our hut, Ali made it clear that she wanted to try and sleep off her sickness alone, so I set off on the bike again, exploring the trails to the north. There were quite a few hills and with only one gear on my bike, some were a real challenge. I passed through lush green paddy fields where I was greeted by waving children wherever I went. The carvings on some of the old Batak houses were intricate and beautiful and after about three hours on my boneshaker I have to admit that my backside ached. When I got back Ali, was obviously feeling better and we were able to start the next day by leaping into the crystal waters of Lake Toba before a late and enormous breakfast of avocado salad, mixed fruit pancakes, noodles and vegetables, and guacamole chapattis – heaven!

Leaving Tuk-Tuk-Timbul, we took the boat to Parapat, followed by a taxi to the station, only to discover that our bus was full. The only alternative was a minibus that was quite a lot more expensive. This sent economical Ali into a regular strop which resulted in her accidentally leaving behind our box of twelve music cassettes; I bit my tongue and tried to be patient. There were only five seats on the minibus and we were in a bad mood, so I abandoned any vestige of English Gentlemanly behaviour and made a determined and successful move towards the best seats which were recliners with loads of legroom - the most comfortable transport on the trip so far and a great aid to restoring harmony. It was a long trip, and we finally got to Bukittingi around 2.30 in the morning. The first two hostels we tried were full. However, third time lucky, and the Yogya Hotel, which looked expensive, turned out to be quite reasonable (less than a pound each). Ali and I had a large room to ourselves, equipped to accommodate six. Boy, were we glad to hit the sack after a long and stressful day!

After a good night's sleep we headed, fresh-faced and enthusiastic, to explore Bukittingi. We started off with the Panorama Park where we had a sensational view over the spectacular gorge. We wanted to send cards of the scene to family and friends and when we stopped at the post office, we had to stick on our stamps using the communal glue pot. Unfortunately, we'd not anticipated such huge stamps and some recipients of the cards would have had to steam them off to read the greetings.

We hadn't intended to visit the zoo, being against the very concept in principle. However, the ticket we had to get into the park also covered the zoo, so hypocritically, in we went. Most of the cages were small and though the animals all looked as if they were in pretty good physical health, their spirits were not high; they all looked extremely sad and listless. I was particularly moved by a black gibbon - the same as the ones I'd seen in the jungle. His eyes were deep, watery (seemingly tear-filled), brown pools pleading for freedom. His beseeching looks were accompanied by a heart-rending plaintive repetitive squeak. The giant orang-utan was pitiful too; such a magnificent, animal, so intelligent, in such a small cage quite brought one's buoyant feelings down. It confirmed all our reasons for disagreeing with zoos as a form of public entertainment, even if they do have a legitimate role in conservation.

Later, we found a shady spot to settle down for a while to write our diaries. Three sweet Sumatran teenage girls came over to us and engaged us in conversation; one of them asked Ali 'Is he your darling?' Of course she had to say 'Yes'! Our next destination was to be Bungga beach. On one of the buses a young man called Genius (seriously!) chatted to us for an hour or so and insisted on exchanging addresses. At the beach we managed to find a cheap room in Carlo's Guesthouse. It had a friendly atmosphere and we spent the evening jawing to two American lads, Dale and Jochan, over a few beers.

A memorable day began when we boarded Carlo's boat at nine o'clock. It was a deep-hulled, narrow craft with outriggers on both sides. We were joined by Dale, Jochan, an Italian couple, two Dutch guys, a Dutch girl, and four of Carlo's brothers who had just come along for the ride. It took just over an hour to reach the first island, Pulau Secquan. As we skimmed along we had tantalising glimpses of coral and brightly-coloured fish darting through the limpid water as well as monkeys frisking on the beaches. The island was rather like something out of a *'Bounty'* chocolate bar advertisement, with palm-fringed beaches of dazzling white coral sand and azure waves gently lapping at the shoreline.

My first taste of snorkelling here was mind-blowing; what a buzz! I spent an hour marvelling at the heart-stopping beauty of the fish, their vivid colours and extraordinary shapes and sizes. I was amazed at how close I could get to them. Most of the coral appeared to be dead, though there were brilliant patches of colour here and there which showed living examples. Back on the beach, we drank coconut milk straight from the shells and then split coconuts, straight from the tree, and hungrily devoured the sweet flesh. Carlo's brothers had been fishing and we had a midday barbecue on the beach, cooked over burning coconut husks. Later, replete, we ambled along the coast, beachcombing, and sunbathing from time to time. Lovers in paradise.

In the afternoon, we went to a second island, Pulau Pagon. If anything, the fish there were even more spectacular. I was hooked and snorkelled for a couple of hours before we had another barbecue. We finally left, reluctantly, in the early evening. On our way back, we saw huge shoals of tiny fish leaping out of the water, almost like a continuous wave of shimmering silver. As we neared Bungga Beach, a storm was brewing and we became enveloped in a black cloud, which soon burst around us and we got soaked.

Yochan and Dale invited us to join them on a visit to a series of waterfalls a few kilometres north of Bungga. After a quick *bemo* ride and half an hour's walk, we arrived, having acquired the usual entourage of lively inquisitive children on the way. The waterfalls were stunning, in a setting a million miles away, it seemed, from the heavily-trodden tourist paths. The children were in their element, jumping into the water, splashing, and swimming like fish. They were so genuinely and simply happy with their flashing smiles and cheeky chuckles and laughs' their joy was infectious and we had a great time jumping in and swimming around too.

On the road again, we were twenty people squashed into a *bemo* the size of a Bedford Rascal! Our attempts to locate a travel agent in Padang were fruitless, so we headed for the airport, but we drew a blank there too. However, we were assured that there was a good chance of our getting a flight if we turned up early the next morning.

Sadly, the minibus we took to the airport next morning broke down four times in the first ten minutes of the journey. This didn't bode well and we should have cut our losses and turned back, for when we arrived at the airport, we found that all of the flights were full. After putting ourselves on a couple of waiting lists, we hung around on standby for five frustrating hours. Nobody could tell us about the availability of flights for the following few days, so eventually, we got fed up and set off for Pedang where we eventually found a travel agent and our worst fears were confirmed; no flights for a week! It turned out that we'd managed to choose to travel on the day when the university exam results were to come out and there was a holiday. In despair, we decided to investigate getting a bus, only to find that all of the express vehicles were full, so we gritted our teeth and paid 25,000Rp (about £7.50) each for the daunting prospect of a thirty-two hour journey without air-conditioning which would, we trusted, end in Jakarta.

The bus was an hour late and absolutely packed. We got an undersized double seat, with Ali next to the window. We stuck to the vinyl seats in the humid heat. We dozed fitfully between the toilet/food stops every four hours. Oh, the relentless grind that is long-distance bus travel - the constant hawking up of phlegm and spitting on the floor, the all-too-soon-to-be used pink plastic sick bags provided for the vomiting children, the chokingly-strong cigarette smoke, the excruciating, brain-jangling Java Technopop song that blared out of the stereo - the only tape the driver had. We stopped to collect even more passengers every now and then and little plastic stools appeared so that they could sit in the aisle.

Every time the bus stopped, we watched cockroaches emerging from the ripped seats in front of us. It was impossible to get comfortable. We slogged on. Whenever we stopped, we were invaded by vendors selling water, drinks, snacks - and an odd selection of combs, cigarette lighters, and unlikely trinkets. They breezed through the bus, shouting their wares and then they were gone and we were off again. We couldn't face eating much at the pit stops - a few bananas, some *sate* served on a leaf, some sweet corn. Our stomachs shrank, our bottoms became numb, our limbs cried out for release from the confines of hell on wheels - the K.M.S. Padang-Jakarta bus run!

Initially, we were dubious about arriving in Jakarta at one in the morning with nowhere to stay, but our worries proved to be groundless as we waited at the K.M.S. bus station until dawn. We enjoyed this weird little window onto Jakartan night life. There were ten others waiting with us, only one of them able to speak any English and we had only a few words of Indonesian. Once again, a photo of my family was an instant hit and was passed around with great curiosity and interest. Even after the guy who spoke a bit of English had gone, we were able to share smiles and laughter with the rest of the gathering. It was interesting to see how friendly the people were with each other; particularly their kindly attitude to an incredibly ancient leathery-faced man without a tooth in his head. Total strangers happily chatted to one another - so natural in Jakarta, yet I couldn't help feeling it would be rather unlikely that an entire waiting-room full of people would behave this way in England. It's a sweeping generalization, I know, and of course there are always many exceptions to every rule, but I'd never realised how stand-offish and suspicious Brits could be until I experienced the friendliness of strangers on my travels abroad. Despite having read and heard a few horror stories about Jakarta - muggings and so on - we felt safe and very welcome.

Ali slept for a while and when she woke we took a taxi to the airport in yet another effort to track down my rucksack. The Aeroflot office was closed - no flights on that day, but the information service told us to go to their office in a hotel in town. Sighing heavily, we eventually found the office in an elegant hotel where I explained the loss and how much of my holiday time and money had been wasted. This was met with stony-faced indifference and I was told that the situation could only be sorted out back in London. Another wasted journey - infuriating! What was most annoying was that we'd been misinformed on our arrival in Bangkok when we'd been told to go to Kuala Lumpur and then to Jakarta where we could either collect the rucksack or £24 cash compensation at Kuala Lumpur or £110 at Jakarta. If they'd only given us the correct information in the first place, we wouldn't have wasted several days of the trip in expensive cities which we hadn't even planned to visit. The only option at that point was to put the whole unfortunate incident behind us and get on with enjoying the last two weeks of our trip.

We couldn't get out of Jakarta quickly enough and took a bus to Bandung where we found somewhere to stay and had a much-needed shower, scraping off the ingrained grime of several days on the road. Later, chatting with three other travellers staying at the guesthouse, Sandy, Liz, and Janet, we arranged to visit a volcano the following day. It transpired that Janet's folks used to work with Ali's mother and that Liz had been at the same college as Ali – I've never ceased to be amazed at the frequency of coincidence while travelling!

The next morning I woke to find sixteen mosquito bites in an area of four centimetres square on my ankle - Ouch! After a leisurely breakfast, we all set off with our local guide to visit the

Kauah Papandayon Volcano. The minibus was another mechanically-challenged affair and after an hour and a half we had to stop at a garage for essential repairs. Unfortunately, the driver appeared to be as mad as a hatter. Miraculously, we had escaped several head-on collisions on assorted blind bends and crests of hills - at least seven by my petrified reckoning. Luckily, we survived the journey. The 2,622m high volcano was the southernmost of a long group. There were hissing and gurgling jets of steam, acid sulphurous fumes, bright yellow masses of exquisitely delicate sulphur crystals, and pools of boiling mud. As a geologist, I was in heaven and embarked on a serious photographic spree. Even Ali, usually bored rigid by anything remotely geological, seemed genuinely fascinated and we finally left after about three hours of rewarding exploration.

On the way back, we stopped off at some hot springs and in the evening Ali and I set off for Yogya on a comfortable bus - I got seven hours' sleep - so this was how the other half lived! The travel agent had told us that the bus arrived in Yogya at six o'clock in the morning, but we found ourselves disembarking at half past three, so we settled down to sit in 'Gang 2' Street and watched the day begin. Around six, a trickle of travellers started to arrive and I stayed with the luggage while Ali went off in search of accommodation. Hotels in Indonesia are rated by the government into a number of categories, *losmen* being at the lower end of the list. Ali came up trumps with the Utar Pension Inn, a very good losmen offering a clean room, a fan, and tranquillity.

We sorted out some laundry that could have practically walked off by itself and went to explore the city. It was interesting to walk around an 'academy' where we were shown how batik is made. We then spent ages browsing through a huge collection; the best examples shown off effectively by backlighting. Ali and I ended up buying a couple each - worthy souvenirs that you can actually put on the wall instead of trinkets that gather dust or end up in the back of a drawer. They were light and easy to transport home too.

After shoe-horning ourselves into a *'becak'* (a front-loading pedal rickshaw), we set off on a tour of the town. We visited a workshop where amazing puppets were being made for shadow theatre performances and a silver workshop where Ali bought some sensational earrings. Later, we went to the Water Castle, the site of a former Sultan's garden. The main attraction was the bathing pool and tower from which the Sultan was said to have gazed at his concubines. An irritating guide latched onto us and eventually dragged us to his batik shop where we were ripped off by local standards – though, to be fair, the small Batiks were still good value by UK standards.

Eventually, we escaped and looked around the bird market where hundreds of brightly-coloured little feathered creatures hopped, fluttered, sang, and squawked in bamboo cages. Captive birds are popular with Indonesians; most families have cages hanging from long poles outside their homes. When we got back to the Gang 2 district we were more than ready to scoff an excellent *Nasi Goreng* (fried rice dish) from a street vendor – one of the best meals of the trip and it cost us the princely sum of 10p!

In the evening, we went to the Prambanan temple to watch a two-hour Ramanaya ballet performance - this time it was Ali the professional actress, rather than Ben the geologist, who was in heaven! The event was wonderfully atmospheric, bathed in the silvery light of the full moon. The show was spectacular in every sense, with amazing colourful costumes and two hundred dancers. Sitting on concrete seats in an open-air amphitheatre however, we were glad we had Ali's Thermarest sleeping mat with us!

From the light of the full moon to an amazing sunrise. We had to make a dawn start the next day to get to Borabadur in time to see the sun rise over the largest Buddhist stupa (dome shaped shrine) in the world. We arrived to find that the gates didn't open until six o'clock. However, the quality of light was gorgeous and approaching the stupa was awe-inspiring, especially with the full moon setting behind it. A strenuous 35m climb straight to the top was rewarded by vast views and it was calming to sit and enjoy the early cold light of dawn becoming the warm light of a new day as the mist on the lowlands was burned off by the rising sun. It was best around five o'clock when we had an electrifying view of the active volcano, *Gunung Merapi* (Fire Mountain), smoking from its mouth, with a deep orange and red sky as a backdrop. There were serene statues of the Buddha everywhere, gazing out imperturbably over the mist. Crowds of tourists arrived at about eight o'clock and we beat a hasty retreat to consume a hearty breakfast before returning to Yogya. Back at the *losmen,* Ali continued her meticulous financial calculations; so far, we had spent £330 each which included our batik extravagances. We agreed that that was pretty good going.

The bus set off for Gunung Merapi at half past ten that night. This volcano is the most active in Indonesia and has been erupting regularly since 1548. By midnight, I could see the profile clearly in the moonlight and as I watched, I saw four minor eruptions glowing red on the 2,911m summit - exciting stuff for me in full geology mode! When we arrived at a *losmen* at the base of the volcano soon after midnight, we were given sandwiches with - would you believe it? - a filling of chocolate hundreds and thousands!

There were twenty people in the tour group, but with six guides it was possible for us to split up and walk at our own pace. Leaving at one in the early morning was an eerie experience with the air of a pagan pilgrimage. We trudged up the volcano by moonlight so bright that we hardly used our torches. The route was quite a scramble at times; steep ground with bone-dry volcanic dust providing distinctly dodgy footing at best. Breathless, we stopped for a break at the plateau at about four. The sunrise was exquisite; no clouds, just a clear sky with a pure and simple gradation of delicate hues from red through orange to yellow - glorious!

We arrived at the summit at about six in the morning; there were clouds below us and distant volcanoes seemed to float like castles in the sky. Below in the crater, it was possible to make out the malevolent dull red glow of cooling lava. The acrid smell of sulphur made us wrinkle our noses and our eyes stung while the stink of hydrogen sulphide turned our guts. The ground was hot, emitting plumes of steam. There were plenty of sulphur deposits and fumaroles emitting steam and gases, though not as spectacular as those we had seen at Papandayan. Eventually, we set off on the three-hour descent, arriving at the *losmen* to be met by a delicious pineapple breakfast. On the bus ride back to Yogya I fell asleep and fell off my seat, much to the amusement of the rest of the passengers!

Our next destination was Pacitan Bay, a perfect crescent of golden sand without a tourist in sight. A short search for accommodation led us to the Happy Bay Losmen, which had only been open for four months. It was run by an amiable Australian guy called Eric. It was clean and well-built with bamboo and cane furniture and offered the best room we had stayed in so far, costing 12,000 Rupiah (3,860RP to £1). There was a balcony above the restaurant with comfortable hanging basket chairs. It didn't take long to settle in and we meandered along the beach which was littered with hundreds of little jellyfish, their 10cm air sacs tinged with blue and green and long blue translucent tentacles hanging down below. In the evening, we splashed out on an extravagant meal of lobster and grilled snapper - the fish was particularly delicious. Our long day ended with us paddling in the surf by moonlight - maybe a touch of Mills and Boon, but it was a very special evening for these two young lovers.

We added yet another mode of transport to our trip the next day when we took a pony and trap to the bus station where the bus back to Solo awaited us. After a spicy nasi sayur (vegetables and rice in a hot peanut sauce), we boarded a non air-conditioned night bus to Denpasar. The lack of air-conditioning wasn't a problem, but the loud, badly dubbed kung fu movie with subtitles in three languages, was 'entertainment' I could have happily done without.

Bleary-eyed after our overnight trip, we arrived in Denpasar just after eight in the morning and squeezed ourselves into a *bemo* full of Germans and set off for Kuta. Kuta is to Australians what Benidorm is to Brits. The accommodation was correspondingly expensive compared to everywhere else we'd been. We settled for 'Jensens III' which was pretty costly. After a rest, we hit the centre of Kuta, only to find that practically every shop was a tourist trap, but however sniffy we'd been about such places, I gave in and bought a really wild Bulldog Fish T-shirt. We realized that the beach was simply awful after the briefest of visits; I guess we'd been completely spoiled by the deserted spots we'd become used to. This, unfortunately, was like an advertisement for 'Club 18-30'. How snobbish we had become!

In the evening, feeling extravagant, we went to a large restaurant and watched a Legong dance as we ate. We were told that this was a dance originating in the nineteenth century as royal entertainment. We were fascinated by the intricate movements of the girls' hands, the complicated footwork and their eloquent gestures and facial expressions. After a couple of drinks, we went from the sublime to the ridiculous. We went to see the film, *Batman Returns*. The cinema was huge with efficient air-conditioning, comfortable seats, and a good stereo sound system. It was total escapism and we forgot where we were until the warm night air and sounds of street life washed over us on the way out.

After a leisurely start, we ended up in Ubud the next day and quickly found a good room at the Detri Inn. It was clean and very quiet - a relief after the bustle of Kuta. It was fun visiting the nearby

Monkey Forest, a small area where temples are surrounded by trees. This was home to three troops of monkeys. They were obviously used to being fed. The babies looked cute, with little Mohican hair styles. Some of the older males were real bruisers though, with fresh battle scars to prove it. A few of the really elderly monkeys were grizzled in appearance and we had a lot of fun taking photographs. Later, no doubt inspired by the monkey coiffure, I found a place to get my hair cut short in the front and at the sides, but keeping a long plait down the back. I have to say, this was an unusual event, as in those far-off days, I tended not to get my hair cut very often, usually sporting a look akin to Jim Morrison from the Doors. On this occasion, though, I enjoyed a pleasant hour in the hands of a skilled barber with the added bonus of a head massage. I felt I could get used to such luxury!

In the evening, we took a minibus to Pelatan where we watched a Kecak dance. This was definitely the best dance we saw on the trip. It told the story of the Hindu Prince Rama and his rescue of Princess Sita who'd been kidnapped by a wicked king. The only lighting was a pillar covered in candles. There was no instrumental music, but a 'choir' of about fifty men shouting, chanting, and rhythmically beating their chests and thighs with the palms of their hands. It was an hour of entertainment of the highest quality. Ali was in raptures.

The next morning, we took a bus to Padangbai where we soon found the Topi Inn. Here we were given a splendid room at a reasonable price with a picture window looking out across the bay. The food was great too, especially the grilled barracuda. We were glad to slow down and took a pleasant evening stroll over the oolitic beach sand, composed of tiny, light-brown, perfect spheres which felt wonderful beneath our feet. Later we had a long game of Scrabble on the balcony.

We enjoyed the next few days snorkelling and lazing around the tranquil Blue Lagoon Cove. Once, we heard the tinkling of cymbals and the beating of drums and a Hindu cremation procession came into view. For the third time, death had wandered across my path, during my recent travels. I remembered the funeral pyre I'd witnessed in Nepal and the body of a small child being committed to the Ganges in India, and now again here in East Bali.

On a happier occasion, we had a four o'clock start to go out on a local fishing boat. The 'Prahu' was a narrow, deep-hulled boat with bamboo outriggers and a triangular blue sail that looked like a bedspread or a tablecloth. As we sailed out of the bay, we saw three shooting stars and made our wishes - romantic or what? As we sped along, the bows spat back showers of brightly-shining silver-green phosphorescence; it was eerie and exciting. Although the sunrise was brief and unspectacular, the first light made the sea shine like burnished copper. After almost an hour, our local fisherman, Yoman, set out his 150m long and 3m high net. We trolled a hand line with about twenty simple feather lures for about an hour. A shoal of tuna passed, the water boiling as they broke the surface and occasionally one or two leapt out of the sea. However, we returned to shore fishless but rich in memories.

Finally it came – the day I'd been avoiding thinking about - the last day of our travels together. We woke early, but got up late.

When we got to the airport the vagaries of Indonesian travel continued to the end.

Garuda airline official: Your flight has not been confirmed, it is not on the   computer printout.

Me: I confirmed the flight a week ago in Kuta.

Garuda airline official: Where are you staying?

Me: I'm not staying anywhere. You are flying me to Jakarta

at 1.55pm.

Forty minutes later, I was handed my ticket and boarding pass, then Ali and I said our last goodbye. She cried; I honestly don't think the enormity of what she'd put in motion had struck home until then. She planned to continue her travels to New Zealand and Australia where she hoped to find work. We agreed that we'd be reunited the following summer. How could I have been so naive? There were big hugs and long kisses as we parted. I felt surprisingly calm as I boarded the plane. I didn't look back - our swansong was over, though I didn't realise it then. I didn't even cry - though I made up for that with a million tears during the next two years when I suffered a clinical depression which descended following Ali ending our relationship only a month later.

PS: Thirty-two hours after leaving Kuta, I arrived back in London. It was no surprise to find that Aeroflot had lost my luggage yet again. I filled in the paperwork and headed for the Aeroflot office.

Me: I want to see the manager please. Now.

(A brief hesitation and then the old bloater shuffled in)

Me: I sent you a letter ten days ago with reference to the loss of my luggage

          six weeks ago in Bangkok - a copy of which I have here. It seems that

          you have managed to lose my 'new' luggage too!

Manager: You aren't doing very well are you?

Me: No, YOU aren't doing very well!

I left empty handed, but my bags (old and new) arrived a couple of days later!

    Ali and I had flown out from Heathrow to Bangkok the day after my school term had ended. It had been the first day of a wonderful trip; the best times we'd ever shared, though sadly, it was the last time we were to spend together – truly a 'Swansong in Paradise'.

Chapter 14 JUMPING HIGH AND DIGGING LOW

A Freefall Parachute Jump and a Busman's Holiday.

I've always had a *penchant* for jumping for joy and in 1993, I had the opportunity to jump for charity. March was not a sunny month and it was only on my third visit to Shobden airfield (near Leominster, Herefordshire) that the weather cleared enough to attempt a freefall tandem jump. Anticipation grew as my instructor, Pete, went through the equipment check and briefing. We squeezed into the tiny twin-prop plane with half a dozen qualified solo freefall parachutists and before long, we were up and away. For a while, it looked as though I was going to be disappointed yet again and have the jump cancelled at the last minute, but suddenly, there was a break in the clouds.

The side door was opened and the other parachutists shuffled eagerly towards it and leapt out, one by one. Finally, it was our turn. Strapped together, Pete and I scuttled, crab-like, to the door and positioned ourselves on the edge. This was it! With a glorious rush of excitement we rolled forward and plummeted out of the plane. The noise was crashing and the rushing air made it hard to breathe, especially as my cheeks were being turned inside out by the wind. We fell (or did we fly?) spread-eagled to maintain stability. The freefall seemed endless - in fact, it was probably less than thirty seconds - and I was gratified that I'd opted to do the 3,700m freefall jump (even if it was in tandem), rather than a static line jump from only 1,000m.

When Pete deployed the main parachute, our descent shuddered to a stop with a jerk and suddenly, it became almost silent as we began to drift down. However, our staid progress became somewhat less than sedate when Pete let me steer. Inevitably, I cranked on the control cords with too much enthusiasm, the result being a fairground-like experience, the two of us spinning like a Catharine wheel. Pete was unfazed, laughed, and encouraged me to do it again in the other direction; what a blast!

Sadly, the descent took only a few minutes and in no time, the ground came up to meet us. I was impressed by how easily we landed with no more impact than stepping down off a couple of stairs. We shook hands and I thanked my intrepid trainer before heading for home to start collecting my sponsorship money for Multiple Sclerosis (£350).

Well, what goes up, must come down! It was now time to revisit the depths under Wales. It took me forty-five minutes to drive from Coleford in the Forest of Dean to Whitewalls, the Chelsea Speleological Society 'hut' that nestles at the foot of the Llangattock escarpment. I had had to get up horrendously early to be there by half past eight in the morning. When I arrived, however, I wondered why I'd bothered as nobody else had turned up! The weather had definitely taken a turn for the better. It was a glorious spring morning and I found myself pondering on how else I could be spending the day when an hour later, Martyn, Gareth, and Peter finally arrived. Hmmm - how I could have done with an extra hour in bed!

Daren Cilau is a very difficult and arduous cave with a long, tortuous entrance series, which follows a small and very cold stream for about 600m and requires crawling, squeezing, wriggling and thrutching for most of the way. Two particularly challenging squeezes are The Vice and The Calcite Squeeze (both of which I negotiated with a cracked rib a few years later!) The four of us entered Daren and made fairly slow progress through the entrance series; neither Peter nor I were feeling particularly 'cave fit'. Having then followed the main cave through Jigsaw passage to the Big Chamber Nowhere Near The Entrance we signed the logbook and followed Epocalypse Passage into Antler Passage. Here we struggled up an awkward 6m climb and slithered over 600m of slippery boulders, real ankle grinding stuff.

A couple of hours after reaching the end of the entrance series we arrived at the first dig site, about thirty minutes' distance before the final choke of Antler Passage. Here, the plan was to continue banging our way along a narrow tube in order to gain access to what appeared to be an open passage below. We'd brought in two 6v batteries for the Bosch drill and were suitably frustrated when we found that one of these had absolutely no charge. Consequently Martyn was only able to drill three short shot holes. By the time this was done and Gareth had set the charge, Peter and I were feeling seriously chilly. Peter decided to start making a slow exit. I almost joined him, but when Martyn and Gareth announced that they were going to have a look at the terminal choke I couldn't resist. We set off the charge and all agreed that it sounded like a 'good- un'. About ten minutes later, my Apex 10 light died - it seems that all of the recent trips to this part of the cave had been plagued by lighting problems. Luckily, I was well equipped with a fistful of photons - I had a Petzl with a fresh battery, plus a spare, so I was able to carry on.

After about three hours of pretty tough caving from the entrance, and having a stop to bang the first dig site, we finally reached our remote destination at the end of Antler Passage; I have to admit, it looked pretty hair-raising. Martyn and Gareth had demolished the choke on a previous expedition by using a crowbar carefully wedged into place and then pulling on a rope from a safe distance; this resulted in tens of tons of boulders rumbling down as they successfully dropped the entire choke!

They suggested (again, from a safe distance) that they now needed a climber and turned to look at me! I obliged and clambered up to investigate, it certainly didn't look very stable. There were two huge Fiat Uno-sized boulders with no visible means of support that had to be negotiated in order to evaluate the results of the last major crowbar-induced rock fall. I managed to climb over them without too much difficulty and then spent several minutes chucking down the worst of the teetering loose blocks around and above me, before tentatively venturing further up through the choke.

After climbing about 10m, I was sure I could see blackness between the boulders. I tried shouting and was excited to hear a good echo which indicated that there was a large passage ahead! I called back to the others and advised waiting a couple of minutes, as many of the blocks looked dangerously loose. My first attempts to excavate a route through the boulders were frustrating. I managed to create a sizeable hole, but couldn't quite squeeze through, even after removing my lid (helmet). Looking up into the obviously spacious passage above was tantalising. Then, I found that I had a solid wall to my right and that some of the larger boulders against it could be moved, even if only a fraction. I spent the next few minutes wrestling with one awkwardly-wedged rock about 50cm x 50cm; one last grunting effort and it came loose and tumbled down through the choke below. The next few came out easily and, in moments, I'd broken through. I shouted to Martyn and Gareth to follow carefully; the whole choke looked decidedly loose.

I was standing in a lofty passage some 3m across and 5m high with a hopeless choke to the west, but a large open passage leading off to the east. While the others were making their way up, I explored the latter for about 30m. It looked as though it might stretch far into the distance, but of course my length of vision was limited, so I couldn't be sure. I returned to the breakthrough to find Gareth climbing a boulder slope to another 20m passage that 'looked like easy digging'. We then set off along the main passage; it seemed lengthy - though we expected it to close down at every turn. This was my first big breakthrough and in my excitement, I'm ashamed to admit, I hogged the lead for the first 100m. After this, we shared it; there was much to explore, most of it really big stuff.

The main passage connected some large chambers up to 15m across, some of which contained good formations, including one pretty grotto. There were potential leads everywhere! We half expected to pop up in Pen Eryr on the Llangattock side of the mountain or Craig a Fynnon on the Clydach Gorge side. In 2002 the chamber we had called Price's Prophecy was reached via Price's

Dig by the Chelsea Speleological Society, creating a formidable through trip, one I've made several times since. Between us, we explored the most obvious leads, including one rather desperate climb which I managed to negotiate in order to enter about 12 to 15m of 1.5m wide phreatic passages which had been formed when completely full of water and therefore had an almost circular cross section; this tube ended in an attractive grotto. I held my breath as I climbed back down; it was 'necky', that is, dangerous, requiring delicate and awkward movements.

When the most obvious leads had been explored, we started back with Martyn pacing and estimating the distances so we could evaluate the discovery. At one point, we struggled up an awkward climb; Martyn and I had to retrace our steps to manhandle Gareth upwards - definitely a spot for a hand line. By the time we got back to the breakthrough, we reckoned we had in excess of 800m of new passage with the potential for more. After gingerly passing through the choke we made a pretty slow exit. On the way out, we found Peter waiting for us in the dark - to add insult to the injury of missing out on the breakthrough, poor lad had had lighting problems.

I was weary as I struggled through the punishing entrance series, emerging barely able to stand after eleven strenuous hours underground. Gareth, though, had found a 'second wind' and had got out first. He was shivering outside Whitewalls – we'd been locked out of the caving hut! Twenty minutes later, Martyn and Peter arrived. We were all freezing by the time a group who'd been down Aggy turned up with a key. It was a relief to get changed and have a much needed mug of tea.

The three of us have made many digging trips in Aggy together. When Martyn first invited me to join him on a dig in Daren, he had described it as 'a bit of a busman's holiday for Aggy diggers', so this seemed an appropriate name for the new extension. On subsequent trips, we produced a basic survey and pushed various leads including Tony Donovan's discovery of about 30m of big passage which he named Orange Blossom Way. There, a particularly stubborn boulder was eventually moved and a further 55m of passage discovered, heading towards Craig a Fynnon, but we were disappointed to find that it closed down into a hopeless crack. During another trip, a determined digging effort at the extreme southern end of the Busman's Holiday was finally pushed by Gareth who squirmed up an awkward squeeze leading to a further 150m of passage, but again we were disappointed to find no potential lead.

A few months later I managed to negotiate a tricky climb in Bridge Cavern, only 100m or so from the original breakthrough point into Busman's Holiday. I walked into about 40m of 'A'-shaped passage with clean scalloped walls and a smooth mud floor - exciting stuff! Then the passage closed down. I returned to tell the others and they came up. Our main digging tackle was quite a way off, but as luck would have it, I'd brought along my new toy - a tiny crowbar that just fitted into a big BDH (a plastic drum used to carry kit underground). Although this had caused much mirth back at Whitewalls, it now came into its own. We spent the next few hours digging in firm mud in a low passage that alternated between being tolerable to being decidedly nasty. Initially, progress was rapid, but we ended up at a flat-out section that took longer to dig as there was only enough room for one of us to dig at a time. The draught was strong; consequently, we all got pretty cold, so the extension was named Exposure Passage.

Though the obvious leads had by this time been examined, with such a large new extension to the system, closer scrutiny would surely yield further passages. There remained a strong possibility of breaking through to Craig a Fynnon or Pen Eryr, and who knew what else awaited discovery. At the time, none of us had expected a breakthrough into such large new passages. The fact that the Llangattock was riddled with caves was beyond dispute, so we were inspired to keep digging and find some more!

Chapter 15 WHITE ADRENALIN

Winter Mountaineering in Scotland

Paul Roberts, a colleague from work, and I had reached the dreary point of February half-term. We'd been caving and climbing partners for some time and we'd always fancied trying some serious winter mountaineering so we seized the moment. As we had a healthy respect for the hazardous environment, we decided to go on a course before setting off on our own snow and ice adventures. Paul contacted Mick Tighe of Nevis Guides who promised to give us a challenging week of instruction in Scotland.

We shared the driving on the way up to Fort William and completed the 800km journey in good time. There were four others on the course; three solicitors who'd come along together and a computer chap. They'd all been winter mountaineering in Scotland before and were well-equipped, moderately experienced, and extremely fit.

On the first day, we were blessed with superb weather conditions. The others said they'd never had it so good over the previous five years! There were clear blue skies, bright sunshine, and clean crisp snow.

We started with ice axe arrest practice, an essential skill if you're to survive a fall on steep ground. It also proved to be highly entertaining as it resulted in ludicrous antics as we slid around on the ice. Wearing crampons took some getting used to, but they really did a good job and enabled us to walk over snow and ice we wouldn't otherwise have contemplated approaching.

Climbing the Forcan Ridge was an easy, but nonetheless, spectacular and enjoyable route. It was a rewarding introduction to winter mountaineering. I was wearing hired plastic boots and on the way down I discovered that they were not quite as good a fit as I'd first thought. By the time I got to the bottom my big toes hurt like crazy. The pain continued throughout the week and a month later I lost both my big toenails - bleagh!

On the second day, we made our way up the Inglis Clark Route which was considerably harder. Grappling with rocks wasn't easy wearing plastic boots and crampons! I had my first attempt at 'front pointing' which is climbing steep ice and snow, using a pair of ice axes and kicking the spikes on the front of the crampons into the ice or snow with each step. It was strenuous, but thrilling at the same time. Now, I felt, I was doing the real thing - the 'big boys' stuff' we'd all come for.

The weather deteriorated the next day, so we went for a serious gorge walk. We scrambled over snow and ice-clad boulders and accomplished many difficult little traverses and short climbs. Trying to follow Victor Saunders , a respected mountaineer who was there training as a Mountain Guide, was a real challenge - especially under snowball fire! The year before, he'd reached 8000m on K2, a Himalayan mountain with a very dangerous reputation. He was later to climb Everest in 2005! Interesting company indeed. Paul, however, had managed a spectacular plunge up to his chest in the icy river. He carried on regardless, much to the amazement of the others, who obviously hadn't met sturdy Welsh cavers before!

Perfect, positively Alpine weather greeted us the following morning and, in ideal conditions, we did a marvellous route called Rayburn's Gully. The only tricky part was negotiating the cornice at the top of the climb where the snow had been blown over the ridge. Paul demonstrated his cave-digging abilities to good effect here, by cutting through the cornice. On the way down, we took a fairly easy walking route and even had a couple of good poly-bag runs, hurling ourselves on top of the plastic bags and using them as if they had been toboggans. Paul and I did a duo run, cackling manically as we sped over the snow head-first.

Day five was the big one. We set off at dawn to tackle the North East Buttress of Ben Nevis, a grade 3 to 4 snow and ice route - serious stuff! Unfortunately, Paul couldn't join us as he'd injured his ankle the previous day. Mark couldn't make it either, as he'd been vomiting half the night. So I set off with Andy, Tim, and Phil. The leader was Mick Tighe, a hardened mountaineer with a background in training marines in Arctic conditions. He didn't suffer fools gladly, but he had a great sense of humour.

When we'd reached the climbing hut and the route had been pointed out to me, I thought 'No way, you have got to be kidding!' But they weren't. It was made up of 400m of snow, ice, and rock, along with ten pitches of some of the most demanding conditions I'd ever experienced. I found it very hard and there were several times when I doubted I would make it, but I did, despite a few desperate moments.

The ultimate section was a veritable dream. We stormed up a steep snow and ice slope on front points with good solid ice axe placements. Reaching the top was a euphoric moment, not to say a great relief! An added bonus was the glorious sunset as we descended, though my toes were absolutely agonizing . . . .

On the last day, we did a route called Hidden Gully. It was moderately short, but it gave us the opportunity to practise new techniques and included some testing climbing sections. These would have been a doddle in rock boots but were extremely 'necky' in crampons.

During the course, Mick Tighe had been involved in filming a programme for BBC2 about the history of Scottish mountaineering and had re-enacted some of the first ascents of routes wearing the old-fashioned gear. On the last night, we went out for a good meal and then to an interesting lecture given by a member of the previous year's Irish Himalayan expedition who had reached the top of Everest. What with Mick's descriptions of the early pioneers of Scottish winter climbing, the Everest mountaineer's accounts of contemporary expeditions, and our recent experiences, we were overwhelmed by a new sense of awe and respect for all dedicated mountaineers, past and present.

Chapter 16 LECHUGUILLA

JEWEL OF THE UNDERGROUND

Caving in New Mexico

I was editor of the Cwmbran Caving Club Journal and shortly before the Easter Break, Bob Savidge, the club's tackle officer, phoned and asked if I had his atlas. A small group of us from the club were planning a caving trip to New Mexico. Ade Fawcett, our treasurer, fell about laughing with visions of us navigating our way across the US using a single page from a school atlas . . . . I wasn't quite so amused, remembering my earlier experience without a compass in the Sahara!

There were spectacular views of icebergs as we flew over the Labrador Sea followed by a four-hour stopover in Houston. Alan got a lot of attention from a sniffer dog that eventually found the contraband it was after – an apple! Our onward flight was overbooked and we had a nerve-wracking twenty-minute delay before we boarded. Finally, we got to Albuquerque and collected our hire car – a Chevrolet 'Blazer'. After ten minutes of trying to figure out how the lights worked, we were able to set off to find our motel and to get a few hours' sleep.

After a cheap yet filling Mexican style *'burrito'* breakfast at a diner around the corner, we left for Carlsbad just after eight. The scenery reminded me of southern Spain; dry and dusty with scrubby vegetation, prickly pear cactus, and tumbleweed. In the Valley of the Fires National Park we stopped for a while to have a look at the spectacular *pahoehoe* (ropy lava flows) which were about 2,000 years old. As we drove south through vast open spaces, there was a 360 degree vista of the distant horizon. This was a region of big roads, big distances, big cars, incredibly big mobile homes, and monstrous trucks, including huge Machs and Kenilworths. The speed limits were ridiculously low, however.

We arrived at Carlsbad Caverns around 5 p.m. and soon found the cavers' hut where we were to stay for the next week. The beds were an experience! They had metal frames with canvas stretched across them, a bit like saggy trampolines and they certainly sounded like them whenever anyone turned over in the night. Noise at night was quite a problem as everyone snored, but no one managed to snore like Adrian. He was the undisputed champion!

In the evening, we drove into Carlsbad and went to a popular Mexican restaurant called Lucy's, where we met most of the other members of the expedition and started to get to know a few of them. If we'd been in UK, I'm sure that everyone would have had vast quantities of beer, but this didn't seem to be the custom with American cavers. I had a couple, but found the beer to be like pop and wasn't terribly impressed.

In the morning there was a talk by Dale Pate, the Carlsbad National Park Specialist. He outlined the rules and regulations for our stay. This wasn't as tedious as it might sound. His coverage of the problems of killer raccoons, scorpions, and rattlesnakes gave pause for thought, but prompted quite a few laughs as well. Pat Seiser, the LEARN (Lechuguilla Exploration and Research Network) chairperson told us about standard procedures for the expedition after which there was a buzz of excited anticipation as thirty wide-eyed cavers waited to find out which sections of the cave they would be visiting and for how long.

Adrian and I were allocated a day trip into the North Rift area accompanied by Jim Erikson, a caver from Colorado who described himself as an ex-climber. We later learned that this was rather an understatement as he was a highly respected mountaineer who had published a number of climbing guidebooks. He gave us some useful advice about what to take into Lechuguilla Cave which had an environment with a constant temperature of about 20°C and consisted mostly of dry walking passage. This was to be a new experience for British cavers. A short drive in Jim's 4x4 and a twenty-minute walk through bone dry scrub and cactus took us to the entrance. The cave was named after the abundant viciously spiky rosettes of the Lechuguilla cactus found in the area.

The three of us descended the dry and dusty 18m-entrance pitch. At the bottom, Adrian asked 'What's that noise?' He was referring to a sound akin to that of an approaching train on the London Underground. It was caused by the draft (up to 50kmph), but referred to by cavers as the roar of the 'Lech Gorilla'. A short descent took us down to the impressive gate - a solid lid that provided a pretty efficient seal to a 6m corrugated iron tube. A howling gale blew dust in our faces when we opened it. It had to be closed after each person descended. When the draught was at its strongest a glove could be thrown down, only for it to be blown straight back!

The cave quickly opened up to a large passage and it wasn't long before we were standing at the top of Boulder Falls. We abseiled down the 50m pitch into a massive chamber, with the bottom 30m free-hanging. My Petzl Stop descender, which I had used to abseil down the pitch, made me jump when it brushed against my leg as I walked away from the bottom of the pitch - the friction break had really heated it up on the way down. We soon arrived at Glacier Bay where there was an enormous block of gypsum, maybe 60m across and 20m thick, with fluted tubes going down through it where water had dripped. They looked like moulds for Roman columns.

For a geologist like me, one of the greatest attractions of visiting Lechuguilla, sometimes described as 'the jewel of the underground', was that the cave was renowned for its varied and beautiful formations, including many unique types of speleothem. Most are composed of the mineral calcite. They're deposited by water supersaturated with calcium carbonate derived from limestone which has been dissolved by carbonic acid at higher levels. When such water comes into contact with cave air it loses some carbon dioxide and precipitation of calcite results. Calcite precipitated in this way produces the wide variety of speleothems we're familiar with in the UK - stalactites, stalagmites, curtains, and flowstone.

In places, the walls were entirely coated with a crust of pure white crystalline gypsum that looked very much like snow. Gypsum also forms stalagmites, columns, 'chandeliers', 'flowers', thin threads, and strangely bulbous chalky forms known as 'popcorn'. Underwater, the gypsum had settled in layered masses up to 10m thick. Lechuguilla contains more gypsum than any other limestone cave known. Examples of speleothems unique to the cave were the amazing subaqueous helectites (contorted depositional speleothems which develop in any direction) which were up to 45cm long and varied from 2mm to 7mm in thickness. Some of them looked just like bean sprouts! These are thought to form where water that has just trickled over gypsum enters a pool already saturated with limestone, causing the less soluble calcite to precipitate.

In summary, Lechuguilla and its speleothems were a constant source of surprise and fantastic beauty. At times, I felt I'd reached 'speleo-sensory-overload'; there was simply too much to take in - an unforgettable experience.

But, back to the caving! When we arrived at the beginning of the North Rift we noticed some flagging tape with the message 'Welcome to the plush and luxurious North Rift'. 'Plush and luxurious', soon became a catch phrase for all that is squalid in caving as this was the Lechuguilla equivalent of Priory Road in Aggy, South Wales. The North Rift certainly wasn't as pretty as other parts we visited, but to be honest, it wasn't really all that bad and had served as useful acclimatisation.

The purpose of our trip was to flag a clear route to the further reaches of the rift to enable exploration teams to reach those areas more quickly. All of the main routes in the cave had been marked with orange tape. In the more recently discovered sections, cavers had had to follow the blue tape which had been placed by surveyors at survey stations along the route as they mapped them. Leads, promising potential routes yet to be explored, had been marked with blue and white striped tape. Delicate formations were flagged with the familiar red and white used by cavers in UK.

After rigging a 10m hand line to make the descent down a very loose slope easier, we proceeded to flag our way through the North Rift. This route involved some slightly awkward traverses and one very thrutchy, extremely awkward contortion on a 12m SRT (single rope technique) pitch which narrowed to a slot at the top. This meant I had to remove my tackle sack and generally get a hefty sweat on. I had learned SRT in preparation for the trip, as it was a requirement for expedition members. It proved to be a useful skill that I was able to use in future caving trips in the UK and abroad, adding a new dimension to my underground experiences.

Our trip took us to Fawn Hall and to the Hub, then we made a short detour to Kryptonite Hall where we admired some exquisitely delicate bushes made of the mineral aragonite. We didn't see any of the super spectacular stuff, though we saw more than enough to whet our appetites and to make most British formations pale into insignificance. In Kryptonite Hall, we met the 'Durango Dudes' raving about a 'Fat Fissure' they were about to descend, hoping that it would lead to 'Booming Borehole'. The Dudes were a group of cavers in their early twenties who had a lingo all of their own and could have walked straight out of the 'Been There, Done That' over-the-top outdoor activity 'Pepsi-max' advert! They were amusing - in small doses.

On our way back, we followed an 'escape route' to the beginning of the traverses via a couple of short pitches. The rope on one of these was as stiff as a steel cable making it impossible to use a Petzl Stop. I was glad I'd brought a steel karabiner which we

British cavers called a 'krab', but called a 'biner' by the Americans. Using the steel krab with an Italian hitch worked really well with the stiff rope.

My impression of the cave after this first short trip, was that the sheer scale of the place was daunting. As a geologist, I was interested in the character and origin of the cave which was very different from the caves I'd explored in UK. Most caves form as a result of the action of weak carbonic acid dissolving limestone combined with the erosive action of water flowing underground. This isn't the case for Lechuguilla and other caves of the Guadalupe Mountains which had been formed in a particularly unusual way. As the rocks of the region were uplifted in the Tertiary (65 million years ago) period, many fractures had formed which allowed the upward migration of hydrogen sulphide. This originated in rocks rich in carbonaceous organic remains. The organic carbon reacted with oxygen to form carbon dioxide; when all the free oxygen had been used up, the carbon attacked the oxygen in sulphates such as gypsum, reducing them to hydrogen sulphide. When the hydrogen sulphide mixed with the oxygen-rich groundwater near the water table, it oxidized to form sulphuric acid; this led to extensive dissolution of the limestone and subsequent cave development. This unusual situation helps to explain the labyrinthine complexity of caves such as Lechuguilla, with its extensive maze-like passages that branch and interconnect in such an unpredictable way. You can't simply 'follow the stream' here. This makes exploration of new areas both exciting and frustrating. The different levels of the cave were formed during periods when the groundwater level remained stable, or when there was an increase in the amount of hydrogen sulphide present. The shape of the passages was largely determined by the presence of fractures which tended to lead to rift development and bedding which, in turn, were prone to lead to the development of wider passages.

Most of the North Rift was dry and dusty, though some sections were like being in a giant sugar cube with pure white aragonite frosting the walls. There wasn't much mud in Lechuguilla, though we did find plenty of the rusty reddish-brown corroded limestone known as 'gorilla shit'. I didn't find the temperature to be as much of a problem as I'd anticipated and I seemed to have got the gear about right. I wore a lightweight 'Duofold' thermal top and leggings with tough shorts over the top, along with Hi-tec Trail lightweight walking boots and a pair of kneepads which I didn't use very much. Twenty degrees Celsius is quite pleasant when you're sitting around or just pootling along at a leisurely pace, but boy do you sweat when you start something strenuous, like 50m of SRT up the Boulder Falls pitch.

The ascent up Boulder Falls took me, a rank amateur at SRT, fourteen minutes, while Adrian zipped up in about ten. When we got back to the gate, the draught had reversed; it was even stronger than before and it was quite a struggle to open. After eleven hours underground, we finally got back to the hut at two in the morning. I had a quick shower, only vaguely aware of the brown water flowing off me, and then crashed out big-time. I was completely burned out.

In the morning we took it easy. Kevin Glover, who works for the Carlsbad National Park, came with the four of us Brits for a short drive to Rattlesnake Springs down on the plain below the escarpment where we were staying. In the afternoon, we visited the Carlsbad Caverns show cave. As members of LEARN, we didn't have to pay an entrance fee. The cave had been discovered when cowboys thought they could see smoke and went to investigate, only to find that what they had thought was smoke was a vast cloud of millions of bats leaving the enormous entrance!

This was undoubtedly the most breathtaking show cave I'd ever visited. The sheer scale of the place was awesome and the prolific formations were colossal as well as beautiful. In one chamber, I spotted a rope dangling 100m from the roof. It turned out to have had a remarkable history in that it had been placed by using a helium balloon! Unfortunately, when the innovative and daring explorers had ascended the ingeniously placed rope they only found about 25m of passage. It amused us all to take a far easier route out; we left the cave by going up 230m in a lift! An evening of caving-talk and a slap-up steak dinner finished off an immensely satisfying day.

The next day, Adrian and I returned to Lechuguilla, this time with Kevin and Jim. We poked around for a while in the Sugarlands area looking for leads off the main room. Our search proved fruitless, so we pushed on to the end of the known passage. Here we examined some superb sub-aqueous helectites (twisted formations with poorly understood origin) and other bizarre and interesting formations. I took quite a few photos. Jim took his boots off to avoid damaging the formations and did an awkward little climb over some flowstone (precipitated calcite that looks like a waterfall, but is made of rock) in his socks. However, he found that the lead couldn't be explored any further as there was a river of pure white flowstone that couldn't be passed without, as Jim put it, an 'aqua body stocking'. Meanwhile, I found a hole in the floor and, hanging upside down, found some amazing ex-sub-aqueous helectites – an unusual discovery.

Then the fun and excitement really started as we explored a narrow rift in the floor that led to a promising-looking tube, that is, a passage with a smooth surface which would be roughly circular in cross section. LEARN policy was to explore no more than 10m or so without surveying, so we acted accordingly. There was an alcove full of 10cm long calcite dogtooth spar just after the rift which was awkward to descend, so Kevin invented the name 'Spargatory' for our discovery. The passage was quite different to most we'd seen and much more like the phreatic tubes (formed when the caves were full of flowing water) that we were familiar with in the UK. There were some really gorgeous formations with pure white gypsum, stalactites, flowstone, and clear blue pools. The passage was small by Lechuguilla standards as it was mostly only about a metre high and a metre wide.

As a surveying team, Adrian placed the lead tape, Jim used the compass clinometer to record direction and slope, Kevin sketched the passage profile, and I helped out with the back sights to confirm Jim's readings. After about 70m we came to a well decorated chamber which we christened 'Sparadise', followed by two more beautiful blue pools. We could see a way forward and there appeared to be a draught, but here our exploration had to end. Because of their importance to scientific research, no pools may be disturbed without permission from the National Park Authority. About sixty types of microbes have been discovered in the pools of Lechuguilla and some of them appear to have important potential with regard to their use in cancer research.

We made our way out, checking leads as we went. Back in the Glacier Bay area we surveyed about 55m of what is known as 'Boneyard' which is strange labyrinthine stuff, just like being inside bone marrow. It was horrendous to survey. There were legion delicate gypsum flowers, some looking as though they had squirted from the walls.

Back at the bottom of Boulder Falls we found two other parties waiting to climb. This meant a two-hour wait. We were kept entertained by cave chat and the enthusiastic photographic antics of Val, who was putting together a collection of portraits of cavers. By the time I could hear the grumbling roar of the 'Lech - Gorilla' back at the entrance, we had been underground for about fourteen hours. I didn't get to bed until three that morning.

On the fifth day, there was a LEARN meeting at which each team reported back on its achievements. It sounded as though there were some exciting leads down the Western Borehole, so Adrian and I thought we should head out there for a few days. Unfortunately, there didn't seem to be much constructive work to be done in the South West area where the most spectacular formations were, although earlier in the week it had been suggested that we might have an opportunity to go there. However, the Western Borehole itself was reputedly pretty impressive, so we weren't too disappointed.

In the afternoon, Adrian and I went into Carlsbad to buy some provisions for our long trip. We did our own version of shopping for a calorie controlled diet - we wanted as many as possible! When we got back, we found Bob and Alan, both rather sunburned and dejected, after having spent several hours looking for the entrance to Chimney Cave without success.

The next day, I was pleased to be able to pack all of my gear for a trip to the Western Borehole area of Lechuguilla into a small tackle sack weighing about 15kg, including two litres of water and all of my food for a few days. The tackle sack was ideal for the expedition and I was surprised to find that most of the Americans used rucksacks which had a tendency to get snagged a lot. We made our way into Lechuguilla around midday with Steve Koehler and Rand Pipp, two Californians. Steve was a Lechuguilla veteran with several expeditions behind him. Rand was a newcomer like us. He'd seen the same 1991 *National Geographic* magazine article about Lechuguilla which had inspired us to visit and had decided to take up caving as a result, with the specific goal of one day visiting Lechuguilla, so this was the fulfilment of a personal dream for him.

On this, the sixth day of our visit, The Lech Gorilla was really howling and sucking rather than blowing. I had to climb down the tube with my eyes shut to keep out the swirling clouds of dust and sand. It took us about four hours to reach the Western Borehole camp, passing through Windy City, E.F. Junction, The Great White Way, Deep Secrets, The Fortress of Chaos, and the Christmas Tree Room. There were quite a few photo stops and we were fortunate that the bigger passages were spectacularly illuminated for us by

Pipp's powerful video light. There was also quite a lot of rope work, so we were all pretty sweaty by the time we got to camp.

Soon after arriving, we went to fetch water from Lake Louise, five minutes away. This proved to be even more beautiful than it looked in the *Jewel of the Underground* book. The incredible 'Lech Gorilla', the mighty draught in the entrance tube below the gate, was responsible for many of the features of the cave. The transfer of moisture by airflow leads to condensation on the walls; this moisture attacks the rock, leaving a fluffy brown residue, the aforementioned 'Gorilla Shit'. Changing water levels have redeposited this residue in places such as Lake Louise, giving the walls orange, red, and yellow coatings. During the later stages of cave development, thick calcite crusts coated the walls of isolated pools, producing curious bulbous mamillated (covered with rounded protuberances) crusts. Back at camp we rested for a while and ate. I had some foil-sealed army rations which tasted far better than I had expected.

Later, we went off to investigate leads in the Red Seas area. This was probably the highlight of the whole expedition. The floor was deep red calcite with raft cones rising up, red at the base, but pure white aragonite above the old water line. The cones were formed by floating rafts of calcite piling up to become pillars. The walls were bristling with fragile bushes of aragonite needles. It was an 'aquasock' area and so, in the interests of conservation, we explored particularly carefully. Unfortunately, we didn't find anything new, but it was well worth visiting the area and I was thoroughly impressed. Back at camp, we slept fairly early, anticipating a long day of exploration and surveying to come.

I woke from the best sleep I'd had in the US so far. It was strange to look up at the mammillated forms of the rock overhead. It was like waking in a Salvador Dali painting. I had rolled oats and hot chocolate for breakfast; unfortunately, it was rather like eating wet cement. We left camp in search of 'Booming Borehole' at about nine, passed Lake Louise, the ABC Room, West Manifest Destiny and The Three Amigos, The leaning Tower of Lechuguilla, and Hard Daze Night Hall. We ended up in an area above The Chocolate Factory where we explored and surveyed about 50m of boneyard. Later, we continued past a huge echoing chamber called The Planetarium, up Willy Wonka's Wiggly Way (honestly!), to a short climb that led us to another little area to explore and survey for about 40m. There were many exquisite formations with delicate aragonite bushes and 'Cave Popcorn' (small nodes of calcite, aragonite, or gypsum that form on surfaces in caves, especially in limestone conditions). We finally returned to camp around ten at night, tired and hungry.

There were excited discussions in the morning when we heard that one of the other teams had made a major discovery the previous day - about 1.5km of big new passage! Needless to say, all three of the Western Borehole teams eagerly went off to explore and push leads. We set off to Hard Daze Night Hall and then turned left into Widowmaker Hall. From here, there was a short mild squeeze under an unstable boulder which led us into the new area.

A 5m climb took us into a beautiful white tube encrusted with gypsum and aragonite. After a series of short climbs we popped out into a chamber sloping at about 45°, 3 to 6m high, 50m wide and at least 120m long - a real 'Fat Fissure' as the Durango Dudes would have said! We soon found and surveyed a lead with a spectacularly beautiful roof festooned with large aragonite bushes and giant gypsum flowers and I was amazed to find some gypsum hair (incredibly fine delicate threads of gypsum) which I'd never seen before.

Adrian and I both worked on instruments when we were surveying and felt we were really getting the hang of it, though the level of accuracy required by LEARN was sometimes difficult to achieve when we were precariously balanced above a gaping chasm and trying desperately not to damage any of the formations. Later, we descended to the lower levels of the main passage and found a stunning room bristling with gypsum and aragonite. We also saw, at about 4m high, the biggest raft cone we'd seen which, as a bonus, was crowned with an aragonite bush.

I led a pretty tricky lead climb for about 15m without ropes or harness, but eventually bottled out, not because I couldn't get any higher, but because I was getting concerned about not being able to climb down. Discretion being the better part of valour, I took up Steve's offer of a short length of 8mm rope and rigged it on a small bridge of rock. It was impossible to tell if the bridge was solid or not, so when it came to my descent the rope was more of a confidence line than anything else and I certainly didn't want to put any weight on it if I could avoid it. We decided to call it a day and headed back to camp. It was on this evening that I sincerely wished I had been taller so that I could be further away from my feet which stank!

The next day, we steamed on, making it to Boulder Falls in two hours. I'd been dreading the prospect of the big pitch, but it wasn't as bad as I'd feared; in fact I made it in the same time as on the shorter trips when I'd been carrying a lighter pack. We finally got back to the surface after a total of seventy-one hours underground to be greeted by a glorious day with warm sun and a cool breeze. It was such a relief to have a dry back again, the only disappointment was that two of the beers we had stashed to celebrate our exit had frozen at night, then exploded and soaked my jeans in the process. Back at the caving hut, it felt good to get cleaned up as gritty gypsum and aragonite seemed to have got into every crack and cranny.

In the afternoon, we went for a short drive to a small quarry nearby where we collected some excellent specimens of large, clear selenite (a variety of gypsum) crystals. Back at the hut there was a euphoric atmosphere as we tucked in to big portions of spaghetti Bolognese. The expedition had been a great success. We had discovered, explored, and surveyed just over 4km of new cave which was the biggest extension for several years. Our discoveries had brought the total surveyed length of Lechuguilla to about 120km! Later, Peter Jones gave us a brief but excellent slide show on Lechuguilla. By way of contrast, we then gave a slide show on the caves of South Wales. Thoughts of the 'plush and luxurious' flat-out wet entrance crawl of Daren Cilau seemed a very long way away - Lechuguilla had spoilt us!

We spent most of the morning of the following day, tidying up and cleaning the hut in preparation for the next expedition team.

Having experienced the otherworldly alien nature of the environment at the limits of exploration in Lechuguilla, it was no surprise to learn that the next expedition team exploring the cave was for NASA research into early life forms in the remote pools of Lechuguilla. We then went off to Carlsbad to do some shopping before visiting the Living Desert National Park exhibit. We'd timed it well and arrived as a video about Lechuguilla began. The film gave quite a good impression of the cave, but what we found most amusing was the commentary, parts of which had been done by one of the members of our expedition team. Donald Davis was a real character with a ponderous American drawl and a dry sense of humour. When he had broken through from Widowmaker Hall into 1.5km of new passage a few days earlier, he is reputed to have said 'I had been trying to break through a collapse to connect up with a known cave and was gravely disappointed to find that I'd found my way into virgin passage'!

The previous night Bob had been chatting to American cavers Pat and Bill Jablonsky and they had invited all four of us to go and stay with them - an offer which we very gratefully accepted. In the evening, we went back to the Carlsbad Caverns hut, where I read about the early exploration of Spider Cave in the 1930's. Apparently, the original explorers had had to crawl through thousands of spiders at the entrance; it sounded like something out of *Indiana Jones*.

We set off to visit Spider, for which, like so many caves in the area, we needed a guide and a permit. Access to many of the caves was restricted to one or two visits a month, so we had been extremely lucky. Our team comprised the four of us Brits together with American cavers, Mark, Melanie, Walt, and Steve, along with our guide, Julia Cronk, from the National Park.

Our trip only lasted two and a half hours and we didn't go very far, but we didn't need to, for the formations we saw were fantastic. They were curious and extraordinary in a different way to the splendours of Lechuguilla. Many of the formations looked like dripping plaster, white and chalky, in contorted shapes. We all went wild with our cameras. Walt had an amazing lighting system with a fluorescent tube powered by 24 AA Duracell batteries strapped around his helmet - batteries are cheap in the US. Walt also had a UV light which allowed us to see the eerie greenish fluorescence of some of the formations after they had been zapped with a flash unit. It was a great trip and excellent fun. Although our good humour was tested on the way home by a brief encounter with a 'Smokie Bear' (police control car). However, we got home eventually without being arrested.

Our mission for the next day was to go in search of Gunsight Cave. The instructions we'd been given by the National Park were extremely detailed - after thirty-one of them, each with a compass bearing and paced distance, we eventually found the cave. The entrance was a spectacular and imposing arch, allegedly large enough for a helicopter to fly into. It didn't extend back very far, but it was worth visiting nevertheless; the enormity of the entrance arch was simply awesome.

Our walk back to the truck was an hour quicker than our route to the cave, but even so, we were running late. We'd arranged with

Pat and Bill to show some slides and have a meal with them and some of their caving friends that evening. After phoning to let them know we'd be late, Alan proceeded to surpass even Bob's exploits by driving us back with poor headlights, no road markings, numerous bends, and the added interest of a motley collection of deer, cattle, foxes, and rabbits wandering over the road. All this combined to give us a hair-raising ride. By the time we got back, some of the guests were already leaving, but we still had a slide show and a discussion with those who remained.

Adrian, Bob, Alan and I, together with Bill and with Kevin as our guide, went to Pink Panther Cave in the morning. It had an easy entrance pitch of about 20m. The formations were impressive from the start. Kevin showed us the calcified remains of a bear skeleton that had been mistakenly identified as a panther when the cave was first discovered, hence its name. The pink came from the pink rock, or maybe because the legendary Pink Panther was notoriously difficult to find! A short climb and the tightest squeeze we had encountered in US caves led us to the incredible Speleogasm room. This was as bizarre as it was beautiful, bristling with myriad medusa-like helectites in every hue from pure white to blood red. It was difficult to decide where to point the camera first, it was such a spectacular finale to our caving exploits in the US. In the evening, Adrian did a long hard drive which took us to Alamagordo where we found a motel and our first real beds since Albuquerque almost a fortnight before.

On our last day, we visited Whitesands National Park with its blindingly white dunes of gypsum sand before driving back to

Albuquerque and booking into the motel we had stayed in when we first arrived. After a celebratory meal at the end of our fantastic trip, we prepared for the long haul home.

Chapter 17 EXPLORING EGYPT

The Nile - Red Sea - Sinai

I'd been teaching for about four years when I decided to treat myself to a sociable trip rather than a solo expedition. I chose to travel with Explore, a company specialising in small group adventure holidays. I felt it was time to head back to Africa.

It was almost midnight when we arrived at Cairo airport, yet even that late, I was struck by the humidity as I left the plane. In the bus on the way to the hotel, it soon became evident to our group that in Egypt there's as much, if not more activity at night as there is during the day; even at that time, families were picnicking on the broad grassy central reservation of the wide road which was teeming with traffic. There seemed to be armed soldiers or military police on every street corner. They looked numb with boredom. The drivers seemed not to use specific lanes; they wove in and out of the general flow using the horn as an indicator of intent. Traffic lights were often ignored and as a result, the numerous traffic police appeared to spend much of their time dicing with death. However, the huge volume of traffic managed to keep on the move, which is more than can be said for some British roads during the rush hour. After checking in at the President Hotel, which was rather grand for one who'd usually travelled as a trekker, I had a pleasant couple of beers with some other members of the group, quite a number of whom were teachers like me. We were to get to know the locally brewed Stella lager pretty well over the next couple of weeks!

The next day, it was important to make an cruelly early start to visit the pyramids at Giza for two reasons, to beat the crowds and the heat, but it was worth it. They looked strangely incongruous as I caught my first glimpse through the modern buildings on the outskirts of Cairo, but when we got closer it was easy to see how all of the photos in the guidebooks make them look as if they're in the middle of the desert, as the green belt that hugs the banks of Nile stops so abruptly, and then suddenly, there's sand.

We were told that the Great Pyramid of Cheops was 137m high and made of nearly 2.5 million gigantic stone blocks weighing between 2.5 and 15 tonnes. It was mind-boggling to consider that it had been estimated that it took 100,000 men twenty years to build these monuments, and incredible that such impressive and advanced engineering techniques were being employed in about 2,600 BC. Going into the Chephren pyramid was exciting. It was easy to imagine the anticipation and trepidation that the first people to enter in modern times must have experienced, especially as occasionally, we had to stoop low and descend steep slopes in complete darkness. The Sphinx was not as big as I'd expected, though it was still imposing and beautiful - even if its nose had been shot off by a cannonball! The nearby temple of Cephren was a marvel of engineering in both scale and detail with immense blocks of polished granite cleverly interlocked with ingenious joints.

The Egyptian Museum was a feast of the wonders of ancient Egypt and it was worth having a knowledgeable guide to pick out the most interesting and beautiful exhibits from the vast and bewildering collection. For me, it was fascinating to see some of the more everyday objects of ancient Egyptian life as well as the glory and splendour of the Pharaohs. The treasures of King Tutankhamun were beyond belief, a glittering array of exquisite artefacts. It was, unsurprisingly, the largest amount of gold I'd ever seen in one room since visiting the Katopi Palace in Turkey. The amazing opulence of the treasures made me wonder what the lifestyle of an ancient Egyptian king must have been like, especially as he'd died so young.

The city was full of contrasts between ancient and modern, east and west. Contemporary western-style high-rise buildings were under construction in all directions, but wooden scaffolding lashed together with hemp ropes was used, rather than up-to-date metal supports. In the teeming traffic, donkey carts mingled with battered black and white taxis and gleaming Mercedes and in the side streets many parked cars were covered with tailor-made 'car cosies' to keep off the dust. It was never long before a 'wide boy' would target me with his individual persuasive patter, whether selling perfume, carpets, camels, or *galabaya* (a traditional long-sleeved white shirt that reaches below the knee). It was easy to be seduced into visiting shops, and often awkward to leave, but it was all part of an endless game that both the vendor and the customer could enjoy, if blessed with a good sense of humour, that is!

Egyptian food was not a particular highlight of the trip, though there were some good dishes. I particularly enjoyed using the flat unleavened bread to scoop up *tahina* (a Middle Eastern paste) or *baba ganoug* (tahina with a puree of baked aubergine, lemon, and garlic). *Falafel* (spiced chick peas made into small balls and fried);

kofta (meatballs) and kebab were also good, though rather variable in standard. Tea and coffee always came with a huge amount of sugar. Even when I asked for none, the waiters didn't seem able to comprehend, so they would usually slip a little in anyway. The fresh fruit juices were very good, especially the lemon and guava. *Karkaday* (hibiscus tea) was a refreshing alternative. However, nothing could compete with an ice-cold Stella when the midday heat hit forty degrees!

It was a surprise to learn that the Suez Canal had by no means been the first project of its kind, an attempt having been made to build a canal as early as 600 BC. I found it somewhat unnerving to drive through the tunnel beneath the leaking canal in 1994. For obvious reasons, there was a lot of repair work going on. We drove south into the desert towards Sinai. There were no big dunes, just lots of dry stony land with heavily weathered outcrops of pinkish granite which probably gave the Red Sea its name.

It was hard to see how people in poor small villages of single storey adobe mud-brick huts in the middle of this harsh wilderness could make a living. Increasingly, it seemed that tourism was becoming the main source of income for many Egyptians in one way or another. As we reached the coast, there were many established and even more embryonic towns and villages that had turned to serving tourists from all over the world. The Germans, in particular, seemed to favour Egypt as a holiday destination. It was amazing to listen to some of the vendors in the tourist markets, haggling in five or six different languages.

A memorable evening in Na-ama Bay was spent in a Bedouin tent on the beach. Although it was a cafe set up to cater for visitors, the musicians and dancers were obviously genuinely enjoying themselves and this, along with the strong sweet smell of the tobacco in the *'sheesha'* water pipes (and a couple of bottles of Stella), created a great atmosphere. Smoking a *sheesha* led to great amusement for everyone. The smoke was really cool and mild after being bubbled through the water and we were led to believe that the water also removed a lot of the tar.

Snorkelling in the Red Sea was fantastic. Shark Bay, a few kilometres along the coast from Na-ama Bay, was a beautiful spot with only the smallest beginnings of tourist development, though it was easy to see how spoilt it might become in the future. The land behind the beach was barren - the beauty in this region was beneath the waves. The hired snorkelling gear was excellent and I could swim for half an hour before I needed to drain the mask. The water was comfortably warm and the visibility good. There was plenty of living coral and a stunning number and variety of fish with an infinite range of colours. I bought the *'Red Sea Fish Watcher's Guide'* and identified the following species: Sergeant Major; Whitetail dascyllus; Blue and gold fusilier; Coral grouper; Bluespotted grouper; Sweetlips; Sailfin tang; Checkerboard wrasse; Threadfin butterflyfish; Bluecheek butterflyfish; Twoband anemone fish; King Solomon fish; Emperor angelfish; Parrotfish; Garfish; Barracuda - and lots more that I couldn't find in the book. It was marvellous simply to float for a while, and then fin along the edge of the reef until I chanced upon something interesting. At one point, I spotted a bundle of scraps that someone had thrown in from the beach, swam up to it, and found myself in the midst of hundreds of brightly-coloured fish that seemed oblivious to my presence.

We got up at 1.30 a.m. to climb Mount Sinai by the light of a half moon. I was pleasantly surprised to find that climbing in sandals wasn't as bad as it sounds. There seemed to be a never-ending stream of people all the way up. Camels loomed out of the gloom, their owners plying for trade by calling 'ride cameeel?' The region was particularly interesting because of its importance to Christians, Jews, and Muslims alike, The Judeo-Christian connection stemming from the Old Testament story of Moses receiving the Ten Commandments from God and the Muslim interest coming from the belief that Jesus was a prophet. As we climbed the mountain, we were accompanied by an enthusiastic group of Christian Korean pilgrims singing hymns and shouting 'Halleluiah!'

It was cold and windy on the top and very crowded by the time dawn arrived; there were groups of both locals and tourists who were huddled together in an effort to keep warm. It was good to watch dawn break and the atmosphere was companiable. The first glimpse of the sun was greeted with a bedraggled cheer and the clicking and whirring of hundreds of cameras. The early morning glow added warmth to the pink and orange rocks which looked as though they might support some wonderful climbing routes. We descended by the steeper path into which hundreds of crude steps had been carved.

Although it was seething with both tourists and local people, Saint Catherine's Monastery was worth a visit. Its namesake,

Catherine of Alexandria was the Christian martyr who, legend has it, was tortured on the wheel (hence the firework, Catherine Wheel) and then beheaded, poor soul! According to tradition, angels took her body to Mount Sinai where the Greek Orthodox monastery bearing her name now stands. Documents going as far back as the fourth century testify to a church having been on the site. The monastery has one of the largest collections of fabulous ancient illuminated manuscripts in the world, as well as one of the most important collections of icons, but tourists are only allowed into certain parts of the complex.

At a lunch stop in a tiny village near the monastery, there was a group of smiling children with brown eyes as big as saucers. They were dressed in brightly-coloured clothes and asked for *baksheesh* (a tip), pens, and sweets. Bill, one of our group, gave an entertaining display of card tricks after lunch, both baffling and delighting the children, the Egyptian bus driver Hussein, and the guide Yemeni.

The temple of Hathor at Denderah was our next stop, impressive in its size, completeness, and the minute detail of the numerous hieroglyphics and relief carvings. Hathor, the goddess of pleasure and love, mother of the gods and wife of Horus, was portrayed as a beautiful woman whose head was topped by a pair of graceful horns bordering a solar disc. In the dingy rooms within the temple, swarms of tiny bats, many with their tiny young clinging to them, hung from the ceilings and the smell of guano really got up our noses. In some of the rooms, the original colours of the reliefs could still be seen. To my mind, the best was a ceiling framed by the sinuous body of the celestial goddess Nut who symbolized the sky.

There was a dramatic change in scenery when our bus approached the town of Luxor where, after so many miles of monotonous desert, the greenery of the Nile floodplain was a welcome sight and the journey became more varied. The irrigation canals that led off the Nile were a hive of activity. There were people fishing, children swimming, and women washing and collecting water in enormous earthenware jars. There were more people riding donkeys than there were driving cars. The animals were small and their silhouettes looked comical from behind, with the comparatively large turned-out feet of their riders dangling to within centimetres of the ground.

Luxor was a good example of the incongruous mixture of ancient and modern that was so typical of Egypt. Many of the temples were on the east bank of the Nile, nestling amongst new buildings. The bazaars were a curious mix of stalls for tourists and those selling everyday goods and food to local inhabitants who went about their daily business seemingly oblivious of the crowds of foreigners wandering amongst them. However, there were plenty of 'wide boys', though on the whole they seemed to be a lot more relaxed and good-humoured than the more aggressive salesmen had been in Cairo. As a result, a browse through the bazaar was pleasantly entertaining. Haggling is a way of life in Egypt and it was important not to take it too seriously or get wound up by it; with a sense of fun it could result in a deal that was mutually beneficial. It didn't take me long to get used to the stock phrases of the vendors:

'You buy carpet?' (or spices, antique, *galabaya*, T-shirt and so on.), 'Top quality!'; 'What is your best price?', and even the surprising 'Luvverly-Jubberly!'

I learned many ways to haggle effectively. Possibly the first rule was never to bargain for something you couldn't walk away from, or at the very least, never to let a salesman know how much you really wanted any of his wares. The first price quoted was usually ridiculously high and was to be met by laughter or better still 'Mish mumpkin!', meaning 'No way!' After a while, the price would become more realistic, and a variety of techniques could be used to get it down even further. Undoubtedly, the most important of these was to master the 'walk-away' which usually produced a good result. 'Tag-team haggling' involving working with a partner who had to stand around looking bored and trying to get you to leave.

Karnak was an amazing place to visit with a vast complex of temples which had grown up over a period of 2,000 years. The two colossal statues of Rameses II were staggering and a taste of the many images of this vain king that we were to see all over Egypt; the guy really fancied himself something rotten! The great hypostyle hall was stupendous with its 134 gigantic columns (up to 23m high), many still showing the original colours of their decoration. One of the most impressive sights was the 29.5m high obelisk of Hatshepsut, the fifth pharaoh of the eighteenth dynasty of Ancient Egypt. It was carved from a single block of granite from Aswan and decorated with ornate carved hieroglyphics. I could just about absorb the fact that the ancient Egyptians had the engineering skills and ingenuity to carve, move, and erect such a structure, but I remained baffled by how they managed to work such a hard rock with such precise and exquisite detail.

Next to the Sacred Lake (a green and slimy pool), there was a carved scarab beetle about a metre long. Legend has it, though I suspect this may be a tale cooked up for the entertainment of both guides and tourists, that if you walk around it three times you'll have good luck, five times you'll get married, and seven times you'll have children. The guide was informative and amusing. His funniest tale concerned a relief showing a chap with a prominent 'stiffy' and with one arm and one leg missing. The story goes that the country was at war and all of the men went off to fight, leaving one behind to look after the women and children. Five years later, the army returned to find every woman in the country pregnant or with young babies. It turned out that the virile young man left to protect the women had been making love one hundred times a day. The king punished him first, by cutting off his arm, then later his leg. The man died, giving the rise to the expression 'giving an arm and a leg'. However, I reckoned that the guide had left out an obvious detail and I'm sure that, considering the crime, an arm would not have been the first thing to be chopped off!

The streets of Luxor were full of *'caleesh'*, a type of horse-drawn carriage. Such a mode of transport proved to be an excellent way to have a good look around the bazaars and take photographs without getting endlessly bothered by people wanting to sell things. It was good to clip-clop away from the bustle of the city for a leisurely trip around some of the small villages on the outskirts.

The fertile floodplain of the Nile was farmed intensively in this region. The main crops seemed to be maize, sugarcane, sesame, dates, bananas, okra, and a variety of others that I couldn't identify or get anyone to translate. All the houses were made of mud-bricks that had been left to dry in the sun for six months before use. Apparently, these houses are cooler than modern buildings by several degrees. The modern buildings, however, all seemed to have air-conditioning, operating with varying degrees of efficiency and noise. It was interesting to observe the daily life of the *Fellahin* (peasant farmers) who lived in such houses. Their ancestors had provided much of the labour used to build the monuments of the pharaohs and many of their cultural and religious beliefs and practices are said to have had roots in those times. Now they were struggling to feed Egypt's population. The women wore long-sleeved black dresses and some covered their faces with a veil. On market days and special occasions they wore colourful jewellery made from glass beads, silver, and copper which made an attractive tinkling sound as they went about their business.

If you wanted to go donkey trekking to the Valley of the Kings on the west bank in Luxor you had to start early (by 3.15 a.m.). After a bit of initial wobbling, donkey-riding is easy and I soon got used to controlling my biddable mount by calling '*Yella*' (go) and '*Hoosha*' (stop). The winding trail climbed high above the Nile, over rocky ground and along the edge of precipitous cliffs. The image of the donkey riders preceding me, silhouetted against the skyline as the first deep hues of the sunrise appeared was unforgettable. The tombs in the Valley of the Kings were good but, to be honest, it didn't take long to feel 'templed out', despite the amazing richness of the colours still preserved on the hieroglyphics and reliefs. I chuckled at the temple of Hatshepsut, though, where every time the guide said 'Hatshepsut' it sounded like 'hedgehog soup'. At the end of the day, it was very pleasant to ride back to Luxor on our docile donkeys along quiet dirt tracks and through verdant fields.

If you wanted to visit Abu Simbel from Aswan guess what? - Another 3.15 a.m. start! A three-hour drive in an air-conditioned coach seemed rather long, but when we saw the splendour of the four colossal (20m high) statues of Rameses II bathed in the soft rosiness of the early morning sun, it was immensely gratifying. If I'd not already known that the twin temples originally had been carved out of the mountainside in the 13th century BCE as a monument to Ramesses II and his queen Nefertari, and the complex moved in its entirety, in 1968, to a man-made hill to save it from being submerged by Lake Nasser as a result of building the Aswan High Dam, I could never have guessed it in a thousand years.

A doorway to the right of the facade led to the amazing interior of the dome of the huge artificial mountain that had been made to accommodate the relocated temple; it was like something out of a James Bond movie. The ingenuity of modern engineers was dramatically displayed, but the wonders of the ancient Egyptians' skills were even more impressive. In the innermost chamber of the temple is the sacred sanctuary where the four gods of the Great Temple sat on their thrones carved in the back wall. The incredible thing is that the temple is aligned in such a way that only on two days a year do the first rays of the rising sun reach across the Nile, penetrate the temple entrance, move along the hall, through the vestibule and into the Sanctuary where they illuminate the figures of Rameses II. How on Earth did they work that one out? The secondary complex of Abu Simbel, the rock-cut Temple of Hathor, fronted by six 10m high standing statues was also quite overwhelming. The unique key to the wooden door of this temple was a giant bronze *Ankh* (life symbol).

On the way back to Aswan, the bus stopped at the High Dam which was absolutely gigantic – 11m high and 3.8km long, creating Lake Nasser, which is 550km long! It was surprising to see that the desert went right up to the edge of Lake Nasser; I'd always assumed that there would be a green fringe of vegetation around it. Once in the city, I enjoyed wandering along the back streets. Frequently, youngsters, noticing that I was curious to see more, would invite me to accompany them down narrow dusty streets crowded with mud-brick tenements to show me their school, their mosque, or where they played football. A walk along the Corniche Road along the banks of the Nile, was interesting, though I had to shrug off countless *'Hello, Felucca?'*, men trying to persuade me to take a trip on a *felucca* (a traditional sailing boat used on the Nile), with an almost automatic *'La shuke-rahn'*, meaning 'No thank you'.

Getting to Philae was quite an adventure, involving a ride in a taxi that didn't appear to have any brakes. This was followed by a trip on a boat with a worryingly 'spluttery' outboard engine. The main temple complex was another relocation after the High Dam was built; this time from the island of Philae (now submerged underneath Lake Nasser) to the island of Agilika. The history of the buildings stretched back through the Greco-Roman era to the Pharaonic era. The principal deity represented was Isis, but Philae was also a seat of the Christian religion. Amazingly, the sculptures on the columns, ceilings, and walls were still bright with paint which had survived for centuries because of the dry climate. The 'son et lumiere' performance, at the temple was a must. It was a well-designed affair that gave an interesting and dramatic view of the temple. During the performance actors playing the gods and goddesses recounted their stories. The performance began at the great entrance and proceeded through the complex with the histories of each building. The relocation was also described. The atmosphere under a spectacularly starlit night sky was otherworldly.

A 6 a.m. start was necessary to catch the ferry across the Nile and then to take part in a camel trek. Inevitably, there was much comic behaviour as we clambered onto the beasts, especially when they lumbered up to a standing position. Plodding along in the early morning sun in the absolute peace and quiet was restful. On arrival at the 6th century Monastery of St Simeon, we were met by our guide Old George, who proved to be quite a comedian, combining mime with Pidgin English and animal impersonations throughout the tour. He was also extremely photogenic with a face like an old prune. I found the different domestic areas of the monastery for cooking, washing, and sleeping rendered particularly fascinating by George's lively running commentary on everyday life in the ancient world.

Nearby, we visited the Mausoleum of the Agha Khan, an elegant modern construction of domed granite and sandstone. It was an oasis of cool tranquillity and commanded a wonderful view. We then took a short boat trip to Kitchener's Island, a relaxing botanical garden in the middle of the Nile. On Elephantine Island, it was interesting to descend the steps of the Nileometer (steps that measure the level of the River Nile). We returned to Aswan on a *felucca* where there was much merriment and chat with fellow passengers, both local and from many parts of the world.

In the evening, another relaxing sail led to a drink in the lap of luxury at the Cataract Hotel, complete with exotically uniformed flunkeys; the whole establishment dripped with opulence. The night was still young and after a reasonable meal at the Promenade Restaurant, we boarded a boat to cross the Nile to one of the Nubian villages on Elephantine Island where a walk through a maze of streets took us to the home of our boatman. We were shown great hospitality. Tea was drunk, *sheesha* smoked, family photos handed around, and then we were given a guided tour of the house which was essentially a collection of single storey mud-brick rooms built around a courtyard.

Later, another walk through tangled streets took us to the wedding of a relative of our boatman who told us that it was considered good luck to have as many people as possible at such a celebration, even more so if some were foreigners. As we waited, the atmosphere gradually escalated to fever pitch. However, the poor bride and groom looked dead on their feet, the wedding ceremony having lasted for four days already! When they arrived at the courtyard where the crowd had congregated, they sat on a small stage. It was bizarre to spot a large picture of dogs playing snooker behind them - a picture I'd seen in a number of British pubs! They were presented with many gifts (including what I thought was a rather tacky clock from our group, but which we'd been assured was exactly what young Nubian newlyweds would want). We all played with the many children who were over-excited and having the time of their lives. Then it was off to the real party where an Egyptian band played very loudly through a rather dodgy P.A. system to a huge crowd who danced as though there was no tomorrow. I finally fell into bed at two o'clock.

The first stop as our group cruised along the Nile was at Kom Ombo. We visited the well-preserved temple shared by two deities – Sobek, the crocodile god and Haroeiris, the god of war. Many of the carvings seemed to have more pronounced relief than others I'd seen; the belly buttons were particularly exaggerated – I wondered what they could reveal about early midwifery - weird! Cruising was a welcome break from land-based site-seeing and one could sit around doing absolutely nothing without feeling guilty about not using every available minute to visit the wonderful treasures of the ancient world whilst the chance was there. It was refreshing just to sit and watch the world go by, lounge out in the sun for a while, and write a few postcards.

The next morning, I woke to see the beauty of the delicate shades of sunrise reflected in the perfect mirror of the Nile. Later, in the intense heat of the day, the boat moored for half an hour so that we could all cool off with a swim. We took enormous pleasure in jumping from the upper deck into the sparkling water. In the afternoon, we stopped at Edfu, where we visited one of the best-maintained temples in Egypt. It was dedicated to the falcon-headed god of the sun, Horus, and the goddess Hathor. The sheer scale of the two great tapering towers, each topped by a cornice, was stirring in its immensity.

The boat moored up around seven in the evening. During the day, I'd soon become oblivious to the chugging of the engine, but it was a great relief when it stopped at night. The peace didn't last for long though; as the sun went down the frog and insect chorus started and the U.V. lamp fly killer began to crackle as it frazzled the bugs. There were very few mozzies I'm pleased to say - I don't remember having been bitten once.

The next morning we took an early ferry to the west bank and hired some bikes. Cycling was an ideal way to travel; it was cool as we rode along, but boy, did the sweat pour when we stopped. The Valley of the Queens (wives of the pharaohs) was something of a disappointment to me, maybe I was just 'templed out', though the tomb of Nefertiti, the favourite wife of Ramesses II, was rather special. I found the Valley of the Nobles more rewarding. Here were much the smaller tombs of civil servants, generals, and other well-to-do people. They were carved in rock and decorated with drawings very different to those on the royal tombs. These paintings shed light on the daily life of wealthy, but not aristocratic, ancient Egyptians. There were scenes depicting rural life - farming, hunting, and fishing; others showed festivals with musicians and dancers, and yet others illustrated the lives of servants, craftsmen, and artisans. My personal favourite was the tomb of Sennefer, the overseer of the gardens of Amon, its bumpy ceiling covered in painted vines. In some of the tombs, the guards would illuminate the paintings by reflecting the light from the entrance with a battered mirror.

It took a long day on a coach to get from Luxor to Cairo. It wasn't possible to take the night train, as there'd recently been some nasty incidents with bandits – a sobering thought. The long drive was broken up by a welcome stop on the coast of the Gulf of Suez where we enjoyed a good swim and some beachcombing for pretty shells and 'sand dollars' (the remains of flat sea urchins). Finally, when we arrived in Cairo, it took quite an effort to go out for a meal, especially as we were so tightly crammed into a taxi, but it was worth it when we arrived at the Felafela Restaurant.

Our last day in Cairo was particularly good, chiefly due to our superb guide who had a degree in Egyptology and a great deal of enthusiasm. He also spoke excellent English. Our first stop with him was the Step Pyramid at Sakkara, which is reputed to be the oldest complete stone building complex in the world. We visited the nearby tomb of Mere Ruka where our guide drew our attention to the most interesting features and offered explanations at just the right pace. The tomb of Seropeum, carved out of the rock, housed thirty-three huge granite sarcophagi that apparently contained mummified animals. How the ancient Egyptians manoeuvred the enormous sarcophagi into the tombs is yet another mind-boggling mystery concerning those consummate early engineers. It didn't seem worth paying to see the alabaster Sphinx in Memphis, as we got a good enough view by looking through the railings!

A change from temples and tombs was a visit a carpet factory. Many of the workers were very young children, perhaps eight or ten years old. It was amazing to see the speed at which they worked, their little fingers moving so fast they were just a blur. It was a complete contrast to go upstairs to the carpet showroom where beautiful wares were on sale at prices that were a world away from the meagre wages of the children below.

Later, we visited the oldest church in Cairo as well as the impressive Mohammed Ali Mosque where the guide gave us some valuable insight into the Muslim religion. On the way to the large bazaar of Khan el-Khalili, we stopped briefly to look out over the 'City of the Dead', where hundreds of thousands of people were living in and amongst the tombs, some of which dated from the 12th century.

We planned a farewell evening at the Cairo Hilton Hotel. It turned out to be rather more lavish than we'd expected as we chanced upon a high society wedding with no expense spared. Wow! I had ever seen such magnificence. We went up to an open-air bar to have a few (expensive) drinks and watched a cabaret which included belly dancing by a woman with a very ample belly.

After such a night, it was time to pack our bags and redirect our thoughts to the world of work. We'd had an active and adventurous tour with our camel and donkey treks, bike rides, and boat trips, as well as a significant number of expeditions on foot. It had been a far cry from a 'package tour' looking out of a coach window and being herded swiftly in and out of historical buildings all the time.

After a five-hour flight the next day, it felt a bit of a come-down, in more ways than one, to land back in the UK - and yes, although it was August - it was raining, grey, and just a tad gloomy!

Chapter 18 A WEEKEND UP NORTH AND A PEAK PERFORMANCE

Iceland and Three Peaks

Not many perks accompany a teaching career, despite the perception of some of the general public that teachers have short working days and long holidays. Of course, people can't help but consider themselves to be experts on all to do with education; after all, they've been to school. As pupils, however, they didn't have to spend every hour God gives preparing and marking lessons, planning field trips and extra-curricular activities, attending countless meetings, and using much 'holiday time' to supervise challenging groups of engaging but overly energetic youngsters on the aforementioned trips, albeit that we do it, for the most part, with enthusiasm and commitment. Enough said – rant over!

Occasionally, however, great opportunities do present themselves and teachers have to grab them with both hands. Fifty-four teachers of geography and geology seized one such chance, having been contacted by an Icelandic field study centre, Arctic Experience. We were to go on a subsidised (!) promotional weekend 'taster' trip to the Hjardarbol Centre in Iceland. I wondered how many of us had any realistic hopes of ever using the centre for our own schools, particularly those from a comprehensive school like me, as the cost would be beyond the means of the families of many of the children. However, for geographers and especially geologists, Iceland is something of a Mecca that few of us ever have the opportunity to visit; it was too good a deal to miss and, without doubt, our own experiences and learning would feed into our teaching in the future. So, having paid the princely sum of £99, I found myself flying to Iceland.

We arrived at the tiny airport in Keflavik where the wind cut to the bone. On our coach journey to the field study centre, however, we were lucky enough to see the mysterious spectacle of the Northern Lights.

The following day started early when we set out on a site-seeing tour. We drove through varied scenery; there was a flat coastal plain, a raised beach formed by the isostatic rise of Iceland due to the removal of the weight of several kilometres thickness of ice following the last glacial period. The raised beach was backed by black craggy mountains; everywhere we went I felt an enormous sense of space. Our first stop was a visit to the Nesjavellir geothermal power station, a space-age type of installation which was so incredibly quiet and clean that it felt like being in a laboratory. We were given a tour and gleaned some impressive facts and figures; for example, water piped 20km to Reykyavik at about 89°C only loses a couple of degrees on its journey.

Later, we stopped at the spectacular Sevalandsfoss Waterfall, a 30m high, natural living sculpture of water and ice which was surprisingly quiet, considering the volume of water that cascaded down in a complex pattern of sheets and rivulets. Lunch was in a community hall near the waterfall, Scogfoss, at the base of which, I found strangely contorted ice that had been sculpted by the wind to form blobs and fingers that looked like something out of a science fiction movie.

Our next stop was Solheimajokull, a glacier which is an extension of the Myrdals-Jokull ice cap. It was thrilling to see the textbook glacial features that so many of us had taught for years, but had never actually beheld with our own eyes. The braided outwash channels snaked silver and bright across the black sand of the plain, a stunning sight. However, this was Iceland and we were soon to be spoilt even further by the beauty of the coast at Kapp Dyrholaey, the southernmost tip of the country. Here we I found jaw-dropping columnar jointing, classic examples of lava flows, and beautiful black sand beaches met by creamy surf as the sun got lower in the sky; this would be an enduring image of Iceland.

Our second day was shorter, but no less exciting and interesting. It started with a visit to the volcanic explosion crater at Kerio. 55 metres deep, it was formed in an explosion 3,000 years ago. It's now extinct and forms a deep lake. Then, it was on to the awesome spectacle of the Gulfoss Waterfall, where a seething maelstrom of water crashed between rocks and ice into a steep-sided canyon.

Of course, we had to witness geysers. Though the Great Geysir itself is now rarely active, the surrounding area is peppered with many smaller active hot springs. Having checked the wind direction first, we witnessed the Strokkur Geyser strut its stuff, spraying 120°C water up to 20m into the air! Later, we wandered amongst the bubbling steaming pools of the smaller geysers – magic!

Our last stop was the Blue Lagoon, just outside Reykyavik, where a pool of hot water from a power station provided an unusual outdoor swimming bath. It was extraordinary to stand muffled in warm clothes in sub-zero temperatures and watch bathers bobbing about in the steaming turquoise water.

All too soon, we had to set off on our homeward journey to the UK. After a tedious wait at the airport, my patience was rewarded with a window seat which gave me spectacular farewell views of a fascinating island.

We'd been Up North in Iceland, so to speak, and now I was to go Up High in the UK. I did the National Three Peaks Challenge with my best mate (later to be my best man) Ade and his father Ron, who was in his sixties, along with hundreds of other walkers, as a sponsored event to raise money for Cystic Fibrosis. The challenge was to climb the highest mountains of Scotland, England, and Wales within twenty-four hours, the peaks being Snowdon (1,085m) the highest mountain in Wales, Scafell Pike (978m) the highest mountain in England, and Ben Nevis (1,344m) the highest mountain in Scotland.

There are many arguments both for and against the organisation of such large-scale events in the mountains and I confess I felt worried embarking on this venture when I thought of the damage so many feet could wreak when trudging at the same time along any mountain path. However, the merits of the good cause triumphed over concern about the natural world and we experienced what proved to be a challenging and rewarding weekend.

Our coach arrived at Pen y Pas around two in the afternoon and we set off up the Pyg Track to begin the hard mountain walk up Snowdon in scorching sun with good, though rather hazy views from the peak a couple of hours later. We descended via the Llanberis track and on the way, Ade kept us entertained with tales of his former climbing escapades in the crags of the area. In Llanberis we had a quick pint in the Victoria Inn, though we couldn't sit still outside for even five minutes as the midges seemed determined to eat us alive. Later, we went to soothe our feet with a soak in Llyn Padarn before having a stonking meal at Pete's Eats Cafe, the climbers' Mecca in North Wales. Ade and I reminisced about our many climbing adventures in Snowdonia over steaming pint mugs of tea. Needless to say, this helped us to catch a few hours' kip on the coach journey to the Lake District.

We arrived at Seatoller around four in the morning and set off, bleary-eyed, fifteen minutes later. It was a fairly long slog up the road to Seatoller Farm, then an easy angled rocky track up to cloud base around 300m which was grey, wet, and miserable. We plodded on through mist, crossing a boulder field with about 20m visibility. As a result of an accident when climbing down a waterfall with detachable handholds whilst exploring the newly discovered cave Ogof Draenan, I had had a fall that had resulted in a collapsed arch in my left foot. This was giving me a few problems so I experimented with methods of walking that would reduce the stress and found that trying to walk without making a sound worked well as it forced me to place my feet carefully, minimising impact and moderating my pace to a steady, but reasonable speed which never left me out of breath.

We were at the top of Scafell Pike, after about three hours, surrounded by cloud, though the sun did break through for a few light-hearted moments, giving us a tantalising glimpse of the Lakeland scenery below. I found a sheltered spot and got into my little bivvi shelter and had a picnic breakfast. I was so hungry that I polished off about a pound of Lardy Cake, the food of champions. It was a long slog down and the road section seemed interminable, so we all felt we'd earned an ice cream by the time we got back to the coach.

After a few hours sleep at Fort William we were rudely awoken and after a quick breakfast were off to Ben Nevis where we started climbing at three, just as it was starting to get light. It was a long, but steady climb in perfect conditions, accompanied by a dramatic sunrise with infinite tones of red and orange and an ever-expanding horizon of spectacular mountain scenery. It took us about four hours to reach the top where we had a team photo standing on the snow (at Ade's wedding he gave a large copy of this to his father as a thank you present).

I found the descent to be easiest when half running, keeping my knees bent to absorb the shock of the rocky path; I got down in an hour and a half. Ade and Ron joined me three quarters of an hour later. Back at the hotel, we had a couple of celebratory pints (at ten in the morning!) to help us snooze on the ten and a half hour coach journey home.

The next day I started a week at Trefil outdoor pursuits centre, supervising sixteen fourteen-year-olds. . . .

Chapter 19 BRITISH CAVER SEEKS EXPEDITION

Ukraine: Caving with the Kiev and New York Caving Cubs

Soon after the Three Peaks Challenge, my old school friend of mine, John Elliott, came over from London to the Forest of Dean. I'd taken him caving about four years previously and he was keen to have another go. We enjoyed an excellent trip down Slaughter Stream Cave where his joyful enthusiasm made it clear that he was well and truly bitten by the caving bug. He'd logged on to the Internet before our meeting and had brought over a few pages of caving information, some of which looked pretty interesting. In those days, I didn't have access to the World Wide Web, so he put a message on the online caving notice board for me which read 'British caver seeks expedition in August 1995, anywhere in the world considered'. A few weeks later, he called to say that he'd received a message that Chris Nicola of the Met Grotto (The Greater New York city area chapter of the Speleological Society in the US) was arranging an expedition to the Ukraine. Over the following months, John was good enough to act as middle-man and relayed messages between Chris and me. After he'd sussed me out by contacting Chris Howes in Britain and Kevin Glover in New Mexico, Chris Nicola was encouraging and seemed confident that it would be possible for me to join the expedition, but it wasn't until the end of June that my place was confirmed.

On Sunday, 13 August, I was up at four in the morning to start a trip which, despite being a shot in the dark, I felt good about. Not knowing the people I was going to be with, having no idea about exactly where we would be going, or the character of the caves, all added to the excitement and anticipation. I arrived in Amsterdam and looked for the members of the Met Grotto whom I'd loosely arranged to meet there. I found the boarding area for the flight to the Ukraine. It was teeming with crowds of Americans off on a Christian mission. Eventually, I spotted three guys and a girl who weren't wearing Jesus Army T-shirts and overheard them talking about caving. I introduced myself and met Chris Nicola, Bob Zimmerman, Jay Jorden, and Becky Jones.

After a flight, during which I read *Descent* (the UK caving magazine) and the latest copy of the Royal Forest of Dean Caving Club newsletter, we arrived at Kiev airport which was grey and miserable. As we collected our luggage, I was astounded by the enormous towering frame-pack Bob wrestled off the conveyor. Equally amazing was the rat's nest of straps that was Chris's pack. Once through customs, we were met by the beaming gold-toothed smile of our host, Valeri Regoznikov. We also met Ed Kehs who had flown in from Germany (via a stopover in Budapest) and one of Valeri's students, Alex Klimchouk (who was later involved in the exploration of Krubera Cave, the deepest cave in the world, located in the Western Caucasus. We all piled into the back of a small van and headed off to Valeri's home in a suburb of Kiev. There was much animated conversation and laughter as we all got to know one another and Valeri started out as he continued for the whole trip, filming everyone on the video with the command: 'Repeat for history'…

Arriving at his address, we wedged ourselves into the lift and went up eight of the nine floors to his flat, one of two hundred apartments in a complex of thirty blocks. We were given a warm welcome by his wife Luda and daughter Sasha. There was much jollity as we tucked into a buffet lunch and many toasts were made; something that would become almost a routine as time went on! We soon learned that we'd arrived on Valeri's 54th birthday and in the evening we all trooped off to celebrate in a small restaurant owned by one of Luda's friends. Shortly after we arrived, we discovered that it was also Andre's (Valeri's son) fourteenth birthday, so it was a double fest. There was a really good spread of food; it seemed that each time I thought the meal was over, another course appeared.

The toasts were beyond counting, both with champagne and LOTS of vodka and many were accompanied by speeches about hospitality, gratitude, and caving. As the evening progressed, the dancing started and the speeches got longer (especially the one that Chris gave). After the meal, Valeri and Chris were keen that we should repeat a ritual they'd performed the year before; we were drunk enough to agree and a few minutes later found ourselves swimming in the river Lurpin which, I think, was only about 70km downstream from Chernobyl! I almost expected to glow in the dark! It had been a long day for all of us, especially the Americans, so it wasn't surprising that Becky fell asleep on the beach. We woke her up and all walked back to Valeri's flat, before Jay the moustached man, and I headed off to stay at Alex's.

The following morning we all became millionaires! Ukrainian currency was like Monopoly money and for every $10 we got 1,000,000 Ukrainian coupons. It was mind-boggling - I never got used to thinking in such large numbers. We went for our first vertical training session at a 25-30m high fortification wall in woods in a park in Kiev. Three ropes were rigged in a combination of ingenious routes involving both the wall and big trees next to it. We all enjoyed the course which proved to be strenuous, but satisfying, with everyone struggling at some point in the proceedings. While 20m above the ground, Becky was heard to utter the worrying statement: 'I think I have done a bad thing', which became something of a mantra during the trip.

Jay seemed to spend an extraordinarily long time on one rope. This was his first experience of using the Frog system of SRT and he was remarkably circumspect in his comments as he struggled with the technique - we were expecting at least a few swear words. He had his feet in a loop attached to his harness with a chest jammer by his belly button and a hand jammer again attached to his harness. As he slid the hand jammer up, then pushed repeatedly with his feet, he did indeed look exactly like a frog. Bob sweated his way through a few rack problems. Chris managed to get into a position where he had jammers on the rope facing in opposite directions, so he couldn't go anywhere, and I managed to get well and truly hung up with my foot in a Girth hitch, much to everyone's amusement (my own included). Meanwhile, Ed zipped up and down ropes with sickening ease - he was a real professional.

It was while at the wall that I met the only British tourist I saw in the Ukraine - a girl from Manchester who had come for the climbing. When we stopped for food, Vitale from the Kiev Caving Club and his friend Sasha amazed us with their magic lamps. These were carbide headsets each with a photoelectric cell that set off an ignition spark if it detected darkness. They were like those trick birthday cake candles that you just can't blow out. They were a clever Ukrainian innovation and I was sufficiently impressed to buy one for myself and another as an unusual present for Niki, my girlfriend at home who would have loved this trip.

After the training session, we stopped briefly at a bar where we drank local beer out of glasses that looked for all the world like jam jars. On any trip, a lot of time seems to be spent planning the next one and this was no exception. As we travelled back to Valeri's on the metro, Chris and I enthused about the possibility of Valeri coming to the UK sometime and of my going over to the States at Easter. In the evening, a party atmosphere prevailed and we all embarrassed ourselves by playing the usual repertoire of caving games - even down to Ed getting stuck while trying his party trick of trying to squeeze through a toilet seat - thankfully it wasn't attached to a lavatory at the time! Needless to say, Valeri was there with the video, as always . . . .'My American friends - repeat for history!'

On the next day, after lining our stomachs with rice pudding for breakfast, we made for a site near the Moskawski Bridge where there was a large concrete tube-like structure called a *caisson*. The *caisson* was apparently part of a fifty-year-old airshaft for a metro line that had never been finished. Several ropes were rigged in order to give everyone practice with a good variety of SRT problems to negotiate. Bob was struggling at an awkward edge and when given some helpful advice from below was heard to say 'I don't think so, skin is important to me' – there was no doubt that making that move would have meant losing quite a lot of his epidermis!

There was some questionable rigging and I was climbing a route up within the structure when Ed, above me, commented I've got something to tell you, but I think I'd better wait until you get up here first. I got to the top to find a steel krab loaded right across its gate, so it was pretty dangerous as the krab could have broken. I was impressed by Alex who'd only been introduced to vertical techniques four months earlier. He led up a bolted route that quickly changed from vertical to horizontal and overhanging. In order to tackle this, he had to use etriers (foot loops). When he'd finished, Valeri suggested that I might have a go. I'd never tried anything like this before and didn't rate my chances very highly, but, in the event, I didn't do too badly. It took almost half an hour and hanging from the roof was strenuous, but it was incredibly satisfying to reach the tenth and final bolt!

The afternoon was spent packing for a three-day trip to visit the gypsum caves of the Podola region in western Ukraine. We also went shopping with Luda, walking through a market where vendors stood in the street touting their wares which included anything from a fistful of dried fish to a few bottles of shampoo. The stalls sold a bewildering array of produce, often in bizarre combinations. I noticed how quiet it was on the streets compared to home - people didn't seem to talk much on the metro either.

In the afternoon, all fifteen of us met at the train station and during the journey, a party atmosphere developed and all fifteen of us crammed into one compartment to eat delicious stuffed peppers and drink wine and vodka.   When we had arrived at our destination, we were collected by a small twenty-seater bus that looked like something out of the 1950s. Chris practically worshipped Valeri for having arranged this transport - apparently he hadn't been enamoured of Ukrainian public transport the year before. We went to the tourist centre in Ternopol where we were met by Vladimir (who had taught Valeri SRT). We were welcomed and given a good breakfast followed by much enthusing about cave surveys. It took a few hours to drive to the Podola region where the roads deteriorated into farm tracks as we approached the site of Ozernaja Blue Lakes cave.

After pitching our tents and getting our kit sorted, we walked over to a huge sinkhole where we found the gated entrance to the cave. It was a six-metre drop down a 75cm metal tube on a slippery ladder that was simply made of thick sticks and baler twine! The trip had been arranged by the Ternopol cavers, led by Serge and Tanya. None of us was used to caving in such a large group of over a dozen cavers. The first hour or so was slow-going with many stops for smoking which appears to be standard practice in the Ukraine. We stopped for a break in a big chamber about 12m across, the walls variegated with layers of white and orange-brown gypsum. A narrow passage led off this chamber with a small metal cross above the entrance.   Serge told us that the forthcoming traverse section of the cave took about an hour with tackle bags, but could be done in seven minutes wearing trainers. In fact, he'd once had to self-rescue with two broken ribs and a twisted ankle! Something was lost in translation when Serge explained what was ahead and there was a fair amount of whingeing when we found ourselves embarking on a 420m traverse over a deep rift. Some of the Ukrainian cavers actually wore butt pads for traversing. At times, it was pretty tricky and at one particularly wide point Serge provided a human bridge. It was here that we discovered that gypsum is *Ochin skolska* (very slippery) - it was like caving on greased glass.

About an hour later, we reached the end of the traverse and were treated to a sit-down snack, complete with a table dug out of the floor. Ed, Becky, and I went to look at the Blue Pools which were a delight. We caved for a couple more hours and found chambers that had walls bristling with gypsum crystals. We saw some really breathtaking stuff which got us all pretty snap-happy with our cameras. The long traverse was pretty tiring on the way out and I don't think I've ever seen anyone sweat as much as Nikolai, one of the Ternopol cavers. Bob suffered with cramp and Sasha was overtired - it had been a challenging trip. Sasha slipped and hurt her knee about ten minutes from the entrance and needed help to get out. Once at the surface, Ternopol cavers Luda and Svetlana bandaged her knee. Becky's assessment was: 'I'd rather crawl through half a mile of racoon shit than do THAT again!'

After our ten-hour trip, we sat around the fire hungrily eating and drinking with a spectacular thunderstorm as our backdrop. When trying to explain how he'd got the description of the trip so wrong, Chris said It's amazing how easy it is to confuse massage

273

with massacre in Ukrainian!

The next day started when Valeri greeted Becky with 'Good morning Becky, how are you?' to which she replied 'I'm fine, but my knees aren't happy'. She certainly had an impressive collection of bruises - her legs were as spotted as a leopard's! As we struck camp it became obvious that the reason why Chris had an extension on his rucksack and so many straps was so that he could continue to accommodate his ever expanding load of clutter. After breakfast, we drove off to Cristalnaya cave for an excellent three-hour trip in part of the 32km system. The beginning of the cave was run as a commercial enterprise and the first decoration we saw was man-made - a Christmas tree! However, the natural formations after the first 3 km were far more beautiful. Many of the gypsum crystals sticking out from the walls were a few centimetres long and there were large numbers of swallowtail twinned crystals amidst countless tiny gypsum roses. The orange gypsum crystals that made up the rock were often as much as half a metre long and were usually curved. In many places, the rock had been sculpted naturally into delightfully curvaceous roof pendants. Sometimes they hung down low, as Bob, who was a huge two metres tall said: 'This cave is far too short – it's a headache for a tall person'.

After the caving trip, the cave owner and his wife prepared a wonderful meal for us - delicious borscht and boiled sweet potatoes washed down with, of course, vodka. Nikolai referred to gherkins as Russian lemons. There were many toasts and once more, a number of long speeches. Chris got pretty drunk and was swept off his feet by the cave owners' daughter, Nadia. After some dancing with Nadia, Chris was whisked away by Nikolai in the sidecar of a huge old motorbike! We pitched camp nearby, next to the Lost Gypsy River. Valeri commanded: 'My American friends, go get tree' (fetch firewood), so off we went.   The next day, there was ribald humour on the bus from Crystalnaya to Slavka, because Nadia was sitting on Chris's knee:

Chris: 'It will take a crowbar to get this smile off my face!'

Ben: 'No Chris, it will take a crowbar to get Nadia off your lap'

Chris: 'It's okay; I have a bar on me'

Ben: 'Yes, that's WHY you need a crowbar!'

We arrived at the Slavka Cave after a long drive on rough tracks and were met by Natasha, a leading light in the organisation of young cavers in the Ukraine. We were a little concerned to see so many people around the entrance which was in a big sink hole in the woods. Thankfully, however, we were split into sensibly sized groups. I was amazed to hear from Natasha that the year before, one hundred and sixty young cavers, aged between twelve and sixteen, had attended a week long vertical caving training workshop in western Ukraine and that one hundred and twenty had attended a surveying workshop in the Slavka region that year. Why, I wondered, was caving not as popular with youngsters in the UK and the US? Before we entered the cave, she gave us an interesting talk about the discovery and history of its exploration and showed us the incredibly complex survey. The cave had been discovered in February 1992 by a group of five young cavers from Kiev who were only ten, twelve, sixteen, seventeen, and nineteen years old.

The first 100m had been a fairly comfortable crawl. The big breakthrough had been made on 7 November 1992 after a series of seven digging trips, in which Valeri and Natasha had also been involved. Nine kilometres of cave passage were discovered and it had taken a year to survey the complicated labyrinth. The survey had to be seen to be believed! The cave consisted almost entirely of dry fossil passage, though there was a small stream in the south-east of the system which had potential for future extensions. The whole area was peppered with caves. There were over one hundred, of which fourteen were more than a 1km in length.

I caved with Ed and Becky, along with Luda, Svetlana, Vitale, and some young local cavers called Romasha and Baton. Natasha's fourteen-year-old son, Pelman (who caved without a lid), also came with us. Our leader was the delightful Tanya, who spoke excellent English and wore a very neat butt pad.

Ben: 'In such a complex cave you can only learn to lead from the front, not from the back.'

Chris: 'Yeah, you just end up looking at the butt in front of you'

Ben: 'Hmmm . . . that's not always such a bad thing!'

The cave started with a damp mud-floored crawl which led to a moderate squeeze into Half Baton Chamber, so called because Baton, one of the original discoverers, couldn't quite push the squeeze. Throughout the cave, there were small paper signs showing the name of each chamber accompanied by some excellent cartoons. We continued to a major junction called Octopus, followed by Three Old Cavers, and then to Hedgehog.

Hedgehog was incredible, the walls bristling with countless well-formed spiky gypsum crystals 3 to 4cm long. After an enthusiastic photo stop we continued to the Passage of 120 Steps which had some pretty laminated clay formations. This was followed by Hole of USSR (sic) and Lenin's Mausoleum, which was a 7m by 7m chamber with beautiful walls of convoluted bands of orange, brown, and white gypsum. Milky Way was covered with white powdery needles and the North Star was incredible with 15 to 20cm long, clear-bladed crystals of selenite gypsum, many exhibiting well-formed swallowtail twins. Our next stop was the highlight of the cave, the coyly named Love Oven! This was the only place where there were copious calcite formations and boy, were they gorgeous! They decorated a small but exquisitely beautiful chamber, about four square metres, with stalactites and stalagmites aplenty. The formations ranged from pure white to a rich, deep orange. Needless to say, I went wild with my camera.

From the Love Oven, we followed the Passage of Priests, its walls glittering with sparkling gypsum crystals, to Big Turtle - a wide low chamber containing a well-preserved mud bank with excellent desiccation cracks. The next section of the cave, a large bedding plane (a boundary between two rock layers) chamber called Suitcase, had a small section known as Peoples' Square where there were some huge translucent gypsum crystals in the roof. These were over a metre long and fluoresced with an eerie tinge of green when we turned out our lights and I zapped them with my flash unit.

In the Versailles chamber there were 10 to 15cm long gypsum crystals sprouting from the walls. Tanya asked if we wanted to stop for more photos, but I said 'No thanks, we've seen better than that' – we'd been thoroughly spoiled already! From Versailles, we headed off to the Wild West and Klondike where part of the wall was covered in 10cm balls of sparkling white needles of aragonite rather than the usual gypsum. We exited the cave after a thoroughly enjoyable and frequently breathtaking three-hour trip.

Lunch was a good buffet spread which included what was becoming the standard fare - bread, tomatoes, cheese, salami, and peppers. Inevitably, there was much toasting in celebration and gratitude, with wine, champagne, and some chilli vodka. Strong vodka has been described as being rather like paint stripper - but this was something else; it could have stripped the tarmac from a motorway! Chris tried to impress Nadia by showing her his NYPD badge. Before long, however, he was having to try to extricate himself from his efforts to dazzle, for fear of a proposal of marriage!

Later, we drove up to the little town of Cricha, where, as we were walking to the church, we met a hefty countrywoman with a glistening gold smile, who was carrying an enormous axe. She showed us around the church which she was helping to renovate along with the other seven Baptist families living nearby, then she and her friend sang an enchanting hymn for us. Valeri videoed it and I can safely say that it was the best, most touching three minutes of the many hours of video tape he recorded during the whole of our stay. After the church, we bought a large supply of kiwi fruit juice for the rest of our journey. When we got back to the bus,

Nadia grabbed Chris, and with deepest feeling, in heavily-accented English said: 'I love you Chris'. Chris, startled, was at rather a loss to find a suitable response and only managed to produce the rather feeble: 'Would you like some kiwi juice?'

On the two-hour drive back to Ternopol, Becky and Vitale must have demonstrated every knot known to humankind! When we arrived, we all freshened up and went for a pleasant walk down to the park by the river where we were able to enjoy a beautiful sunset. Ed presented Sasha with a large bunch of flowers for her sixteenth birthday. Chris had noticed that she'd looked upset at lunchtime and at first, he assumed it was because she had thought that the group had forgotten her birthday, but then he realised it was because her best birthday present (Ed) would be leaving in two weeks' time. Altogether too much romance! Back at the centre for tourism there were the usual toasts and speeches before we headed back to the station to catch the late night train back to Kiev.

It was good to wake up and lie on my bunk looking out of the train window at the trees which seemed to glitter in the early morning sun as we rushed by. We got back to Valeri's home around ten in the morning and spent a few hours sorting ourselves out. After an excellent meal of chicken, potatoes, and red wine, we took the metro over to Old Kiev to do some sightseeing.

Old Kiev, with its broad cobbled streets and old buildings, was a huge contrast to the modern suburbs where we'd been staying. The churches had gorgeous gilded spires and crosses that looked spectacular against the green roofs. Becky found a little souvenir shop and bought a small clay figurine of an old woman and announced 'She's splendid; I'll wrap her in my dirty socks to take her home safely'. Later, we sat in the street for a while listening to an accomplished busker, before enjoying a pleasant cold drink at a street side cafe. It was good to walk slowly up the main street, marvelling at the splendour of St Andrews church, an eighteenth century Baroque building perched on the top of the hill. Its large single dome and five small decorative gilded spires looked wonderful silhouetted against the sky and its unusual aqua blue colour made it stand out from all the other buildings. The street was lined with stalls selling souvenirs and craft goods. Most of it was pretty good particularly the delicately hand-painted eggs; there was really not much of the tacky trash you often find wherever tourists congregate. Chris and I each bought Russian army hats. Mine was a stereotypical bearskin hat complete with a red star badge for $15, minutes later; of course, I found one for only $10 - sod's law.

St Sophia's cathedral (eleventh century) was imposing, but we could only see it from the outside as it was locked. Later, we visited the Ukraine Mountain/Cave Rescue base where we were met by Vladimir, a highly respected caver with plenty of good stories to tell. On the way back, I bought four films. It took me ages to sort out the enormous wad of cash as I needed to hand over 2,700,000 coupons! Back at Valeri's home, we watched the video he'd filmed of the trip up until then. I've never really been very keen on the idea of taking along a video camera; it can be intrusive and you always end up doing a lot of 'repeat for history' shots, but I have to admit much of Valeri's film was interesting and amusing too. In the evening, Vitale gave us a slideshow about a seven-day trip he'd taken part in to make a video about the Krashna (Red) Cave. The slides whetted our appetite for our planned visit to that cave towards the end of our stay.

After another rice pudding breakfast, we took a tram to the Pushka Vodize forest park where there was a 35m high metal fire lookout tower with a fixed ladder up through the middle and four hefty anchor cables secured from the top. Alec, Andre, and Vitale quickly rigged three rope routes that included every SRT situation imaginable, plus a few I hadn't even thought of, including all manner of rebelays (re-anchoring ropes usually to avoid rub points or split long pitches), deviations, and traverses. Everybody worked hard practising their vertical techniques in the morning and by lunchtime we all wished we'd had better padding on our leg loops! Later, there was a flurry of on-rope rescue when Andre demonstrated his own technique after his mate got his hair caught in his own rack and Andre zipped up to sort it out. In the evening, we watched a long video of the Red Cave after which Jay made a toast 'to the wonderful, hardworking Ukrainian women' - Valeri had to be cajoled into joining in as Svetlana and Luda wanted the toast in writing!

Unfortunately, Jay was unable to join us the next day when we began our journey to the Crimea. He had to return to the States to sort out house-buying problems. The train left at half past nine and we were due to arrive at our destination almost twenty-four hours later at half past seven the following morning – a long haul. Sasha and Valeri kept us entertained by singing and playing Ukrainian folk songs on the guitar. Whenever the train stopped, it was mobbed by vendors selling melons, tomatoes, crayfish, dried fish, roasted sunflower seeds, and drinks. It was hot and humid, quite unpleasant at times, because hardly any of the windows would open. On the evening of the first day, we joined the young Ukrainian caver contingent in their third class carriage with three-tiered bunks, for a sing-song and a one or two drinks.

On arrival, we were relieved to find a private bus waiting for us. It took about three hours to reach our campsite on the Karabi Plateau. The roads deteriorated steadily as we journeyed on and it wasn't until watching the video later that we realised just how much the bus had squeaked. On the way, Chris regaled me with tales of his escapades as an undercover cop in the US, while Vitale and Becky studiously completed crosswords. The scenery was classic limestone karst – spectacular! Suddenly, the bus screeched to a halt; Sasha jumped out and ran like hell. She returned carrying a head-sized puffball mushroom. This enthusiasm for fungi was to be a taste of things to come.

We arrived at our campsite soon after midday and pitched our tents in a broad sink backed by a limestone crag a few hundred metres from the old mountain rescue post on the hill. After lunch, we set off on one of Valeri's 'short go' walks (i.e. a 10km 'spotholing' walk looking for cave entrances). The karst scenery was pitted with innumerable deep sinkholes, some as much as 100m across. The ground was covered with dainty flowers, but apart from hosts of noisy insects there wasn't much evidence of other wildlife. We walked to the edge of the plateau and stared out towards the Black Sea. On the way back Becky said 'I can see our tents', to which Bob replied 'I can see my laundry' and Chris chipped in 'I can

SMELL your laundry!' He had a point. Cavers get dirty! When we got back we had soup with diced puffball for supper. Reinvigorated, Ed and I cut wood until it got dark while Alex spent hours cutting slots in bolts with a hacksaw for us to use the following day. After our labours, while sitting around the campfire, an embryonic plan emerged to join the Met Grotto annual Easter caving trip to West Virginia. Chris also came up with the idea of a Ukrainian/American Youth Caver Exchange Project. More adventures to look forward to!

In the early hours, I was woken by the cold and the sound of bolts being sawn - had Alex been up all night? At seven, I heard Valeri ask 'Becky, you live?' Becky just groaned and continued to sleep until breakfast which was a huge plate of Bulgar wheat - serious ballast. When Chris and Ed went up to the rescue post to fetch water, they were met by a ram which made a determined attempt to but Chris. The animal followed them back to camp and proceeded to steal our apples and generally made a nuisance of itself. In the end, Svetlana had to drag it away and use a heavy block of wood to persuade it not to come back.

It took forty-five minutes to walk to Big Buzuluk, an 80m deep cave with very little horizontal development. It was particularly interesting because it acted as a natural refrigerator and despite it being really hot above ground, (28°C), there was a considerable amount of ice at the bottom of the cave. We all had a try at bolting and had lots of fun hanging around on skyhooks until they popped off and I took an enormous pendulum, nearly knocking Luda over as I swung past. Back at camp, Valeri was trying to find storage space:

Valeri: 'Bob, you in tent on own?'

Bob: 'Yes'

Valeri: 'Bob, we store food in your tent'

Chris: 'Bob in charge of food? Are you crazy? We're going to starve to death!'

That night I didn't feel too good, suffering with bad guts and feeling the cold. However, it was made easier to bear by the absolute silence and being able to gaze at the Milky Way which looked particularly bright.

I woke feeling a lot better, though a little delicate. Despite my fragile condition, I joined the rest of the team to go for another bolting session at Krubera Cave. It was about 50m deep with some big, pretty, and extremely old calcite formations. Bob had a problem with his enormous rack at one rebelay and after much faffing about was heard to say 'It's okay, I'm a super duper!' This was greeted with roars of laughter because *dupah* is Polish for arse.

We went for an evening walk along the ridge behind the campsite. After the sun had gone down below the horizon, it still lit the clouds from below, a dramatic sight. Meanwhile, Svetlana put up a bolted route on the crag by carbide light while Alex did some climbing. In the evening by the fire, Sasha again played her guitar and sang. When a string broke, she demonstrated typical Ukrainian innovation by replacing it with waxed cotton borrowed from Chris who spent most of the evening sewing up the flapping soles of his caving boots. He had assured us all: 'It never rains in the Crim', but he was to be proved wrong that very night. After heavy rain, the morning was very misty, so misty, in fact, that when Valeri asked

Chris if he could borrow his compass, Alex was quick to clarify: 'Valeri wants to go to the toilet'.

It was a 6km walk to Dublanskogo Cave, but we stopped off on the way to look at the entrance to Nahimovskya Cave. Five years earlier, it had been discovered in the bottom of a classic sink after only about 2m of digging. Had it been a British cave it would have been considered a ridiculously easy and extremely rare dig. It was 405m deep and had about 1,000m of horizontal development. Alex and his girlfriend Natasha had already been on an exploration expedition down there with a couple of friends before they met up with us. When we got to Dublanskogo Cave, we sat around eating wild hazelnuts while Alex and Natasha rigged the pitches and Ed did some bolting. While Becky was loading up her lamp, she showed Vitale her carbide. 'Pah! That's not carbide, that's sand!' he said, producing a Crimean caver carbide cobble so big it wouldn't even fit into Becky's generator.

After lunch, we descended the 25m long and 5m wide entrance rift via three rebelays. The lush vegetation around the entrance gave the place a positively tropical feel. The cave was spectacular and had a huge single chamber littered with enormous fallen blocks 5 to10m across, covered in old formations and draped with new ones. This created an unusual pattern of speleothems at a variety of crazy angles forming a spooky maze to explore.

On the walk back to the campsite, we found a few, apparently new caves, but there was little excitement. Any cave less than 30m deep in the Crimea just has a number because there are so many of them. We had an excellent mushroom soup for supper and then enjoyed an evening of red wine, laughter, song, and the music of the guitar.

After a good breakfast of porridge this time, we set off on a 5km walk to the Chokrak Cave and, to Becky's delight, we collected two carrier bags full of field mushrooms and ceps on the way. We arrived to find that the cave entrance was in a massive sink with trees clinging to the steep sides and moss covering the upper walls of the shaft. The shaft was about 85m deep and negotiating the pitch needed five rebelays and one deviation. I was quite pleased that I'd managed to descend smoothly in about twenty minutes, considering I was a rank amateur at the SRT game.

Looking back up at the entrance from the base of the pitch was a striking experience. The chamber was huge, about 100m long and 30 to 40m high. It was well decorated with gigantic old formations. Becky came down after me and we joined Svetlana to explore further. An uncomfortable little crawl, which had been excavated for about 4m, led us to a series of increasingly wonderful chambers with great formations. In places, the mud was dangerously slippery and a chorus was struck up to the tune of 'Rawhide'. We sang 'Skolska, skolska, skolska, ochin skolska, skolska!' (ochin = very, skolska = slippery). After a few short 'skolska' rope climbs we had reached the end and Svetlana entertained us with a humorously outrageous series of mock 'Playboy' glamour poses in front of a well-decorated calcite slope. On the walk back to camp we picked even more mushrooms - mushroom soup for supper that night too!

After a week without a decent wash, we arranged with the guy at the Mountain Rescue post to have showers for $2 each. We were pleasantly surprised to find that something had been lost in translation and what we actually got was a sauna! It was made by placing a large oil drum full of water on a wood burner. There were also several barrels of warm and cold water placed around what was basically just a small bare room with wooden benches and a slatted floor. Being true gentlemen, we let Becky and Sasha go first, and wished that we'd had a tape recorder to record the 'Oohs!' and 'Ahhs!', their giggles, and finally their screams as they doused themselves with water of varying temperatures. After half an hour, it was our turn to revel in a truly luxurious experience. We returned to camp glowing pink and squeaky-clean.

That night, I nearly made Andre swallow the police whistle that Chris had made the mistake of giving him – there's only so much whistle-blowing anyone can take, even a policeman! In the evening, there was much talk of marketing Vitale's magic carbide lamp in the States. It contained a photoelectric cell that triggered off a spark automatically if the flame went out. This was graphically demonstrated by the video he showed us of the lamp in use in wet conditions in Red Cave. Chris also suggested redesigning the carbide generator by putting water in the top and mushrooms in the bottom! I think, by then, we'd had all had enough mushrooms to last a lifetime.

It was a long day on the bus, travelling on some terrifying roads that were etched into improbably precipitous mountain-sides. Our journey was broken by a stop at a place on the coast which translated as Fisherman's Town. We went for a welcome swim in the Black Sea before having lunch on the beach. Afterwards, we strolled around the local market. Chris wanted to get rid of a huge stack of small denomination bills by buying a bottle of wine, but while he laboriously counted out the money, the stall closed behind his back!

Valeri woke us at six with a cheerful 'Good morning my American friends! Blue sky, sunshine, birds in trees, get up and eat!' We were back to a rice pudding breakfast after which we walked up to Krashna Cave (Red Cave) and spent about an hour struggling into dry suits, an experience that Becky, in particular, is never likely to want to repeat!   Shortly after the show cave, we came to the first siphon (sump) which turned out to be an easy 1m duck with 10 to15cm airspace above our heads.   There was quite a bit of swimming and we were glad of the hand line, as in many sections our feet couldn't touch the bottom. It was a relief to get the rubber hoods of our dry suits off and to explore passages decorated with wonderful formations. Some of the best were in the grotto known as Bloody Mary Hall - other-worldly shapes, some decidedly phallic. There were also some gorgeous small formations and a few large stalactites bristling with helectites.

We left the cave in high spirits and we laughed a lot as we got out of our dry suits. Vitale wore his on the walk back to camp, an exceedingly sweaty experience, so we weren't surprised when he jumped into the river as soon as he got back. After spreading out our kit to dry in the sun, there was a flurry of trading caving gear which seemed to end up with everyone happy with his or her lot.

After packing the tents away, we had a bumpy bus ride back to Simferopol where we stayed at the Mountain-Cave Rescue HQ. In the evening, we were given a great buffet meal followed by the usual toasts. Chris announced his proposal for the 'Ukrainian/American Youth Caver Exchange Project' which was well received. Ed and the HQ boss had an arm-wrestling contest and Chris's speeches got louder and more rambling as the evening progressed. In the end, he had to ask for help when he went to bed because he couldn't get the straps off his sleeping bag! Meanwhile, the Ukrainian cavers talked into the night about the pros and cons of nylon rope versus steel cable and ultimately, entered the speleopolitics zone.

The next day, Chris asked: 'Are our hosts still speaking to me?'

Bob replied: 'Yes, but they aren't speaking to one another!'

We spent the morning wandering around Simferopol before boarding our train for the twenty-two hour journey back to Kiev. We were extremely grateful to be in a carriage with a window that opened this time!

Breakfast the next day included wine – well, it was Ed's birthday! Now in Kiev, another round of mutually beneficial trading commenced. In the afternoon, we strolled around the city and I managed to find a bottle of chilli vodka to inflict on my friends at home. Sasha presented Ed with a bunch of flowers for his birthday. Unfortunately, he wasn't in much of a birthday mood as it was then his turn to suffer bad guts. However, he improved enough by the evening to enjoy Valeri's latest video footage.

Most of our last day in the Ukraine was spent sightseeing in Old Kiev again. Unfortunately, the Ukrainian Art Museum was closed, though we managed to visit a different Art Gallery and the Natural History Museum. Sadly, when we took a ride on the underground, Ed was mugged and there was a scuffle on the train followed by a chase along the platform at the next station. We managed to catch one guy, but the main perpetrator got away. Of all the people to get mugged, Ed was the least likely as he had a triangular shape and muscular physique. This was a nasty twist at the end of an otherwise trouble-free trip. Chris stayed with Ed at the police station while the rest of us continued sightseeing as there was nothing more we could do to help.

We visited the beautiful nineteenth century Vladimir Church, built in the neo-Byzantine style where we were delighted to watch part of a triple wedding ceremony which was accompanied by enchanting singing. Later, we went into the catacombs of the large complex called the Lavra, and crept past mummified monks in coffins lit only by tiny tapers. Exhausted, after so much excitement and sightseeing, in the evening, we went to Vitale's home where we were reenergised and inspired by his videos of expeditions he'd made with his mate Luscha. Later, we enjoyed our last excellent meal followed by an extra special toast (after many others, of course!) to 'new caves and new friends'. There was a ceremonial exchange of gifts, then it was time for our goodbyes and thanks to the warm, generous, hospitable, and kind-hearted people who had been our wonderful hosts for three fantastic weeks in the Ukraine.

PS   Ed got his wallet back which was incredible, but more amazing still was the fact that there was only about $5 missing and both his credit card and driving license were still there!

Chapter 20 LES TROIS AMIS SOUS VERCOUR

Caving, Canyoning, Climbing and Mountain Biking in Vercour.

Over the following year, I spent short half-term breaks caving in Wales, England, and Ireland. The discussions we'd had in the Ukraine with Chris Nicola had born fruit and I spent a wonderful Easter caving in West Virginia and New York State with the Andy Clark and Mark Wildin of the Royal forest of Dean Caving Club (RFDCC). This was followed by an exciting summer trip with the Gloucester Speleological Society to the Czeck and Slovak Republics. All great adventures, but probably only of interest to fellow cavers, so I have not included those tall tales of deep exploits here, though you can about read about them on my website www.benchurch.com.

With another school year behind me and summer ahead, it was time for a slight change – a mountain-biking/caving break. Andy Clark, Mark Wildin, and I, all old friends from the RFDCC, were on our way to France – Les Trois Amis. Mark's car was challenged to keep its front wheels on the road on the way to Dover as we were so laden with outdoor gear; nevertheless, we made it to the ferry just in time. We shared the laborious driving across France, breaking up the journey with an unscheduled overnight stop in Francles. We'd hoped to fill up with fuel, but found there was no garage. Rather than continue in the dark, we decided to camp at the municipal campsite.

The first few kilometres the next morning were nerve racking, as every time we braked, we heard the fuel pump buzzing. However, luck was on our side and we made it to a garage before disaster struck. After another long day of driving we found Le Lepaiz, our destination, without difficulty. When we arrived, there was nobody around, but the place was unlocked and knowing that we were expected, we went in. It looked as though there was quite a crowd staying in the bunkhouse and, knowing how noisy and smelly such places could be when full of cavers, we opted to set up camp in the barn instead. This proved to be the right choice.

The intense heat made us all rather lethargic at first, but we managed to pull ourselves together and head off on the bikes for a 16km ride. We started with a 6km long, 400m climb along a little country lane. It was steep and tiring and I was at the back, as usual, realising how unfit I was compared to Andy and Young Mark, as he was known (he was ten years our junior). However, the downhill to Presles was a blinding off-road trail. There were a few dodgy gravel patches and Andy took a tumble, though somehow he managed to land on his feet. A startled French family having a picnic first heckled me and then whooped encouragement as I sped by, grappling with gravity. We stopped in Presles for a beer and some food and returned in the dark. Back at Le Lepaiz we met our host, Hugh Penny. We were also introduced to Ben, Craig, and Paddy, a trio of friendly northern lads who were helping Hugh renovate the place. We chatted over a few beers and felt we were in for an excellent holiday.

The following afternoon, after a fairly painless shopping trip that had included a visit to 'Le Monde du Bier' in a large hypermarket, we set off in search of Gour Fumant. Craig had provided us with a pretty good sketch map, but we still managed to take a wrong turn in the woods before we found the two entrances to the cave. The 'False Gour' entrance was the one we chose, leading to six pitches (17m, 9m, 15m, 9m, 12m and 9m) and a total depth of about 160m. Andy rigged the awkward and exposed fifth pitch which provided Mark and me with some amusement, though I must admit the joke was on me when I struggled to de-rig it on the way out. The whole cave had suffered from a bad case of 'bolt pox', with a lot of unnecessary and often poorly set bolts at the head of almost every pitch. Unfortunately, this was one of those caves where carbide had been dumped and graffiti scrawled on many surfaces. Nevertheless, it had been a pretty good four and a half hour trip and though the cave was nothing special, it had provided a good 'warm up' for things to come.

The booming tones of Les Williams and his mates from the Wessex Caving Club greeted us when we got back to Le Lepaiz close on midnight. They were on their way back from Slovenia and were breaking the journey home with a few days in Vercour. After a gargantuan *chilli con carne*, we got stuck into a plastic barrel of excellent red wine and launched into caving talk. One discussion about the relative merits of lighting systems included references to the short comings of the 'Petzl Gloom' (rather than a Petzl Zoom) and 'FX Poo' (rather than a Speleotechnics FX 2).

Mad dogs and Englishmen (three in particular) went on a 37km mountain bike ride in the midday sun, including about 1,000m of ascent and descent. The ride started well with a 10km downhill to Choranche, accompanied by spectacular views of the classic limestone gorges characteristic of the area. Then we sweated our way up the Bourne Gorge, stopping for lunch at a little cafe at the head of the valley in the village of La Balme de Rencurel. Having bought four baguettes we strapped them across my luggage rack with the ever-ready gaffa tape, much to the amusement of a number of onlookers. Onwards and upwards. We cycled through Rencurel to le Violon where we swung round to the south, climbing to the Col de Pra L'Etang at 1,267m. From the col, it was a glorious breezy descent back to Le Lepaiz. This was in stark contrast to the smell of petrol that greeted us as soon as we approached Mark's car. There was a leak in the fuel tank which led to much crawling about underneath the chassis and an admirable Heath Robinson repair.

One of the greatest highlights of our visit to the Vercour was a visit to the Grotte Gournier, a truly beautiful cave. The large entrance chamber was something special, a peaceful spot where we paused to gaze at the emerald green lake and gnarled old stalactites that festooned the roof. A 40m paddle in a small inflatable dinghy took us to the foot of an exposed climb and airy traverse which led to the start of the main passage. This was a huge tunnel 20m high and 20m across, graced with many fine formations, including stalagmites up to 7m high and some impressive gour pools (pools with calcite rims, sometimes called rimstone). After about 800m we descended into the streamway and the fun really started.

Wow, what a streamway! The pools got deeper and deeper, changing colour through every breathtaking hue of the blue–green spectrum. It wasn't long before the traverses began – and went on and on. I lost count of the number of fixed ropes and rather substandard 4mm wires (looking disturbingly like coat-hanger wire) that we clipped into as we clambered, bridged, and thrutched our way over the pools and up an impressive 12m waterfall. After a couple of hours we finally reached the end of the traverses and looked up a 10m wide shaft that appeared to be about 40m high.

I took loads of photos on the way out, though I knew that it would be impossible to capture the atmosphere of the cave in any really meaningful way. Once back at the entrance, Mark de-rigged the traverse, leaving Andy stranded. He was stuck until he performed a circus-worthy abseil into the waiting dinghy 10m below! On our way back to the car, we passed a number of tourists who were visiting the neighbouring show cave and I'm afraid we yielded, not for the first time, to a little swaggering. Our good mood continued well into the night when we enjoyed a stupendous barbecue.

A leisurely start the next morning gave no hint of the excitement that was to follow when we had our first experience of canyoning (hiking down canyons often requiring both technical climbing and/or technical swims). Paddy and his girlfriend Wendy joined us to spend a couple of hours descending the lower section of the Canyon des Ecouges. Almost immediately, I found myself abseiling down a 15m waterfall in the sunshine. This canyoning lark was 'cabriolet caving' and I took to the sport immediately; it was like caving with the roof off. The gorge continued as a series of cascades and waterfalls of varying heights, including a 25m abseil, a 6m 'toboggan run' (where I slid down a cascade on my bum), and a series of 16m, 15m, and 14m abseils of varying levels of difficulty and varying amounts of water! Afterwards, it took a long hot and sticky slog uphill wearing wetsuits, in the blazing sun to get to the car. Nevertheless, in the evening, eager for even more excitement, we summoned up enough strength to cycle up to the Col de Pra L'Etang and then storm downhill off-road in the twilight.

Another overheated walk took us from the hydroelectric power station in the Bourne Gorge up to the grandeur of the 80m high entrance porch of Gouffre Bournillon, nestling at the base of awesome 400m high cliffs. We'd checked the weather conditions before entering the cave, as in times of flood a staggering 80 cubic metres of water per second can surge through the passages. It only took about half an hour to get to the lake about halfway (1km) into the system as it was mostly large walking passage with plenty of boulder hopping. Some of the boulders were 6–8m across. Much of the cave was coated in black manganese oxide which made the rock appear very dark and it seemed to suck the light out of our lamps. We spent almost an hour getting back to the entrance as we stopped frequently to take photos of the 5m stalagmites.

Despite Mark being somewhat hungover the following morning, we joined Craig and Ben for a great 36km mountain bike ride. Craig had got the route plan from a chap called Phil who ran mountain biking holidays in the area. The day started with a drive over to Rousset, marvelling at the wonders of the Gorges de Goulet on the way. It took us an hour to cycle up to the Col de Rousset, 500m of ascent in about 16km. Even though Mark was still suffering, I remained at the back – but I made it – just!

Once we'd re-filled our water bottles and passed through the welcome cool of the road tunnel at the top of the col, there was a spectacular view south down to a tight series of hairpin bends. However, this mind-bending descent was not for us; we continued onward and upward off road, climbing to 1,470m. The hard part over, the fun began with a of white knuckle descents on mixed surfaces – cobbles, gravel, and pot-holed tarmac. There was some demanding technical riding and enough speed to satisfy the most hardened adrenalin junky. Miraculously, none of us fell off, despite the challenging terrain. Surprisingly, too, apart from Ben having a blow out, there were no mechanical failures and even the wheel that Mark had dented on the previous evening held out after he'd applied a 'delicate adjustment' to the rim with an adjustable spanner. The ride finished with an exhilarating 60kmph burn-up along the road back to the Rousset where we stopped for a richly deserved pizza.

We returned to caving the following day and Ben joined us on a trip to Trois Qui Souffle (quickly dubbed 'tricky souffle') near Autrans, an hour's drive away. A group of cavers from Swaledale who were staying at Le Lepaiz had done the epic ten-hour through trip the day before and we'd volunteered to de-rig it for them. The entrance really was, as the guidebook said, 'close enough to the road to be able to place the first bolt while sitting in your car'. There was a strong, icy draught howling out of the cave; it was cold enough to see one's breath in spite of the heat of the midday sun. I rigged the entrance pitch and we set off on a good four-hour trip, reaching a total depth of about 200m. The 7m entrance pitch was followed by canyon passage which led to a splendid airy 30m free hanging pitch, followed by a series of shorter pitches and a wire traverse. The trip ended at the Galerie des Condensations.

On the way out, we shared the de-rigging and managed to establish a fairly major 'rats-nest' (a tangle of biblical proportions). This resulted in some blasphemous outbursts at the top of the 30m pitch which had been rigged by two other groups behind us. As we left, we passed a group of drop-dead gorgeous young women on a beginners' trip and later their instructor came back in to de-rig. He must have been well-practised; he travelled at suicidal speed, running over the top of 30m rifts with no cows' tails for protection. It was good to emerge into sunlight and it made a pleasant change not to have to walk far back to the car.

Despite a very late night, Mark and I went climbing at Petit Goulet the next day. This was an amazing location, an embayment between two road tunnels in an impressive gorge with a spectacular view of a precipitous ridge. I led four bolted routes, all about 20m high – a V. Diff (very difficult), Severe, Hard Severe and Hard Very Severe. The routes were enjoyable good quality climbs with plenty of variety and no 'epics' (when it all goes wrong). After a while, we were joined by Paddy and Craig whose standard of climbing made my efforts look utterly pathetic.

Later, Andy turned up and we all headed down to the Bourne Gorge, leaving Paddy's car at the bottom and driving up to the top in Mark's. After inflating Andy's little dinghy, we set off on the canyoning trip which lasted an hour and a half. The sporting element was not a patch on the Ecouge trip, but the scenery was more spectacular, with cliffs up to 600m high towering above us. There was only one abseil of about 11m, but we did do an adrenalin-inducing 6m jump into icy water. After all this exertion we headed back to Le Lepaiz for some warming wine.

After a start, delayed by Andy (hungover) staggering a slalom route across the yard with a towel draped over his head, Paddy and Ben joined us on the bikes for an off-road route to Col de Pra L'Etang. Andy struggled not to throw up with all the exertion, though he still managed to overtake me. He and I got separated from the other three by taking a wrong turn which fortunately, turned out to be a superb descent. We decided not to plod back up when we realised our mistake and made up our own route instead.

Our mistake turned out to be a blessing in disguise and we enjoyed an excellent ride. As for getting separated from the others, it was a case of mind over matter – we didn't mind and it didn't really matter. After a good section of off-road riding on the GR9 long-distance trail, we climbed 1,431m to the Col du Mont Noir. Andy was still suffering from his excesses of the previous night and when we stopped for a rest he laid his bike down against a fence and received an electric shock. When he had recovered from his surprise and I'd recovered from my laughter, we lifted his bike off the fence by holding onto the tyres. It certainly got rid of his hangover!

This tomfoolery was followed by a series of good off-road descents, finishing with the ride we'd done in semi-darkness a few days previously. After about 32km, I got a puncture, just 200m from home! Thereafter, I decided to relax in a hammock and read while Andy and Mark set out on a death-defyingly steep 9km off-road descent to Pont. In the evening, we were all absolutely exhausted. When it came to having a beer, it was left to me - Andy and Mark wouldn't touch a drop!

The next day we drove to Le Balcon de Villard with Ben, Craig, and Paddy and took a cable car up to 1,720m before walking a further 10km to an altitude of just over 2,000m. We were above the Pas de Eille and had excellent views along the Arêtes du Gerbier and the towering cliffs at the col which must have been 500m high. The area was one of classic karst scenery with superb limestone pavements and gorgeous alpine flowers. However, there had been a lot of serious blasting and grading (smoothing out the route) to push new ski runs through the area, something that would never have been allowed in a British National Park. Back at Le Lepaiz, I had to fix three punctures before cycling up to Col de Pra L'Etang with Paddy, Hugh, Mark, and Andy. Then we did a mixture of old and new bombing off-road descents back to base. In the evening, a group of eight Czech cavers arrived and introduced us to some fiery Czech spirit; it was about as enjoyable as drinking turps!

As we got kitted up by the roadside the next morning, a car pulled up and a dumpy little bloke with a face like a bulldog chewing a wasp emerged and offered us a tray of peaches. He spoke with a strong local accent and was difficult to understand. Andy asked him for three peaches and gave him ten Francs. He muttered something – I got the impression that he wanted to sell us the whole tray – and then got back into his car with his peaches and Andy's ten francs and drove off, leaving us standing there, gawping and peach-less!

The slope up to the entrance of Grotte Favot, high on the side of the Bourne Gorge, was a punishingly clammy climb. We changed inside the entrance and soon entered the breathtaking Grand Tunnel. It was an amazing pentangular phreatic passage. This was about 5m in diameter which descended, flat-floored, at an angle of about 45° for 70m. At the bottom of the Grand Tunnel, there were some great formations which we explored before heading out. Our trip had lasted only one hour, but we all agreed that the Grotte Favot had been rewarding, despite the arduous ascent to the entrance.

Later, we went to look at the spectacular entrance to Goule Blanche. It was cluttered with metal bridges, walkways, and hydroelectric hardware. It was easy to imagine water thundering through in a flood. We also had a look at Goule Noire where we had hoped to abseil 40m off the bridge to the entrance, but unfortunately a sign advised us that this was now illegal. In the evening, Mark went for a bike ride with Paddy and Ben. When he came back he was wide-eyed with tall tales of terror after having had a close encounter with a wild boar. Hugh put on an excellent BBQ for his birthday attended by about fifty people. It ended at around three in the morning, with a number of revellers sleeping in dishevelled heaps around the fire.

The spectacular climax of our Vercour experience was, ironically, a descent –the descent of the upper section of the Canyon des Ecouges. The gorge was a natural wonder of water-sculpted limestone with a dozen pitches of between 5 and 35m. A decidedly 'airy' hanging traverse on a fixed wire led straight to the top of an exciting 25m pitch. The abseils got better and better. It was exhilarating to stand on the lip of waterfalls that looked like boiling mercury cascading in a torrent and exploding in a turbulent maelstrom of bubbles in the plunge pool below; an absolute frenzy of energetic beauty. On one 22m waterfall pitch I slithered about three quarters of the way down into a slick gully off to one side of the free hang. I did this to delay the inevitable swing out into the full force of the torrent. As I did so, I swung under the arch of a perfect rainbow that had been formed by the spray of the waterfall.

Everything had gone smoothly until we reached the final pitch which was a total drop of 70m with a re-belay half-way down a waterfall. A couple of French guys, who were obviously more experienced than we were, descended first and we were left looking at each other, trying to decide who should go first. I pulled the short straw and gingerly clambered out onto the head of the intimidating pitch, the most exposed situation I'd ever been in. Paddy commented that I had my 'serious face' on – my mind was totally focused as I rigged the pitch, oblivious to the ribald heckling that the others gave me as a diversion from their own apprehension. I abseiled about 20m down to a large ledge where I had seen the French guys stop, but I couldn't see the re-belay below me. Having heard that the Wessex boys had managed to abseil past the re-belay the previous week, I decided to err on the side of caution by traversing across to a small tree that clung to the cliff face. I made myself safe and signalled to the others to follow (they couldn't hear me due to the noise of the waterfall). I can definitely say that we were all gripped!

Once everyone was safely attached to the tree, I abseiled off the tiny ledge. I was relieved to spot the second re-belay which had been hidden by the spray of the waterfall. However, getting to the chain of the belay was decidedly perilous. It involved a tricky 20m diagonal abseil to a very scary, extremely 'polished' 3m long sloping ledge about 15cm wide which was covered in algal slime – to fall off there would have been a catastrophe. I cautiously edged my way along and heaved a sigh of relief when I finally clipped the belay with my cow's tail. This was definitely one of those 'Thank you God' moments.

The final 35m pitch was a joy and involved whoops of the 'glad to be alive' variety. A fitting end to a superb holiday.

Chapter 21 MOUNTAIN BIKING IN THE ROCKIES AND THE MOAB DESERT

The United States of America

I was sitting next to my girlfriend, Maria, with whom I had yet to arrange a holiday, when Andy, without much tact, told me that he'd booked me a provisional place on a mountain biking trip in the US. To add to the awkwardness of the situation, he then announced: 'I don't want to exert any pressure, but I'll have to have a definite answer by tomorrow.' I struggled with my decision for a moment or two, but it didn't take long before I capitulated in the face of Andy's excited descriptions of what might be in store. Maria was understandably unenthusiastic, even though we'd invited her along too (honest!) – it really wasn't her cup of tea. I had to box pretty, so she and I started making plans for a holiday which she would really enjoy and we decided to spend ten days soaking up the sun on the shore of Lake Garda in Italy at the earliest opportunity.

There were moments when timing was dangerously tight on the journey from the Forest of Dean to Breckonridge, Colorado. It was a miracle that our boxed bikes arrived at Denver airport at the same time as we did. However, despite having landed at the largest airport in the world (145 square km), it wasn't long before we were met by Nick and his girlfriend Sarah, the representatives of Rocky Mountain Adventures. I'd expected there to be perhaps ten people on the trip, but due to a few last minute cancellations there were only Mark, Andy, and I, (Les Trois Amis), another Nick, and his wife Kate. Kate was three months pregnant, but they'd booked the trip before they knew.

We soon settled in to the chalet and after assembling our bikes, walked into town to a restaurant called 'Downstairs at Eric's'. Walking back we were surprised by how much we were affected by the altitude. Even though we were only at 2,900m, we were gasping our way up the smallest hills.

Our first day dawned bright and clear with a backdrop of glorious blue skies to set off the spectacular mountain scenery. In the morning, we browsed around the bike shops where I took the opportunity of buying the new bike I'd promised myself for years. The deciding factor was money as bikes in the US cost about two thirds the price of those in the UK and consequently, I was able to afford a much better model (a Kona Pahoehoe) than I'd ever have been able to at home. It was a lean, mean, minty-green machine.

In the afternoon, we were introduced to mountain biking Rocky Mountain style. We were led by Sam, a young geography student with, what seemed to me, to be the best holiday job ever. Early on in the 20km ride, Nick and Kate fell a long way behind and opted for a shorter route, so for most of the time, it was just Sam and the three of us from the UK. Our route followed the Baker Tank Trail with a few extra sporting twists added at the end.

I whooped a few times as I discovered the joys of Mazzochi Bomber 7.5cm front suspension, skipping and jumping over every obstacle the sublime single track could throw at me as we sped through the trees.

It soon became apparent that Sam was an astonishingly competent and sickeningly fit biker with an excellent knowledge of the local trails. His enthusiastic descriptions of the rides that we'd be doing soon had us drooling in anticipation. However, it took a while to get used to the thin air and the enormous volume of water we felt compelled to drink. After a few stops to take photos we screamed down a series of tight switchbacks which took us back down to the chalet. It had been an enjoyable hour and a half and though we were keen for more, it seemed sensible to call it a day and ease ourselves into biking so high in the mountains.

After a leisurely start the next day, we set off on the Sally Barber Mine Trail. Nick and Kate joined us for the whole ride this time, so there were quite a few long rest stops. This wasn't a problem; the scenery was gorgeous and the old mine workings were fascinating to investigate. The trail was only about 18km, so after lunch at the Subway (foot-long sandwiches), we set off with Sam to do the Blue River Trail. It was about 16km there and back along a single track with a good balance between slick mud and pine needle surfaces and technically tricky rocky sections, and with a generous sprinkling of gnarled roots thrown in to keep us concentrating. It was enjoyable even though, despite my new steed, I was still always at the back.

The 37km Peak Trail was a popular one, so we set off early in order to beat the crowds. We'd seen very few bikers on the previous rides, but there were quite a few here. Three and a half hours of challenging technical riding with some difficult descents really put my front suspension through its paces and there were many sections that I wouldn't have even considered on my English bike. The end of the ride was less enjoyable with a long grim slog on a crowded tarmac trail alongside the freeway.

On the way back, we stopped off at the Great Adventure bike shop and I swapped the Shimano Pedalling Dynamics system pedals that cycling shoes clip into with a cleat (SPDs) that came with my new bike, for some more user-friendly pedals that had a bit of a cage on them too. Knowing that they'd take some getting used to, I decided to stick with toe clips for the rest of the holiday so that I could ride to my limit without the inevitable hesitancy and falls that accompany getting used to new kit.

The longest ride of our trip was when the three of us took in about 50km of varied terrain on the Hoosier Ridge Trail and a bit of the Blue River Trail. The ride started with a 15km climb to over 2,000m, much of it both technical and strenuous. However, this was all made bearable by the fantastic views of high mountain pastures and beautiful snow-capped peaks. We stopped in a bleak area near the top where a forest fire had left a desolate landscape of charred and twisted trees. We tucked into bananas which were so good that when Mark dropped his, he simply scraped the thick dirt off with his knife and continued to eat it. We enjoyed a prodigious 6km descent and mixed technical riding - all fearsome stuff. The route instructions we had didn't make sense to us and after a few hopeless uphill kilometres we asked some campers (who turned out to be British) for directions. They soon put us right. A punishing 8km climb up a reasonably surfaced dirt road took us 250m up to Boreas Pass. Our reward was a thrilling 13km descent, polished off by the delights of the Blue River Trail - a really special day of top quality mountain biking!

It took five hours to drive to Moab in Utah where we set up camp next to the Colorado River. Despite the strong current, we managed to swim across, though on reflection this was somewhat daft. There was a spectacular 150m cliff on the other side. It glowed yellow, orange, and finally red as the sun set behind the site which was simple with few facilities and minute tents, but the marvellous location more than made up for the lack of mod. cons. Supper was an excellent BBQ and was followed by one of the best shooting-star-spotting sessions ever.

A very early start took us onto the legendary Slickrock Trail before it got too hot on the Moab Desert plateau. Nick and Sarah opted for the practice trail while Sam took us around the main trail. I can't deny that I was rather disappointed to find that there were wide stripes of white paint every few metres as way-markers. However, by the time we'd finished the ride, I could understand why this had been done. It had first been established in 1969 as a motorbike trail and, as people had stuck to the route, erosion had been kept to a minimum. However, in spite of the way-marks, there was still a wide-open space and wilderness feel about the Moab and it was easy to understand why some scenes in *Star Wars* had been filmed in this weird and wonderful place.

Thanks to the traction provided by the gritty red desert sandstone, the mountain biking rules we were familiar with had to be thrown to the winds. I found myself in 'granny gear' for most of the ride, managing both to ascend and descend improbably steep slopes. Inevitably, the spectacular scenery and stupendous feats of technical biking led to many excellent photo opportunities. It took us about four hours to get round the 20km trail and we all agreed it was mountain biking heaven. After a lunch of giant sandwiches and gallons of Coke to get us rehydrated, we set off for a drive in the Arches National Park. It was a gorgeous evening and the scenery was made all the more beautiful by the delicate hues of the desert sandstone illuminated by the evening sun. Our excellent day was rounded off by a meal at the improbably named Eddie McStiff's, followed by cold beer and more stargazing.

The Arches National Park had been so stunning that we made a second visit the following morning before heading back to Breckonridge. On the way back, we stopped off to do a splendid 13km ride just outside Crested Butte, Upper Loop was a single-track through silver aspen trees and an absolute joy to ride.

As a change from biking, the next day we chose to go white-water rafting on the Arkensaw River in the Royal Gorge. It didn't start well because poor old Sam clipped a car while parking the van for a snack stock-up. Thankfully, it all got sorted pretty quickly and before long we were on our way. The rafting was good fun, but the water levels were quite low, making it technical rather than exciting. It was great though, to follow the canyon for a couple of hours.

When we got back to Breckonridge we decided to round off the day with a short ride Sam had enthused about – the Burro and Wheeler Trails. It was a good ride, but we'd been a bit ambitious setting out in the late afternoon and we finished in the dark with no lights. It was a miracle that none of us fell off and I half expected to plough into a bear lumbering across the track.

The fitting finale to our trip was the exquisite Colorado Trail, 37km of superb cycling, generally on a single track. The ascents were mostly easy-angled and 99.9 per cent rideable, while the descents were twisted and technical, leaving us breathless with a huge whack of adrenalin. On the way back to the chalet, Mark, swayed by my undying praise for my new front suspension, decided to splash out on a pair of Mazzochi Bomber 3s.

Just when we thought it was all over, we had an 11th-hour extension as bad weather delayed our landing in Chicago. This meant that we'd missed our connecting flight. Before we knew it, we were comfortably ensconced in a swanky hotel, courtesy of the airline. After a bonus day of CD shopping, sightseeing in Chicago, and a visit to the fascinating Shedd Aquarium, we finally took off for home.

Chapter 22 ANOTHER FIRST CHAPTER

Would you Adam and Eve it?

A Mountainous Proposal!

This chapter really started when I dangled Maria off a cliff on the end of an abseil rope, part of an end-of-term social event. The following week, I put up a notice in the staffroom which said: 'Ben Church needs a woman for a week'. The small print revealed that this was actually a request for a female presence to help 'babysit' a mixed group of year nine students who were doing a Duke of Edinburgh Award taster. This was to be a multi-activity week at Trefil, the Gwent County Council Outdoor Centre where I occasionally worked with Martyn Farr, the celebrated international cave explorer.

Maria was quick to volunteer, not just for one night, but for the whole week! I was deeply grateful. Soon after that, the summer holiday started and Maria and I began to go out with one another. She was a trifle startled on our first real 'date' as I asked her to bring rubber gloves and wellies. I took her on what was my idea of a good time - a rather wet caving trip. In retrospect, I realise it might not have been her idea of fun, but nevertheless, she was a good sport and we had a great time; our relationship had begun.

Fourteen months later, I woke her up to show her a gorgeous pair of young fox cubs that were playing in the field a few metres behind my house. Then I announced that we were going on a mystery tour. I could sense that she had doubts when I told her that I'd already packed her bags for the weekend, but I was convinced she'd enjoy what I had in store. We drove up to Snowdonia and parked at the base of Tryfan early in the evening. Maria was a little reluctant to pull on her walking boots, but soon we were scrambling up the north face of my favourite mountain.

On the ascent, we met a young lady who didn't share my sentiments – her boyfriend called me over, asking if I had a rope. Maria took off her harness and I performed a simple rope rescue of his hapless (soon to be ex?) girlfriend, who'd had enough. Our climb continued and we had the mountain to ourselves, apart from a few nimble feral goats.

Finally, we reached the summit and I helped Maria to clamber up onto the top of 'Eve', one of a pair of monoliths that crown Tryfan. I climbed onto 'Adam', its twin, and, as the sun went down and the sea shimmered red in the distance, I asked Maria to marry me. She said 'yes'. I popped open a bottle of champagne and we descended the mountain to have fish and chips in Bethesda - the beginning of a new chapter in both of our lives.

Alas, there was no fairy-tale ending in the usual sense of those words, but whatever we did or didn't achieve in our marriage (we got divorced in 2010), we were much blessed with our wonderful son Finn, to whom this book is dedicated with all my love.

The adventure continues….

Printed in Germany
by Amazon Distribution
GmbH, Leipzig